Spain since 19?

STUDIES IN CONTEMPORARY HISTORY

PUBLISHED

SPAIN SINCE 1939 *Stanley Black*

THE ARAB–ISRAELI CONFLICT, THIRD EDITION *T. G. Fraser*

AMERICA AND THE WORLD SINCE 1945 *T. G. Fraser and Donette Murray*

THE ULSTER QUESTION SINCE 1945, SECOND EDITION *James Loughlin*

GERMANY SINCE 1945 *Pól O'Dochartaigh*

THE RISE AND FALL OF THE SOVIET EMPIRE, SECOND EDITION *Raymond Pearson*

THE CIVIL RIGHTS MOVEMENT: Struggle and Resistance, SECOND EDITION *William T. Martin Riches*

THE UNITED NATIONS AND INTERNATIONAL POLITICS *Stephen Ryan*

JAPAN SINCE 1945 *Dennis B. Smith*

DECOLONIZATION SINCE 1945 *John Springhall*

Studies in Contemporary History
Series Standing Order
ISBN 0–333–71706–6 hardcover
ISBN 0–333–69351–5 paperback
(*outside North America only*)

You can receive future titles in this series as they are published by placing a standing order. Please contact your bookseller or, in the case of difficulty, write to us at the address below with your name and address, the title of the series and the ISBN quoted above.

Customer Services Department, Macmillan Distribution Ltd
Houndmills, Basingstoke, Hampshire RG21 6XS, England

SPAIN SINCE 1939

STANLEY BLACK

© Stanley Black 2010

First published 2010 by
PALGRAVE MACMILLAN

Palgrave Macmillan in the UK is an imprint of Macmillan Publishers Limited, registered in England, company number 785998, of Houndmills, Basingstoke, Hampshire RG21 6XS.

Palgrave Macmillan in the US is a division of St Martin's Press LLC, 175 Fifth Avenue, New York, NY 10010.

Palgrave Macmillan is the global academic imprint of the above companies and has companies and representatives throughout the world.

Palgrave® and Macmillan® are registered trademarks in the United States, the United Kingdom, Europe and other countries

ISBN 978–1–4039–3569–4 hardback
ISBN 978–1–4039–3570–0 paperback

This book is printed on paper suitable for recycling and made from fully managed and sustained forest sources. Logging, pulping and manufacturing processes are expected to conform to the environmental regulations of the country of origin.

A catalogue record for this book is available from the British Library.

A catalog record for this book is available from the Library of Congress.

10 9 8 7 6 5 4 3 2 1
19 18 17 16 15 14 13 12 11 10

Printed and bound in Great Britain by
CPI Antony Rowe, Chippenham and Eastbourne

CONTENTS

v

Contents

Contents

Contents

To Pat Doris,
an inspirational Spanish teacher

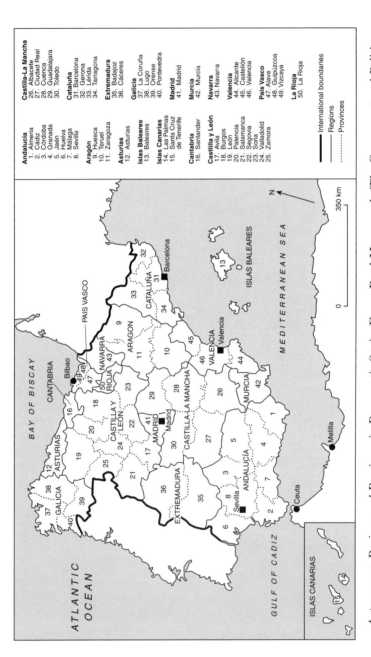

Andalucía
1. Almería
2. Cádiz
3. Córdoba
4. Granada
5. Jaén
6. Huelva
7. Málaga
8. Sevilla

Aragón
9. Huesca
10. Teruel
11. Zaragoza

Asturias
12. Asturias

Islas Baleares
13. Baleares

Islas Canarias
14. Las Palmas
15. Santa Cruz de Tenerife

Cantabria
16. Santander

Castilla y León
17. Ávila
18. Burgos
19. León
20. Palencia
21. Salamanca
22. Segovia
23. Soria
24. Valladolid
25. Zamora

Castilla-La Mancha
26. Albacete
27. Ciudad Real
28. Cuenca
29. Guadalajara
30. Toledo

Cataluña
31. Barcelona
32. Gerona
33. Lérida
34. Tarragona

Extremadura
35. Badajoz
36. Cáceres

Galicia
37. La Coruña
38. Lugo
39. Orense
40. Pontevedra

Madrid
41. Madrid

Murcia
42. Murcia

Navarra
43. Navarra

Valencia
44. Alicante
45. Castellón
46. Valencia

País Vasco
47. Álava
48. Guipúzcoa
49. Vizcaya

La Rioja
50. La Rioja

—— International boundaries
—— Regions
········· Provinces

Acknowledgements

I could not have completed this book without the help of many friends and colleagues. I am indebted to the then series editors, Professor Tom Fraser and Dr John Springhall, for inviting me to write it in the first place. Colleagues at the University of Ulster have been a constant source of support and encouragement, in particular Dr Ian Connor, Professor Graham Gargett and Professor Pól O'Dochartaigh. The library staff at Coleraine are truly wonderful, especially Linda Southall and Christine McGeehan in the Inter-Library Loan section. Other friends and colleagues who have helped in their own way include Dr Xosé María Gómez Clemente, Professor David Corkhill, Miguel Angel Garduño, Professor John Kinsella, Dr Terence McMullan, Dr Chris Ross and Angela Sacnz, and I owe a special debt of gratitude to my students from whom over the years I have learned so much.

I would also like to take this opportunity to thank the editorial team at Palgrave Macmillan, especially the commissioning editor Sonya Barker for her advice, encouragement and inexhaustible patience and the copy-editor Juanita Bullough for her help and guidance in completing the manuscript.

I want to thank my family, especially sisters Ann and Violet, my daughter Rosana, who also helped with the index, my son Christopher and, above all, my wife Chus, for her love and tolerance at all times.

SB

ABBREVIATIONS

ACNP	Catholic National Association of Propagandists, *Asociación Católica Nacional de Propagandistas*
AIC	Independent Groupings of the Canaries, *Agrupaciones Independientes de Canarias*
AP	Popular Alliance, *Alianza Popular* (after 1990 People's Party, *Partido Popular*)
BNG	Galician Nationalist Bloc, *Bloque Nacionalista Galego*
CAIC	Candidatura Aragonesa Independiente del Centro
CC OO	Workers' Commissions, *Comisiones Obreras* (communist trade union)
CD	Democratic Coalition, *Coalición Democrática*
CDC	Catalan Democratic Convergence Party, *Convergència Democràtica de Catalunya*
CDS	Social Democratic Centre, *Centro Democrático y Social*
CG	Galician Coalition, *Coalición Galega*
ChA	Aragonese Regionalist Party, *Chunta Aragonesista*
CIC	Independent Candidates of the Centre, *Candidatura Independiente del Centro*
CiU	Convergence and Union, *Convergència i Unió*
EA	Basque Solidarity, *Eusko Alkartasuna* (1986 breakaway from PNV)
EAJ	Basque Nationalist Party, *Euzko Alderdi Jeltzalea* (in Spanish, *Partido Nacionalista Vasco*, PNV)
EB	Basque United Left, *Ezker Batua* (from 1994 allied with Greens to form *Ezker Batua-Berdeak* (EB-B)

List of Abbreviations

EC–FED	Catalan Left–Democratic Electoral Front, *Esquerra de Catalunya–Front Electoral Democràtic*
EE	Basque Country Left, *Euskadiko Ezkerra* (from 1991 merged with PSE to form PSE–EE)
EE–IE	Basque Country Left, *Euskadiko Ezkerra–Izquierda de Euskadi* (name of EE from 1982 to 1991)
EH	Alliance of Basque Citizens, *Euskal Herritarrok* (from 1998 coalition substituting HB)
ERC	Republican Left of Catalonia, *Esquerra Republicana de Catalunya*
ETA	Basque Homeland and Freedom, *Euskadi ta Askatasuna*
FN	New Force, *Fuerza Nueva*
FRAP	Revolutionary Anti-Fascist and Patriotic Front, *Frente Revolucionario Antifascista y Patriótico*
GAL	Anti-terrorist Liberation Groups, *Grupos Antiterroristas de Liberación*
GRAPO	The First of October Anti-Fascist Resistance Groups, *Grupos de Resistencia Antifascistas Primero de Octubre*
HB	People's Unity, *Herri Batasuna*
HOAC	Catholic Action Workers Brotherhood, *Hermandad Obrera de Acción Católica*
IC–V	Initiative for Catalonia–Green Party, *Iniciativa per Catalunya –Verds*
IU	United Left, *Izquierda Unida*
JOC	Catholic Workers Youth, *Juventudes Obreras Católicas*
KAS	Radical Basque Socialist Coordinating Group, *Koordinadora Abertzale Sozialista*, usually referred to as the KAS Alternative, *Alternativa KAS*
Na-Bai	Navarre Yes, *Nafarroa Bai*
PAR	Regionalist Party of Aragon, *Partido Aragonés Regionalista*
PCE	Spanish Communist Party, *Partido Comunista de España*

List of Abbreviations

PDC	Democratic Pact for Catalonia, *Pacte Democràtic per Catalunya*
PDP	Popular Democratic Party, *Partido Demócrata Popular*
PNC	Canaries Nationalist Party, *Partido Nacionalista Canario*
PNV	Basque Nationalist Party, *Partido Nacionalista Vasco*
PP	People's Party, *Partido Popular*
PSA–PA	Andalusian Socialist Party–Andalusian Party, *Partido Socialista de Andalucía–Partido Andaluz*
PSC	Socialist Party of Catalonia, *Partit Socialista de Catalunya*
PSOE	Spanish Socialist Workers Party, *Partido Socialista Obrero Español*
PSP–US	Popular Socialist Party–Socialist Unity, *Partido Socialista Popular–Unidad Socialista*
PSUC	*Partit dels Socialistes Unificat de Catalunya*, Unified Socialist Party of Catalonia
UAl	Unity of Alava, *Unidad Alavesa* (aligned with *Partido Popular*)
UCD	Union of the Democratic Centre, *Unión de Centro Democrático*
UC-DCC	Union of the Centre and Christian Democrat Party of Catalonia, *Unió del Centro i la Democracia Cristiana de Catalunya*
UDC	Democratic Union of Catalonia, *Unió Democràtica de Catalunya*
UGT	General Workers' Union, *Unión General de Trabajadores*, socialist trade union
UN	National Union, *Unión Nacional*
UPC	Union of the People of Canaries, *Unión del Pueblo Canario*
UPN	Union of the People of Navarre, *Unión del Pueblo Navarro*
UPyD	Union for Progress and Democracy, *Unión Progreso y Democracia*
UV	Valencian Union, *Unió Valenciana*

INTRODUCTION

Although Spanish history in the twentieth century is without a doubt marked, some might say scarred, by the cataclysmic event of the Spanish Civil War between 1936 and 1939, one cannot really speak of a watershed moment or a historical turning point. While the international dimension of the Spanish Civil War has ensured its enduring interest for historians (Preston 1995b: 35), it has long been accepted that the war was not simply the stage for an international conflict, a battle of twentieth-century ideologies or even a prelude to the even greater catastrophe which was the Second World War. It was, fundamentally, as the liberal intellectual Salvador de Madariaga observed, 'a strictly Spanish event' (1942: 367), born out of tensions and issues that, while not particularly original in themselves (issues of class, adjustments to modernity, growing secularization, and so on), acquired a very Spanish hue over the decades, if not centuries. In the Spanish case, the Civil War was not an exorcism of these national demons or an opportunity to achieve some form of national reconciliation. Instead, the war and its aftermath perpetuated and even exacerbated the problems that had given rise to it. In its early stages, the dictatorship was an institutionalized continuation of the war that preceded it. Many of the wounds that it had opened and the underlying causes of those wounds were as real in 1975 when Franco died as when he had conspired with his fellow officers to overthrow the government of the Second Republic in 1936 (Balfour and Quiroga 2007: 39).

For this reason, Spain has never fully recovered from the war. One commentator has said: 'the trauma of the Civil War was so great that it continued to shape the collective psychology of the Spanish people even fifty years on' (Esenwein and Shubert 1995: 265) and, according to Paul Preston, the 'historiography of modern Spain has been concerned with three main issues – the origins of the Spanish Civil War, the course of the Spanish Civil War and the aftermath of the Spanish Civil War' (1995: 30).

A civil war is the most graphic and tragic outcome of a divided society, but in Spain the concept of the 'two Spains' has haunted it for centuries. As Balfour and Quiroga note:

> Two opposing concepts of nation emerged in Spain in the first decades of the nineteenth century when the liberal and the traditionalist models of Spain as an imagined political and cultural community were first formulated ... Since then the confrontation between the two became increasingly hostile and the most extreme manifestation of this conflict of identities was the idea of the 'two antagonistic Spains' promoted by Franco during the Civil War and his forty-year-long dictatorship. (2007: 18)

Almost the whole of the period covered by this book, from 1939 to the present, has in Spain been governed by two kinds of pact, a Francoist *pacto de la sangre*, or pact of blood, whose aim was to ensure that the 'complicity of all parties in brutal repression meant no one group could escape punishment should the political situation be completely reversed' (Esenwein and Shubert 1995: 269) and, since the death of the dictator, a *pacto del olvido* or a *pacto de silencio*, a pact of forgetting or of silence. Paul Preston calls the *pacto del olvido* a 'tacit, collective agreement of the great majority of the Spanish people to renounce any settling of accounts after the death of Franco' (2006: 9). While the 'pact of silence' was a necessary evil, and Preston recognizes its political value 'as a measure of the great political maturity of the Spanish people' (2006: 12) at a critical juncture, it is still undoubtedly the case that it was merely postponing the day when Spain would have to face the demons of division that have haunted it throughout its history.

It is only in recent years that Spain has attempted to do so and it has not been an easy process. In fact, it has reawakened the divisions and rancours that were at the root of the original conflict and, once again, the Spanish Civil War is a central issue in the argument. In November 2008 Esperanza Aguirre, a leading member of the conservative opposition party, the People's Party, chose to attack the Government of Rodríguez Zapatero by invoking what she claimed, citing the historian Stanley Payne, was the 'violent past' of the Spanish Socialist Workers Party (*Partido Socialista Obrero Español*, PSOE). She mentioned in particular the killing of the conservative politician José Calvo Sotelo in July 1936 attributed to the bodyguard of a leading figure in the PSOE, Indalecio Prieto. This assassination, one of the two tit-for-tat murders that sparked the outbreak of the war, is implicitly laid at the door of the current Socialist Party. Such a controversy reveals not only the readiness there is in Spain, and not just among the political classes, to use and abuse history in such an ahistorical way, but also, at a simpler level, it demonstrates how close beneath the surface of Spanish society lurk the old ghosts of resentment, ready to re-emerge, stir up old hatreds and provoke new confrontations.

It also justifies, if justification were ever needed, the continued need not only to study the past but to study the history of the past, the varying ways that that past has been and continues to be represented. For if it is true that the events of the Civil War and its aftermath and their effects on contemporary Spain have never been as relevant and fashionable as they are today, what Jo Labanyi has called 'the increased cultural memorialisation of the Civil War' (witness the popularity of films and books such as *Soldados de Salamina*, or *Las 13 Rosas* or *Los girasoles ciegos*, or television series such as *Amar en tiempos revueltos* or *Cuéntame cómo pasó*), it is equally true that Spanish historiography has itself become an issue in recent years, with a trend towards right-wing revisionist histories attaining both commercial success and academic opprobrium in almost equal measure (Preston 2006: 14; Labanyi 2007: 96).

If the Spanish Civil War was not a watershed in the sense of a before-and-after, it was certainly a high-water mark in terms of the tensions at issue, and the period from 1939 to the present has been a continuous attempt to react and recover from it. That response, as we have indicated, followed several clear phases. For the duration of the Franco regime, Spain was governed by both the victors of the conflict and their attitudes. After the death of Franco, the period known as the Transition attempted to pragmatically progress towards democracy unhindered by a painful and destructive process of recrimination and account-settling. The pact of forgetting was, as Preston indicated, a necessary part of that process. The victory of the PSOE under Felipe González in 1982 was seen as a sign of the success of that process, further confirmed when under his leadership Spain joined the European Community, thus ending a sense of isolation and exclusion that had lasted virtually since the Counter-Reformation. Despite their success and the apparent solidity of democracy, the Socialist Party of the 1980s and early 1990s (and their conservative opponents) were still products of the end of the regime and the mood of consensus that reigned during the Transition. The latter for them was not merely a historical reality, it was, as the historian Javier Tusell rightly says, 'un episodio biográfico ... un esfuerzo vital', an important episode in their biography, a part of their life's struggle (Tusell 2004: 40). Hence they too were governed by the pact of silence, a desire to keeping looking forward towards Europe, monetary union, and so on. The Socialist period came somewhat ingloriously to an end in 1996, mired in scandals that were a sign of their inability not only to cope with the freedoms and opportunities which their successful economic management had brought the country, but also to shake off certain shadier practices inherited from the previous regime.

While the new period ushered in by José María Aznar and his young team of conservatives in the *Partido Popular* (PP, People's Party) no longer had, as Tusell points out, that attachment to the past and experience of the Transition, the nature of their ideological roots made them, while not Francoists at heart, then at least not unsympathetic to some of the values and achievements of the regime. Thus there was no inclination or even any need felt to revisit old grievances and cure old wounds. When the initial moves from those quarters which would eventually promote the movement for the recovery of historical memory were made during the Aznar prime-ministership they received scant support, with the government refusing to fund exhumations and investigations and denying access to military archives (Davis 2005: 876–7).

It has therefore been the period of government of José Luis Rodríguez Zapatero when serious attempts have been undertaken to address, once and for all, the damage done by the Spanish Civil War to Spanish society. Part of the urgency in all of this is the fact that the body of people directly affected by these events is dwindling. The cause of the families of victims of violence and persecution during the Civil War is mainly being promoted by the grandchildren. Still, Zapatero's Socialist government is the first that, as a leftist party and one that is not bound to the *pacto de silencio*, can legitimately take up this cause and seek a resolution. Measures can be taken with greater confidence and magnanimity now. An example is the concession in 2008 of full Spanish citizenship to the surviving members of the International Brigades as final fulfilment of a promise made to them on their departure from Spain in October 1938 by Dolores Ibarruri, 'La Pasionaria', when she told them 'we shall not forget you' (Low 1992: 110). A previous offer in 1996 under Aznar's government had been half-hearted, as it required them to renounce their existing nationalities. Not surprisingly, most refused. Sadly, by 2008 there were only 23 survivors able to accept the offer in person.

In the Spain of today, it is not merely the events themselves but the historical account of them which is undergoing revision. Reference has already been made to the right-wing revisionism which, though dismissed by the majority of historians, is seen by many as part of 'the real coming of age of Spain's democratic culture' (Graham 2005: 146). This affects the historiography not only of the Civil War but also of that other historical high-light of the last 70 years, the Transition. In particular there is increasing debate on the conflicting narratives on the success of the process, depending on whether priority is given to the role of socioeconomic factors from the 1960s onwards, the role of key elite figures, such as the King or Adolfo Suárez, or to the often undervalued part played by civil society. Above all, as Pérez Serrano observes, one can detect a historiographical trend towards a mythification of the agents of the Transition as well as an idealization of its political outcome as represented by the parliamentary monarchy, understandable given the scarcely exemplary nature of preceding regimes which makes the post-Franco era appear to stand out as 'the great collective success of all Spaniards' (2007: 71).

It is beyond the scope and remit of the present book to give these issues the attention they deserve. Its aim within the space available is to provide a general overview of the events that have shaped Spain's history since the end of the Civil War, without sacrificing too much detail or complexity on the way, and drawing as far as possible on the best and most relevant historical research. However, the sheer vastness of the latter has necessitated considerable selectivity. The account will follow a necessary chronological order and the chapters will respect the periodization that has become fairly standard in most accounts of Spain's history, not out of academic laziness but because its enduring relevance would make any alternative approach seem wilfully idiosyncratic. However, rather than a straightforward chronological narrative, I have attempted to incorporate a thematic approach for the separate sections. This has the inevitable effect of producing some repetition which I have tried to keep to a minimum. Likewise, though chronological, I have tried to avoid the accusation of a 'unidirectional' or teleological account which gives an impression of historical inevitability to the events. The conventional view of Spain's successful emergence from a dark past to its current, if not problem-free, certainly impressive and generally optimistic present, can tend to lead to such a mechanistic account. The narrative framework of the book with the Civil War as both genesis and nemesis of Spain's current historical situation is, hopefully, a corrective to such simplistic approaches.

1

SPAIN'S DARK DECADES, 1939–59

1.1 Introduction

The regime that emerged at the end of the Spanish Civil War in 1939 had the unusual characteristic of being not a new post-conflict administration but rather a continuation of a government, illegitimate in every way, that had been constituted during the conflict itself. The Francoist state, an alternative to the legitimate government of the Spanish Second Republic, had been declared by the military rebels themselves by the Decree of 21 September 1936, according to which Franco assumed all the powers of the New State (Carr 1986: 259). Moreover, Franco, by clever political manoeuvring, had made sure that his hold on power would not be temporary. He had been declared 'Head of Government of the Spanish State', but his supporters had made sure to remove the words 'for the duration of the war' that appeared in the original draft document. Gloomily but correctly his military colleagues predicted that, like a true *africanista*, once in power he would never relinquish it (Graham 2005: 71). As his military dominance asserted itself, it was boosted by gradual recognition by foreign powers. This had begun in August 1937 when the Vatican had recognized the Nationalist government and sent an ambassador. Legislation even began before eventual military victory. In March 1938 it had actually 'passed' a Labour Charter, the first of his eventual seven 'Fundamental Laws', in which workers' rights and the principles of the Spanish Falange organization were outlined. The regime's origin in conflict partly explains why, after 1939, it continued on the war through a violent campaign of repression. In fact, the

7

war was not officially declared over and martial law lifted until 17 April 1948.

Franco's vision was to rescue Spain from its enemies and restore it to its former glory, which Francoist ideology, essentially a form of National Catholicism, located in the sixteenth and seventeenth centuries. The fact that those 'enemies' were Spaniards too did not alter his determination to eliminate them. He had no interest in reconstitution since such 'a "healing of wounds" went against the logic of the victors' determination to "purify" Spain' (Richards 1998: 27). As Carolyn Boyd puts it, '[b]y codifying and sacralising a particular interpretation of a particular moment in the Spanish past, National Catholicism invalidated divergence from that model as heretical and "anti-national"' (Boyd 1997: 235).

Thus, the post-war years were a prolonged period of conflict in which the victors attempted to consolidate their victory and seek a legitimacy for their role other than that of force or the 'legitimacy of conquest' (Carr 1986: 259). Franco's victory was so comprehensive and the extent of his powers so absolute that one might have thought, given his undoubted belief in Spanish nationalism and the unity of the state, that this might have led him to some attempt at national reconciliation – in the words of Salvador de Madariaga, 'to forge a united nation in the crucible of grief' (1942: 421) – but instead it merely 'meant the opportunity to impose absolute political control and a series of unilateral policies developed on an individual and ad hoc basis rather than according to any fully conceived grand design or plan' (Payne 1987: 231). Any possible return to normality was complicated by the reality of a major international conflict in the form of the Second World War on its doorstep, one in which Franco, contrary to the myth of his propagandists, would eagerly seek to participate to his best advantage, but unfortunately on the wrong side.

Nonetheless, the success of the Franco regime was its ability to evolve and adapt to changing circumstances, especially on the international front. Broadly, it can be viewed as spanning an arc, with its high point being the year 1959. In the initial period the prevailing ideology is that of autarchy and, while Franco was noted for a lack of any strong ideological views, autarchy appealed to his fundamentally military, authoritarian spirit. In this period, the main groupings in the Francoist camp, or 'families' as they were known, i.e. the Army, the Church and the fascist party, the Falange, with varying degrees of dominance, held sway, though always under Franco's overarching control. After 1957, Spain's move towards neo-capitalism under the guidance of the group known as the technocrats and the changes they helped institute would initiate, albeit not intentionally, both Spain's irreversible journey towards democracy and modernity, and at the same time, the steady, slow decline of the regime.

1.2   The Caudillo Digs In

Franco's aims immediately after the war were threefold: one was to consolidate the regime through a process of institutionalization; another was to root out the vestiges of the enemy, seen as 'anti-Spain', i.e. the supporters of the Republican cause; and the third was to pursue territorial and imperial aims by capitalizing on his alliance with Hitler and Mussolini. However, all of these aims were subsumed within the overall aim of maintaining himself in power.

Franco's emergence at the end of the Civil War as supreme leader with powers that exceeded 'any Spanish ruler since Fernando VII' (Payne 1967: 25) was not without controversy. Many of his senior army colleagues wished him to step down and return Spain to a monarchist system that they saw as an 'authentically Spanish form of government' (Payne 1987: 328). While up to the end of the Second World War Franco could plausibly argue that the time was not right, after 1945 this could no longer be sustained. Part of his strategy was to actively encourage a cult of personality which portrayed him as the messianic saviour of Spain, a strategy in which most of the Church hierarchy was happy to collude, though with some notable exceptions (Lannon 1987: 204–6). The Church's support of Franco is understandable. The modernizing zeal of the Second Republic undoubtedly went further than necessary in its anti-clerical reform and, similarly, the barbaric attacks by Republican extremists on the clergy and church buildings is well-attested, yet it was less the random violence of a radical minority than the progressive loss of privileges that threw the Church and the rebels together. For the Church, therefore, Franco's victory signified the return to its former position of authority and influence in Spanish society and government (Lannon 1987: 218). In fact, under Franco the Church reaped advantages unmatched since the early nineteenth century (Callahan 2007: 183).

The management of his political allies was Franco's other great skill. Nowhere was this more evident than in his careful containment of the Falange. The early fascistization of the regime was principally the work of his brother-in-law, Ramón Serrano Suñer, an admirer of Mussolini's corporativist Italy and to a lesser extent Nazi Germany (Thomàs 2005: 169). However, while Franco shared this admiration and was especially drawn to Fascism's rhetoric of Empire, he inclined more towards an authoritarian regime rather than a totalitarian one, steeped less in Fascist doctrine than in the ideals of Spain's imperial past. While it suited him, however, Franco encouraged his Falangist supporters but he was careful to balance that encouragement with similar entreaties to other groupings to ensure that he neither lost their potential support nor that the power of the Falange threaten his own. It was this mixture of ruthless control and flexibility, an almost chameleonic quality allowing him to adapt to changing circumstances and the scope for playing one 'family' off against the other that gave Franco the context he needed to perpetuate himself in power.

1.3 The Nature of the Regime

There have been various attempts to define the nature of the Franco regime and these usually revolve around its links with

Fascism. Juan José Linz, in a seminal article, argued that Spain was neither a totalitarian nor a democratic system but rather an 'authoritarian' regime which he defined as one 'with limited, not responsible, political pluralism' (Linz 1976: 165). By this he meant regimes where the single party is not so much 'single' as 'unified', a grouping of tendencies in which there was 'some competition for power' (Linz 1976: 166). Linz was attempting to counter the rather facile equation between Francoism and Fascism. Stanley Payne agrees that Franco was never a ' "core fascist" or a genuine Falangist' and indeed in its first decade, his regime was 'much more violent, autocratic, and repressive in every respect' than more traditional models of Fascism such as Italy's (Payne 1999: 477). In a recent general study of Fascism, Kevin Passmore makes clear that while the Spanish Falange shared many of the characteristics of European Fascism it was just one component of the support base for Franco and 'circumstances in Spain ensured that authoritarian conservatives largely won out' (Passmore, 2002: 77). For Romero Salvadó the debate over the label given to Franco's regime can distract from the fact that its 'record of internal suppression … surpassed that of Hitler's Germany and Mussolini's Italy' (Romero Salvadó 2005: 186).

While to the outside the regime seemed like 'a simple monolith resting on police repression it was, like most authoritarian regimes, a Byzantine structure composed of the political groups … "clans" or "families" – that accepted the legitimacy of the dictator's rule' (Carr and Fusi 1981: 21). This inevitably made for certain compromises at the level of policy-making but it had the important advantage of preventing any individual group achieving the upper hand. For Linz, rather than an ideology, what characterized the regime was a distinctive mentality based on 'conservative interpretations of Catholic social doctrine' (Linz 1976: 169). Michael Richards, on the other hand, maintains that a Francoist ideology did exist, 'formed of a complex of traditions', and that this ideology 'systematically promoted certain meanings above others, redefining nation and state as a "purified" body and space'. For Franco, Catholicism was 'the crucible of nationality', the defining characteristic of 'true Spaniards' (Richards 1998: 18). Initially, the combination of National Catholicism (see **1.6**), which harked back to a glorious and seemingly immutable past, and Falangist ideas of a New State, primarily a rejection of the Second Republic and its post-Enlightenment values, allowed the regime to appear both traditional and modern at the same time. Indeed, Guy Hermet notes how the regime evolved from an initial counter-revolutionary movement against the Republic and its progressive reforms to a reactionary one, intent on exalting a mythical past, ending up as a form of authoritarian conservatism, content with minimal reforms all the better to consolidate the status quo (Hermet 1976: 322).

One of the distinctive features of the Franco regime was its longevity, which explains its evolution through differing phases and also its willingness to incorporate elements of different systems and ideologies in the interests precisely of ensuring such longevity. It is this combination of longevity and change which, for Edward Malefakis, distinguishes the Franco regime from comparable authoritarian systems. In his view, while the regime evolved over the years for purely pragmatic reasons, not out of any genuine liberalizing concern, the changes wrought were 'genuine and profoundly altered Spanish society' (Malefakis 2007: 251). And yet, those pragmatic, survival-ensuring changes were precisely what would lead to its eventual collapse, albeit not in Franco's lifetime.

1.4   Franco and the Second World War

The Second World War was important to Franco, but not because he felt an obligation to return any favours to Hitler for his aid during the Civil War. Franco certainly felt no solidarity with the cause of international Fascism, his priority being his own regime's survival, but collaboration with Hitler offered the possibility of advancing Spain's imperial ambitions. However, Franco would only enter the war on his own terms, much to

Hitler's annoyance, which he expressed in a letter to Mussolini, referring to an irresolute Spain which 'will only take sides once the outcome of the war is decided' (Preston 1995a: 437). Still, in the early stages of the war, Franco was eager to involve Spain, a step probably only averted by the two leaders' mutual antipathy and distrust (Preston 2008: 115–17). In March 1939 Spain had both signed a German–Spanish agreement and subscribed to the Anti-Comintern Pact (Leitz 1999: 135). During the course of the war Spain's stance moved from initial neutrality to 'non-belligerence' in 1940, to 'moral belligerency' the following year, to 'vigilant neutrality' by 1943.

The nearest Spain came to joining the war was in 1940, but luckily, during the famous meeting at Hendaye on 23 October, Franco's clumsy attempt to guarantee Spain's entry into the war in return for French Morocco was too much for Hitler, who was keen not to either alarm Italy, for whom Spain was a potential rival in the Mediterranean, nor the Vichy government in France (Carr 1986: 272). When the tide started to turn in 1942 with the entry of the USA into the war after the bombing of Pearl Harbor in 1941, the German defeat on the Russian front at Stalingrad, and allied victories in North Africa, Franco decided to put involvement on hold. Still, Spain's new 'moral belligerency' did allow it to send a volunteer force, the Blue Division, to the Russian front in Germany's aid. Workers were also 'volunteered' and shipped to work in German factories. Such volunteer activity had the double advantage for Franco of currying favour with the Germans should they still emerge as victors, while being 'formally deniable' in the event of an Allied victory (Preston 1995a: 439). Meanwhile, Franco was happy to benefit from the enticements of the Allies, such as Britain's provision of supplies and oil, with the aim of keeping Spain neutral (Tusell 2007: 42).

1.5   The Politics of Repression

At an international level, by the end of the world war, Spain was 'in almost complete diplomatic isolation, the political pariah of western Europe' (Payne 1967: 35). Its only allies were equally unsalubrious dictatorships such as Salazar's Portugal and Perón's Argentina. In 1946 France had closed its border and the UN had formally censured Spain and urged withdrawal of diplomats. Unfortunately, this method of punishing the regime 'also had the material effect of punishing most of those who had lost the Civil War' (Graham 2005: 136). Republican supporters had hoped that the Allied victory would mean the end for Franco. However, the country's reluctant non-belligerency eventually meant that Spain, while an outcast, was left alone. Even so, it was the fleeing Republican soldiers in France who helped create the maquis resistance there to German occupation and back home in Spain their fellow maquisards tried to maintain a guerrilla resistance, especially in the north and east of the country. However, the intense military control of the country throughout the 1940s exerted by Franco and the wavering support they received from a tired and threatened populace meant that no strong resistance movement took hold. Franco kept up the military pressure on the population until the end of the decade, and in the mid-1940s nearly half the State budget was invested in the forces of law and order (Preston 1995a: 549). As Mary Vincent notes, 'the *maquis* never came close to their aim of fomenting a general, popular rebellion against the regime … by 1949 a mute acceptance of the status quo characterized much of the population' (2007: 161).

Reconciliation after the war did not feature in Franco's plan. Instead he enacted a politics of revenge on a grand scale. This even took the form of retrospective legislation. A Law of Political Responsibilities was introduced in February 1939 according to which activities that were legal under the Republic were criminalized under the new regime and the punishments backdated to 1934. The law allowed someone to be convicted of 'serious passivity' towards the Republic (Balfour, 2000: 265). Approximately 500,000 people were accused under this law in the first six years of the New State (Graham 2005: 134). The country was divided between winners and losers and the former had free rein under the Political Responsibilities legislation to use the denunciation, without any great need to provide evidence, to seek revenge or simply settle old scores (Graham 2005: 135; Carr 1986: 258). The numbers of executions from 1939 to 1945 by the regime forces are variously set at between 28,000 and 200,000 (Fusi, 1985a: 79), with more recent accounts supporting the higher figure (Romero Salvadó 2005: 188; Richards 1998: 30; Preston 2006: 302), but most concur on the impossibility of knowing exact figures. What was certain in all cases was the mood of fear and petty vindictiveness that was felt throughout Spain. Nonetheless, this was not entirely mind-less violence on the part of the Francoist regime. It was inspired by an ideological purging of the country of those elements that corrupted the pure-Spanish identity in search of what Balfour terms 'the spiritual disinfection of Spain' (Balfour 2000: 266; Richards 1998: 16–17). These elements were deemed to be 'foreign', i.e. anti-Spanish, and included 'urban workers, the rural landless, regional nationalists, liberal professionals, and "new" women – groups that challenged the established order culturally, politically or economically' (Graham 2005: 129).

The repression was also intellectual, moral and social. In 1938 a Press Law had introduced censorship and control over publications and journalists. A Special Tribunal for the Repression of Freemasonry and Communism set up in March 1940 carried out a purge of artists, journalists and teachers. The clergy became once again a powerful force in society, able to demand that Catholic morality and ritual be upheld on pain of denunciation to the authorities. Priests were especially active in the ideological purging of the educational sectors (Lannon 1995: 276). In the same way, the middle-class members of the *Sección Femenina*, the female wing of the Falange, could exert similar moral and even political control. As Vincent notes, 'its members penetrated society, furthering the state's knowledge of its least visible citizens, gathered information on behalf of the authorities, as did the purge commissions and other institutions of repression' (2007: 172; Graham 2005: 136).

An additional repression occurred at the level of Spain's historic regions. These were the regions that had been given statutes of autonomy by the Second Republic. Catalonia received its Statute in 1932, the Basque Country in December 1935 and Galicia was on the point of approving its statute when war broke out. Given that regional autonomy was one of the motivations for the rebellion against the Republican government it is not surprising that, once in power, the Franco regime should immediately set about revoking the statutes. The regime attempted to eliminate all traces of cultural identity in these regions. The language was prohibited, flags and emblems were banned, public signs, street-names and monuments were destroyed or Castilianized. In Catalonia, notices were erected exhorting the populace to 'Speak Spanish! Speak the Language of the Empire!' Elements within the Church in these regions played an important role in defending the regional identity. In 1947, at a religious ceremony at Montserrat, the Catalan language was used and the flag displayed before a gathering of 70,000 people. The future leader of the Catalan region, Jordi Pujol, started his pro-Catalan militancy within a Christian organization, *Crist i Catalunya*, which led to him being imprisoned for seven years (McRoberts 2001: 41–2).

Something similar occurred in the Basque region, which 'was subjected to a regime of terror with no parallel in its history … even innocuous aspects of popular culture, such as dance and music, were subjected to suspicion, inquiry and proscription' (Conversi 1997: 80–1). The culture and language were stamped on and the promotion of nationalism, which in the eyes of the regime was synonymous with separatism, was rewarded with imprisonment and sometimes execution. Furthermore, as Conversi points out, 'the oligarchic bourgeoisie sided with Franco, thereby stamping a sinister class mark on state repression' (Conversi 1997: 81). As we will see, this bourgeois collaborationism, along with that of the official Church in the Basque region, would be stimuli for the emergence of the Basque separatist organization ETA in the late 1950s (see **2.13**). The Church in the Basque country, like the Catholic hierarchy throughout Spain, sided with the regime. But in 1960, 339 Basque priests, at considerable risk to their own safety, issued a manifesto denouncing the regime's policy as 'reactionary and anti-human to the point of genocide' (Conversi 1997: 95). These forms of 'cultural genocide', in the words of the Catalan sociologist Salvador Giner (McRoberts 2001: 41), would breed a resentment that would underpin the movements of protest against the regime throughout the 1950s and 1960s, though in very different ways. In Catalonia the expression would be mainly cultural, whereas in the Basque Country it would take the form of terrorist violence.

1.6   Franco's Families

In many ways it was the variety within the Nationalist side that permitted Franco to dominate them. No group achieved sufficient grass-roots support to mount a challenge to Franco's personal leadership. This was made easier by the tensions that existed between and even within the different groups. The Falange did not really like their imposed leader, Franco's brother-in-law, Ramón Serrano Suñer, who was not even a true Falangist or *camisa vieja* but merely the intermediary with Franco in the early days. Even between Franco and Serrano there was deep suspicion, with Franco wary of his brother-in-law's ambitions and perhaps envious of his charm and sharp mind (Ashford Hodges 2000: 178). Serrano would eventually fall foul of the Caudillo, not least due to an extra-marital affair. The Army, in turn, resented the prominence accorded the Falangists within the regime and leading generals from the start were bent on destroying both it and Serrano. There was mutual antagonism between Falangists and Monarchists, with the latter resenting the former's hold on the regime which blocked a return of the traditional monarchy. The Falange's implication in the corruption of Spain's thriving black market in the 1940s added to its unpopularity with other groups. But even the Falange had divisions between the *camisas viejas* ('old shirts', i.e. members of the Falange from before the war) and the 'new shirts', those who had joined at the time of the war or after as a way of collaborating with the regime. Franco was happy to use the Falange for his own purposes, and these included certain key organizational tasks, such as marshalling the labour movement, both workers and management, through the Spanish Trade Union Organization (*Organización Sindical Española*) and its 'vertical' trade unions, as well as putting them in charge of the media and the state bureaucracy.

In the early stages of the regime, Franco also exploited the Falange's hostility to the Monarchists, who presented perhaps the greatest threat to his continuity in power. The Monarchist camp was divided between rival dynasties, the Carlists and the Alfonsists, and even within each of these there were rival contenders and alternative options which Franco would not be slow to use to his advantage.

It was, in fact, a clash between several of the main factions, Monarchists, Army and Falange, in the Basque village of Begoña in August 1942 that precipitated Serrano's downfall. At a religious service to honour the fallen soldiers of the Carlist militia, the *requetés*, presided over by a Monarchist Army general, Varela, some Falangists threw bombs, one of which injured over one hundred people. Varela's subsequent complaints tried to break the hold of the Falange but Franco was bent on reconciling the two. At a gathering later in the month, he 'praised the military spirit of the Falange and the Falangist virtues of the Army' (Preston 1995a: 467). Varela represented a movement within the Army that would press for early restoration of the Monarchy. Aware of this and resentful of his attempt to force his hand, Franco resisted, and accepted Varela's resignation but balanced it by dismissing Serrano from his post of leader of the Falange and Foreign Minister. He also approved the execution of the bomb-thrower.

The incident, described by Preston as possibly 'the most serious internal crisis faced by Franco' (1993: 466), is also a good illustration of how, with a blend of ruthlessness and caution, Franco would manage the three main groupings, the Army, the Falange and the Monarchists, on which he would rely; these, along with the Church, would form the pillars of his regime and, depending on the political climate and international political scene, he would favour one or the other. Hence, the early predominance of the Spanish Fascist party the Falange and its leader, Serrano, made sense when it looked as if Spain's future lay in an alliance with Germany and Italy. Aside from the internal tensions between the groups and Franco's feelings about Serrano, the change in the fortunes of the Axis powers from 1942 onwards made practical and therefore inevitable Serrano's displacement as leading light of the regime.

Although, as Preston notes, Franco 'may have had some emotional commitment to the Falange, it did not undermine his capacity for ruthless calculation' (1993: 548), and his instinctive and abiding allegiance was to the Army. Hence, in the early stages of the regime, even when the Falange held sway, the core of his government was in the control of the Army. The Army dominated in the key areas of defence and interior, whereas the Falange was mainly in charge of party organization, labour relations and agriculture, as well as retaining control of the press. While the Falange permeated the organizational apparatus of the state with its anthem *Cara al sol* still being heard in the 1960s (Preston 1995b: 37), its political and ideological influence waned after 1945 and came to a virtual end in the cabinet reshuffle of 1957.

Ideologically, the waning of Falangism as a valuable doctrine on which to base the regime explained the gradual move to closer allegiance with the Catholic Church. National Syndicalism, Spain's equivalent of Nazism, gave way to National Catholicism, a set of values which had its roots in the Primo de Rivera dictatorship of the 1920s and which Boyd describes as more 'a mentality than a formal ideology, it blended the reactionary cultural values of traditional Spanish Catholicism with strident authoritarian nationalism and a smattering of corporatist ideas of mixed lineage' (1997: 168). Like the other Francoist families, the Church was never allowed to overshadow the state apparatus controlled by Franco, but from the mid-1940s it was undoubtedly the case that the 'entire regime, from Franco downwards, was committed to an authoritarian political model in which Church and state stood together against all subversive alternatives' (Lannon 1995: 277).

As was so often the case, a strategy adopted by Franco for purely personal reasons ultimately redounded to the benefit of Spain. The denial of power to any one group in particular was to ensure Franco's position was never in jeopardy, but the frustration of the Falangist ideal was ultimately to the benefit of Spain since 'a mass party on Falangist lines would ... have prevented the gradual emergence of a quasi-pluralistic society' (Carr 1986: 266). Each sector of his supporters, Monarchists, Army, the Church, the conservative classes, the Falange, wanted their own political structure either established or restored. Franco ensured that none attained the upper hand and thus could exploit them to greatest effect. Advised by Serrano Suñer, he had already merged the Carlists and the Falange, the only two groups with some sort of mass appeal, into one body, the FET (*Falange Española Tradicionalista y de las JONS*), popularly known as the National Movement (*Movimiento Nacional*), through the Decree of Unification in 19 April 1937, under the leadership of Serrano Suñer, but this had less to do with strengthening the Falange than defusing the constituent groups and bringing them all ultimately, via Serrano, under Franco's own control (Preston 1995a: 266). Both Franco and Serrano were careful to ensure that, despite the importance conceded to the new single party, it was always to be subordinate to the State, represented by the Caudillo himself (Thomàs 2005: 171). The FET became responsible for the 'political indoctrination of the population and for providing the political infrastructure of the entire system' (Payne 1987: 238), but the more left-wing social aspects of its ideology, such as were included in the 1938 Labour Charter, were ignored in so far as they might conflict with the values of the right-wing elite on whom Franco depended (Payne 1967: 25).

1.7 Institutionalization of the Regime

Despite Franco's absolute powers at the end of the war, and the legitimacy which victory in conflict bestowed, the regime soon felt the need to secure that legitimacy in a set of institutions. This would become increasingly important both as Spain needed to seek recognition from the international community but also to reassure those sectors in society who expected some semblance of civil society to re-emerge after the conflict. For that reason, as Carr notes, 'the constitutional theoreticians of the regime were to talk of a "constituent dictatorship" which would adjust political institutions to the needs of a changing society' (1986: 259).

To this end, a Law of the Cortes (Parliament) in 1942, the second of the eventual seven fundamental laws, reintroduced the parliamentary body, albeit devoid of any real powers as its members (or *procuradores* as they were called) were either *ex officio* delegates of the administration or nominated by the Caudillo himself. In 1945 a *Fuero de los Españoles* (Charter of Rights) was passed outlining Spaniards' 'rights and duties', although as one observer noted, there were rather more of the latter than the former. These initial 'constitutional' measures were little more than cosmetic. According to the *Fuero del Trabajo* (Labour Charter) passed in 1938 Franco could bypass the Cortes should he want to, though this was rarely necessary. Payne called the 1945 Charter 'another dab of icing on the cake of dictatorship' (1967: 34).

Alfonso XIII, exiled in Rome and gravely ill, had on 15 January 1941 abdicated in favour of his third son (the others renouncing their claim for health reasons), Don Juan, and died a month later. Franco teased the heir with offers of a restoration, but they were insincere and politically motivated (Anson: 167–8). From 1943, Franco was pressed from various quarters within his movement to restore the monarchy. Four attempts in 1943 were met with refusal and reprisals against those who were behind them. There was no question of him relinquishing a position which, on one level, he genuinely felt that he had been chosen by God to fill and, on the other, he was clearly relishing (Ellwood 1994: 134–5). His eventual acceptance of the restoration was a result, as always, of the political circumstances and its details were distinctly to Franco's advantage. The person behind the proposal was the man who from 1941 onwards would replace Serrano as Franco's principal adviser, Luis Carrero Blanco (Preston 2004: 36). The challenge for Franco would be to, on the one hand, legitimize the regime, satisfying monarchist aspirations but, on the other, avoid ceding his personal power, above all to someone he trusted so little as Don Juan, the legitimate heir.

Hence, the 1947 Law of Succession determined that Spain was a kingdom but also that Franco was Head of State with powers to propose his 'successor' as King or Regent. Effectively it enshrined Franco as Head of State for life. Don Juan ruined his chances to eventually succeed Franco when he rejected the law in his 'Estoril Manifesto' on 7 April 1947. However, he did try to mount a challenge, and even in August 1948 came close to a pact with the exiled Socialist leader Indalecio Prieto, but in view of Franco's unassailable position he conceded to a meeting with the *Caudillo* on 25 August to discuss Juan Carlos completing his education in Spain, thereby effectively consolidating the law.

The 1947 Law of Succession came as the fifth of the 'fundamental laws' that would eventually constitute the Francoist constitution. The others had been the Labour Charter (1938), the Constitutive Law of the Cortes (1943), the Charter of Rights and the Law on National Referendum (both 1945). Subsequent Fundamental Laws would be the Law of the Principles of the Movement (1958) and finally the Organic Law of State (1967).

1.8   The Hunger Years

In addition to institutionalizing the regime, more immediate challenges faced its leadership. Spain's economic problems in the post-war period were threefold. One was the damage wrought by the Civil War itself, though this was not as bad as might be assumed, since the country's agricultural and industrial base was relatively intact. Carr described the Spanish economy as not so much 'in ruins as was the Russian economy after the Civil War of 1919–21' as merely 'run down' (Carr and Fusi 1981: 49; Tusell 2007: 82). As an economy still largely reliant on agriculture, which at the end of the war employed over half of the active population, Spain suffered both natural and man-made obstacles. Though exaggerated by the regime to excuse underproduction, drought was a problem, especially in 1944–5, but political isolation and autarchy meant an inability to import fertilizers, as a result of which the production of cereals, which accounted for 40 per cent of Spain's cultivated land, stagnated at 25 per cent of pre-war levels throughout the 1940s, surviving on imports until the first good crop in 1951. In addition, the sector was starved of investment as efforts were channelled into industrial revitalization (Carr 1986: 254; Payne 1987: 386; Tusell 2007: 86).

The other problem was Spain's international isolation as a result of objections to Franco's regime. This excluded Spain from the benefits of Europe's post-war economic Recovery Programme, the Marshall Plan of 1948. The UN boycott lasted from 1946 to 1953 and meant that international trade formed a mere 5 per cent of Spain's GNP in 1950 (Salmon 1995: 2). Finally, there was the added factor of the regime's economic incompetence. As Ellwood notes, that 'the economy did not show signs of recovery once hostilities had ceased had more to do with the political choices made by the Franco regime than with the economic structures themselves' (1994: 115).

The solution sought by the regime was autarchy or economic self-sufficiency: state control of capitalism, import substitution, interventionism and protectionism. While this policy might be justified as a short-term response to a crisis, and certainly it was in many ways the only response Spain could adopt in a situation of international isolation and ostracism, it became clear that for Franco it was the most appropriate policy for an 'imperial military state' (Carr, 1980: 156). Towards the end of the war, he was firm in his belief that autarchy was the key to 'full-scale economic well-being' (Preston 1995a: 298). There was also a strong ideological motivation. International hostility was deliberately exploited by the regime to justify internal control, a necessary form of social quarantine from pernicious foreign influence that would aid Spain's return to a state of social 'health' and, to this extent, autarchy was 'seen as not simply an economic response but also as political and cultural' (Richards 1998: 22–3).

Franco's willingness to spend half of his budget on maintaining high levels of militarization, especially during the Second World War, and pandering to the socio-economic elite that had backed him in the conflict meant that the needs of the people took second place. In the aftermath of the war priority was given to returning land expropriated during the Republic, and there was so little investment in agriculture that in the 1940s the population in many parts was close to famine. Food shortages had a devastating impact on the health of the population. In the 1940–5 period there were '200,000 deaths from malnutrition and disease ... pulmonary tuberculosis carried off at least 25,000 a year while in 1941, there were 53,307 registered deaths from diarrhea and enteritis, 4,168 from typhoid fever and 1,644 from typhus' (Payne 1987: 252).

As a result of Spain's policy of economic self-sufficiency it was unable to benefit from foreign loans and investment that would have rescued its struggling economy. At the end of the Civil War per capita income was at nineteenth-century levels. Rationing was introduced in 1939, which was a source of widespread corruption and profiteering. Consumption of meat in 1950 was half its 1930s level and only attained pre-war levels in the 1970s (Sánchez Marroyo: 308; Preston 1995b: 46). Spain's isolation meant that, while the devastation wrought by the Civil War was less than that of the world war on its European neighbours, reconstruction from 1945 onwards was substantially slower (Tusell 2007: 83)

Ideological dogma lay behind much of the economic mishandling. The glorification of the farmer as the archetypal Spaniard led to a misguided emphasis on a return to traditional methods and crops such as wheat as a means of preserving the social status quo in the countryside until the 1960s (Shubert 1990: 209). Even in the 1950s the discourse of the regime still reflected a view 'which considered agriculture less as an economic activity than as a way of life that supported patriotic peasant families immune to the dissolvent influences of the great cities where the working-class supporters of the Republic were concentrated' (Carr 1986: 256). No wonder, then, that agricultural production was slow, failing to reach its late 1920s level until the end of the 1950s (Salmon 1995: 3). These were man-made failures that the regime's propaganda chose to blame on the 'persistent drought'. In respect of industry, the regime did see the need to promote modernization and, to this end, in 1941 set up the Italian-inspired *Instituto Nacional de Industria* (National Institute for Industry) a state investment and holding company, offering incentives to business, encouraging new enterprises and giving support to heavy industry. However, by 1950 manufacturing industry was still a small part of the economy, employing under 20 per cent of its working population, while agriculture accounted for 50 per cent (Salmon 1995: 3). The autarchical framework which meant that the domestic industrial sector depended on a small and poor internal consumer market had a further restrictive effect on industrial production.

Such economic mismanagement led to a thriving black market, as a result of which in 'a context of grinding poverty and near starvation, spectacular fortunes were amassed, often by Falangists and government officials' (Preston 1995a: 466). Food shortages led to rationing and those producers and managers of the system, members of the Francoist oligarchy or the party system, were the first to benefit. At a lower level, too, the shortages and the black market benefited the regime by encouraging the populace to conform. Families with links to the regime could be favoured by the functionaries who distributed aid and cooperation with the authorities was often the price to pay for receipt of help or charity. Rationing became an 'added layer of repression' as Republicans and their families had to resort to the black market to survive (Richards 1998: 139).

1.9　Opposition Inside and Out

Opposition to the regime took the form of both political organization and popular resistance. Until the late 1950s both of
these were in a fairly parlous state. Outside Spain Republican
political formations, defeated in the Civil War, carried on in
exile and ran clandestine operations within Spain. Within Spain
a more moderate, ambiguous opposition was formed by monarchists, either supporters of Don Juan or some more authoritarian monarchical alternative to Franco. There were occasional
attempts at cooperation between these two groupings,
Republicans and Monarchists, most famously in the 1962
Munich affair (see **2.10**), but in the 1940s and 1950s the regime
was unassailable.

At a popular level, serious opposition was unthinkable as the
priority for the vast majority of Spaniards was basic survival.
Nonetheless, as Richards shows, there was some evidence of
'rejection of the dictatorship by the populace', though it tended
to take the form of 'a semi-underground spirit of defiance and
cynicism' which showed through in 'popular stories, refrains,
rumour-mongering and complaints' (1998: 156). Later, during
the 1950s, the workers and university students would become a
focus for protest that would escalate in the following decade.

As with the maquisards, the mistake of the Republican opposition in the early post-war period was to fail to recognize the
extent of popular support the rebellion and ensuing Nationalist
state enjoyed for both reasons of principle and practical survival
(Richards 1998: 21; Preston 1995b: 3–4). The 1940s were a
period dominated by the fundamental aim of survival, so the
majority of the population lacked the stomach for a fight. As
Carr put it, 'a proletariat in a police state concerned above all
with scraping a living in difficult circumstances is unlikely to be
the vanguard of a revolution' (1986: 274; Richards 1998: 24).
Furthermore, the divisions among the Republican forces that
had undermined their prosecution of the war were carried on
into the post-war period. Those Republicans who escaped into
exile were in their own way as uninterested as Franco in national

reconciliation and carried on abroad the same petty ideological squabbles that had undermined the struggle against Franco (Esenwein and Shubert 1995: 271). It delayed the formation of a Republican government in exile until 1945, by which time Fascism had already been defeated at an international level and the looming battle was against Communism. The elusive accommodation between the Republicans and Socialists and their Communist rivals was finally quashed with the advent of the Cold War. Suddenly the Communists were a 'liability' (Carr 1986: 275) and Franco's position became, as a staunch ally of the USA in the fight against Communism, consolidated.

The Monarchists posed a moderate threat to the regime, especially in the early years, when many of Franco's senior army colleagues expected a change of power once the war was over. American attitudes would eventually change with the arrival of Truman in the presidency after Roosevelt's dealth in 1945. Truman was no admirer of Franco but he was an ardent anti-Stalinist and blocked the latter's attempt to facilitate a return of a predictedly weak Monarchy at the close of the war (Anson 1994). The dictator's relation with Alfonso XIII in exile had been deferential at first but then after the capture of Madrid, dismissive. Don Juan had also been kept at a distance, refused permission to enter the war but assured in 1942 that the intention was to restore the Monarchy when the time was right (Payne 1987: 298).

However, as Don Juan had revealed in his Lausanne Manifesto in 1945, calling for Franco to abandon power and promising a broad range of democratic freedoms, his version of a liberal monarchy was too much of a risk to those in the Nationalist camp. Franco was able to reassure them that the Monarchy would be restored in Spain but that it would be one based not on dynastic legitimacy but on the principles of the regime (Payne 1987: 347), for which an appropriate candidate might be Juan Carlos, the son of Don Juan. Despite challenges such as the Lausanne Manifesto, and even one occasion when 458 members of the regime's political elite, including 20 former ministers and the presidents of the five leading banks signed a letter of support for Don Juan (Anson 1994: 248), monarchism never really mounted a serious challenge to Franco. The victory of the Truman doctrine meant that international backing was absent and, in addition, the Monarchists themselves were divided, not only between the rival factions, Carlists and Alfonsists, but also between those among the latter who supported an authoritarian regime, albeit headed by a king, and those who favoured the traditional liberal democracy seemingly promised by Don Juan. As usual, Franco was skilled at nurturing, if not completely satisfying, the hope of a future restoration and so keeping them all on side.

One group which would pose a problem for the regime was the student body, steadily increasing in size and confidence as Spain grew in prosperity throughout the 1950s. Most students were children of comfortable families, a situation determined by the strict rules of attendance that barred any who had to work to support their studies (Blaye 1976: 186), so youthful rebellion against conservative parents combined with growing political awareness. A liberal, reformist Catholic Joaquín Ruiz Giménez had taken over as Education Minister in 1951 but his period saw increasing disturbances in the universities where the student body were dominated by the Falange through the official union, the SEU (*Sindicato Español Universitario*). There were increasing calls from discontented students for a Student Congress independent of the SEU. In February 1956 a clash between supporters of the Congress and members of the Falangist Youth Front (*Frente de Juventudes*) ended with a young Falangist being shot, it is believed, by one of his own. The incident was a major political crisis in a country where increasingly the regime promoted its success based on peace and stability provided by Franco and signalled the university campus as a site of permanent tension for the regime throughout Spain right up to the 1970s. The protesting students comprised different groups, Communists, Socialists and Christian Democrats, and the incident led to the growth of a more confident student protest movement that saw its power to influence internal politics (Tusell 2007: 126). Franco had been forced into another instance of even-handed retribution, dismissing both the liberal Education Minister and the Minister of the National Movement.

The 1950s also saw increasing protests, strikes and disturbances in both industry and agriculture (Blaye 1976: 188–9). It was only a matter of time, especially once the hard years of the 1940s were overcome, that working-class passivity towards the hierarchical Falangist system would end, despite the undoubted though paltry benefits that the system's 'social paternalism' conferred, such as job security (Carr and Fusi 1981: 138). The official trade unions were not intended as organs of representation but rather mechanisms of control. Throughout the regime's existence strikes were illegal. Even the word was banned, substituted by the euphemistic 'labour conflict'. Throughout the 1950s the regime's mixture of pandering to the individual worker, denying collective rights and strict police control kept protest to a minimum. The Barcelona transport boycott over a rise in fares in 1951 and the Asturian miners' strike in 1958 were isolated examples of high-profile incidents. Nonetheless, steady pressure led to the government relenting and introducing a Law on Collective Bargaining in 1958. This and the new economic direction undertaking in the late 1950s would set the scene for increasing worker unrest throughout the following decade.

1.10   Society under Franco

At the level of society, Franco's triumph was the victory of traditional middle-class, Catholic values (Carr and Fusi 1981: 82). This in itself was a check to the advance of true Falangist principles. Minor tensions arose in the early years when the Spanish Primate, Cardinal Gomá, criticized the totalitarian drift of the regime in 1940, but in general Falangist principles were compatible with those of 'anti-liberal social Catholicism' (Carr 1986: 261). Certainly Falangism had no real support base in Spain and Franco had a greater affinity with reactionary groups such as the clergy and landowners than with the forces of radical social change. The original Falange of José Antonio Primo de Rivera would have been scarcely compatible with the ruling elites that supported Franco and sought to rebuild Spanish society and the economy after the Civil War. After 1942, the Catholic ACNP (National Association of Propagandists) held the upper hand and managed to dominate political and intellectual circles in the same way that Opus Dei would a decade later. It was responsible for the negotiation of the 1953 Concordat with the Vatican which gave Franco control over the nomination of Spanish bishops. With few exceptions (the young Basque and Catalan clergy), the hierarchy of the Church threw in its lot with the regime and granted it the moral legitimacy it badly needed.

Still, the early years of the regime saw society dominated by Falangist principles. Its symbolism and insignias, the yoke and arrows, were prominent in all towns and villages. Its movements governed the young and women through the Falangist Youth and the *Sección Femenina*, founded by Pilar, the sister of José Antonio Primo de Rivera. But, as Vincent makes clear, the Falange lost any significant mobilizing force once the war was over; its role became that of policing and administering but never agitating the population. The Falange, operating as the National Movement, the regime's single party, brought a new militaristic discipline to the organization of the state and increasingly this organizational element took precedence. 'As the single party expanded, fascist credentials became relatively unimportant' (Vincent 2007: 163). Spanish society thus became one where Catholic values dominated, the National Movement imposed administrative order on behalf of the state and in which the governing elites continued with their privileges, often joining the Movement as a way of gaining 'influence and preferment' (Vincent 2007: 163).

Censorship and propaganda were the regime's instruments for inculcating the values of the regime and insulating its people from pernicious foreign ideas. This was done by a mixture of shock tactics and sentimental glorification of Francoist values.

Spaniards were regularly reminded through government publications, graphically illustrated, of the atrocities committed by the 'red hordes' (Esenwein and Shubert 1995: 271). Midway through the war the propaganda machine of the new state swung into action and Franco was promoted as a kindly father figure who saved Spain from Communism (Preston 1995a: 289). The creation in 1942 of the NO-DO (*Noticiarios y Documentales*), the state-sponsored news broadcasts shown before every film, *Radio Nacional* in 1937 and, from the early 1960s, Spanish television, ensured that Spaniards were fed a constant diet of reports glorifying the regime's progress, usually in the face of a hostile international community, and escapist entertainment. The latter included historical dramas focusing on glories of Spain's past as well as traditional Hollywood westerns, musicals and romances, all rigorously controlled by the censor through the useful, though often clumsily applied mechanism of dubbing. In some cases lovers or married couples were recast as siblings in such a way that relationships escaped the scandal of adultery while seemingly transgressing an even graver social taboo (Hopewell 1986: 38).

For one important sector of Spanish society, women, the Franco regime signified a major step backwards. They became subject to a form of Catholic traditionalism which relegated them 'to a sphere defined as narrowly, and perhaps more so, than the women's sphere of the nineteenth century' and in which they 'could aspire to marriage and motherhood but little more' (Shubert 1990: 214). This was as much about economics as about morality. The regime was concerned about depopulation after the war and operated pronatalist policies, a 1941 law actually stating that the Spanish state 'wishes and will obtain many healthy and robust children' (Harrison and Corkill 2004: 27–8; Nash, 1994). But women also became subject to an ideology that deliberately fomented ignorance and, in particular, were discouraged from education (Richards 1998: 173). A restored Civil Code of 1889 and Criminal Code of 1870 made them legally dependent on their husbands and legal treatment of marital misdemeanours remained flagrantly discriminatory until 1958. All single women, including widows without children between the ages of 18 and 35, had to complete the six months' social service organized by the Falange's women's section aimed at preparing them for 'their new role as rebuilders of the Spanish nation, the dedicated, self-denying heart of the Catholic family and mainstay of Franco's deeply authoritarian patriarchal regime' (Brooksbank Jones 1997: 1–2). However, it is also the case that many women, unable to identify either with left-wing ideology or with the values of conservative patriarchy, found satisfaction in the alternative ideology offered by Falangism's combination of a programme of social justice and its ideals of patriotism and family values. The *Sección Femenina* encouraged some of its adherents to challenge the restrictions that Francoist society would have imposed on them. From this perspective, for example, St Teresa of Avila became a role model not as a traditional Catholic saint but as an exemplary revolutionary woman (Enders: 1999).

1.11   In from the Cold

It is hard to say how long the regime might have lasted had the hostility of the international community continued. What saved the Franco regime was the turn of international events prior to the outbreak of the Korean War in 1950. From being a pariah quasi-fascist state it became a potentially staunch anti-communist ally. The first signs came when the General Assembly of the United Nations in 1947 rejected a proposal from the USSR that could have led to direct action to remove Franco. France had reopened the border in February 1948 and later that year it and Great Britain negotiated trade deals with Spain. The following year most diplomatic relations had been restored. After intense lobbying, finally a loan of $25 million was negotiated with the Chase National Bank in 1949. The US military were by now eyeing Spain as a possible venue for bases and further loans followed. In addition the UN in November 1950 voted that ambassadors should return to Spain, undoing the 1946 resolution. In 1952 Spain joined UNESCO. Franco's ostracism was almost at an end. As usual Franco and his ministers took the credit, but international acceptance was mainly due to 'Spain's strategic value and to the consistency of Franco's anti-Communism' (Preston 1995a: 601).

By 1953 Franco would manage the double feat of a treaty with the USA over military bases, known as the Treaty of Madrid, and a Concordat with the Vatican. All at once the regime had gained international political and moral legitimacy. A ten-year boycott by the United Nations came to an end when Spain was admitted in 1955. The financial prize for allowing American bases on Spanish soil was worth approximately $625 million over six years (Balfour, 2000: 268). A more important prize was the future security of his regime. After signing the treaty with the Americans, Franco is reported to have said, 'Now I have won the Civil War' (Carr and Fusi 1981: 162).

Spain launched a diplomatic charm offensive, the high point of which was the visit by the US President Eisenhower in 1959. Franco was boosted especially by the propaganda coup of an embrace from Eisenhower at Madrid airport and 'overcome with emotion' (Preston 1995a: 681), but by this stage the relationship with the USA was only part of his plans. In fact with East–West tensions developing and with four American bases on Spanish soil, Franco was uneasy about his position on the front line of the Cold War battlefield and attempts were made to widen Spain's international links, even with the Communist bloc. Franco was waking up to the pragmatics of international relations although, worryingly, the new developments, far from giving him the encouragement to loosen his grip and open Spain up, had the effect of confirming the rightness of his stance all along (Ellwood 1994: 184).

1.12 Crisis and the End of Autarchy

On an economic level the 1950s represented the gradual liberalization of the system and the move away from autarchy. There was still no sign of Franco being moved, despite American pressure, to liberalize politically. This was seen in the 1951 cabinet reshuffle, where the presence of the Falange was reinforced, although, as usual for Franco, it was balanced by the appointment of a liberal Catholic and future focus for the Christian Democrat movement, Joaquín Ruiz Giménez, as Minister of Education. In addition, the apparent backing for the Falange was done in the full knowledge that politically the movement was a spent force and therefore their promotion at this stage both posed no risk and defused their potential displeasure at the American presence on Spanish territory (Preston 1995a: 614). The treaty with the USA in 1953 and the resulting cash inflow, a further more momentous cabinet reshuffle in 1957 that brought in a new generation of economic specialists, and finally the Stabilization Plan of 1959, were the landmarks of the decade that laid the ground for the economic miracle of the 1960s.

The principal feature of the decade was the reduction in state interventionism. Keynesian economics had led to an expansion of Western economies in general. In Spain the emphasis shifted to boosting its flagging industrial sector and abandoning the dominance of agriculture. By 1951 the industrial GDP was exceeding its agricultural counterpart and the watchword of the regime was now productivity (Martínez 2003: 82–3). Throughout the decade GDP rose at a steady 5 per cent and per capita income rose by 30 per cent (Sánchez Marroyo 2003: 321). Industrial production, aided by imports of raw material and machinery, doubled. One of the agreements signed with the USA in 1953 related to economic aid, and although not as beneficial as the Marshall Plan would have been, it still acted as a boost to foreign trade (Sánchez Marroyo 2003: 322). Nonetheless, this stimulated growth was still operating within a basically autarchic system and, as a result, was unsustainable in the long term, and the rampant growth of inflation led to a spate of strikes which, unfortunately, the Falangist ministers in charge tried to quell by offering massive and unaffordable wage rises (Blaye 1976: 195). To make matters worse, a chaotic scheme of public investment had been launched in 1953, funded not by taxes, but by newly created money (Sánchez Marroyo 2003: 323).

So it was the very growth of the economy and the impossibility for the autarchic system to contain it that necessitated the radical change that was to follow. It is not entirely sure that Franco understood the need for the change and, under the guidance of Carrero Blanco, he was even contemplating a stricter application of autarchical principles (Payne 1987: 468). However, a new political elite was rising to prominence which would, luckily, persuade the dictator otherwise.

1.13   The Rise of Opus

After the moral, political and financial consolidation of the regime with the signings of the Concordat and the Treaty of Madrid in 1953, a battle for supremacy took place within the Francoist families between the Monarchists and the Falange. In 1954, Don Juan met once again with Franco in Cáceres, near the Portuguese border, and demanded an end to the restrictions on freedom still imposed by the regime. The result was a joint communiqué which 'recognised the hereditary rights to the throne of the Bourbon dynasty', but Franco was determined that this would not deflect him from retaining power under the terms of the 1947 Law of Succession and resisting any real move towards political liberalization (Preston 1995a: 637–8). The Monarchists, however, saw their cause in the ascendancy and were further boosted by the results of municipal elections in 1954 which strengthened their power base despite intimidation by members of the Falange against their supporters. Such conflict between the two leading groupings within his regime was entirely suited to Franco's purposes, ensuring as it always did that his personal position was never questioned and leaving him with the role he liked to play best, that of ultimate arbiter.

The crisis of the student protests in 1956 and the problems of the economy precipitated a cabinet shuffle in 1957 which saw the Falangists relegated to a small number of lowly posts, thus confirming their decline. This may have been prompted by Franco's irritation at an attempt the previous year made by one of their leaders, José Luis de Arrese, to promote constitutional reform that would effectively convert Spain into a Falangist regime. Not only was he demoted, but the following year Franco presented his sixth Fundamental Law entitled 'Declaration of the Fundamental Principles of the National Movement', in which Spain was confirmed as 'a traditional, Catholic, social and representative monarchy' and any reference to the Falange was conspicuous by its absence (Blaye 1976: 194).

The driving force behind the law was Laureano López Rodó, a keen supporter of Juan Carlos's succession as Head of State. He was the leading representative of the new breed of politicians close to Opus Dei who would from this point influence the regime's development effectively until well after Franco's death. López Rodó had assumed the rather unwieldy title of 'technical secretariat-general of the head of the Government' and his fellow ministers at Finance and Trade were also members of the secretive but highly influential Catholic lay organization.

1.14   Followers of the Monsignor

Opus Dei is a lay religious organization which has often been likened to the Freemasons, not least by the Spanish Falange, who denounced it to the special tribunal for the suppression of Masonry and Communism (Coverdale 2002: 351), and it has also attracted accusations of being 'the Catholic Mafia'. It is a secular apostolic body founded in 1928 by the Spanish priest José María Escrivá de Balaguer and granted authority to practise in 1947 by Pope Pius XII. Members of Opus Dei devote themselves to an apostolate but one carried out very much *in* the world. During the Franco regime its control extended 'either directly or indirectly through its adherents, [to] dozens of establishments of primary and secondary education, a university (Pamplona), several banks, building societies, daily papers, industries and so on' (Blaye 1976: 262). Its members tend to be highly qualified and work in sectors such as universities and government administration so that not only can they control the levers of power but also, through their apostolic mission, try to influence and reach out to their colleagues (Allen 2005: 123). Payne reports that by the 1950s it was 'alleged that as many as 20 per cent of the teaching posts in Spanish higher education were held by institute members', though he admits that is probably an exaggeration (1987: 438). Trythall summed up their approach as being broadly in tune with Franco's: 'It believed in probity and in professionalism, it believed in technical progress but in political and religious conservatism; it was hostile to *aggiornamento* in the Catholic Church, and rejected democracy on the grounds that equality is a dangerous myth' (1970: 227).

Much of the controversy over Opus Dei revolves around the character of its founder, 'reviled by some and venerated by millions more', as the normally balanced Opus apologist John Allen perhaps rather tendentiously puts it (Allen 2005: 43). In Spain, his unpopularity is linked to his supposed pro-Franco sympathies. He founded the organization in the 1930s and during the war, which caught him in the Republican-controlled capital, he 'feigned insanity in a mental asylum run by a friend' then escaped to Nationalist-dominated Burgos (Allen 2005: 47). After a period spent in Rome, in 1952 he founded the University of Navarra, a private, Opus-run institution. After his death in 1975, the speed and appropriateness of his canonization in 2002 under the papacy of John Paul II was the subject of much criticism.

The degree of penetration of the regime by Opus has possibly been exaggerated. Allen points out that throughout the entire period of the regime, out of 116 ministers in 11 governments only 8 had been Opus Dei members and that there had been some members who were high-profile critics of the regime, such as the Don Juan supporter Rafael Calvo Serer (Allen 2005: 59). The problem with Opus is that identifying its members was never easy and its detractors, of which there are many, tended to see its influence everywhere. Michael Walsh, in a highly critical account, noted that 'most commentators would regard the number of Opus ministers [in Franco's governments] at any one time as surprisingly large' (1989: 132). Hence its enemies referred to it as 'Octopusdei'. However, even Walsh cannot deny that the involvement of Opus Dei at the crucial juncture of politics in Spain in the late 1950s and early 1960s was an important factor in the neutralization of the pernicious influence of the Falange, helping, despite their faults, the economic modernization of Spain and promoting a monarchist succession (Walsh 1989: 134–5). It is doubtful if Franco would have trusted any other than the staunchly ultra-conservative Catholic group to introduce the momentous changes Spain needed, since there was never any sign that they favoured any modification in the Francoist system 'beyond establishing a monarchy which they hoped would be its continuation, not its nemesis' (Lannon 1987: 229). On the undoubted negative side, the internal network of patronage that characterized the organization was a further example of that endemic Spanish trait of clientelism (*enchufismo*) that underlay much of the corruption of 1960s developmentalism in Spain, of which the 1969 MATESA (see **2.12**) scandal was the one surprisingly public example. Given that that scandal only broke because of the anti-Opus intriguing of some disgruntled Falangists, one is led to wonder how many other Opus-inspired scandals and corruptions lay unpublicized (Cabrera and Del Rey 2007: 114–20).

1.15   The Technocrats Step in

The 1957 cabinet reshuffle was a chance for Franco to demote the Falange. They were handed the relatively minor portfolios of Labour, Education and Housing. The latter was given to Arrese, a former head of the Movement to chastise him for his proposal of a few months before which would have enshrined Spain as a totalitarian fascist regime (Blaye 1976: 193). The year 1958 saw the promulgation of the Principles of the Movement, and, while these principles had a Falangist colour, Spain ceased to be a national-syndicalist state. It was clear that Franco had accepted the need to change. The introduction into the cabinet in 1957 of the modernizing Opus Dei 'technocrats', such as Mariano Navarro Rubio, who had been a director of the Banco Popular, at Finance and Alberto Ullastres Calvo, a professor of Economics at Madrid University, at Trade as well as Laureano López Rodó (Payne 1987: 450), would be the spur to that change. Vincent describes them neatly as 'combining pietism and theological conservatism with professional training and an enthusiasm for business' (2007: 180). They would be joined in 1962 by another *opusdeísta*, Gregorio López Bravo, at the Ministry of Industry.

This new generation was referred to bitterly by the right-wing journalist Emilio Romero as 'the solvers (*solucionadores*), the managers, the boys who have been to university in the last few years, especially in the Faculties of Economics' (Carr and Fusi 1981: 81). It seems clear that the views of Franco, whose lack of sophistication in economic matters was well known, were closer to Romero's than his own ministers'. Tusell reminds us that when faced with the proposals of the technocrats, Franco's reaction was one of 'do as you like', revealing, on the one hand, his innate opposition in principle to what was proposed but, more importantly, the fact that he had reached a stage where he delegated increasing freedom to his cabinet (Tusell 1988: 134). In effect, he ceased in practice to be Head of Government to assume the role of Head of State. Still, Franco was not only loath to abandon statist autarchy but secretly feared that economic liberalization might lead to its political and social counterparts (Payne 1987: 470).

From 1957 the new government tried a series of measures to stabilize the economy, with little success. The turning point for Spain was integration into international financial organizations such as the World Bank in 1958 and the IMF (International Monetary Fund) in 1959, followed by membership of the OEEC (Organization for European Economic Co-operation). Part of the conditions for entry was adherence to a strict set of economic principles that would be enshrined in the

Stabilization Plan of 1959. The main aim was to reduce inflation and involved lowering public expenditure, reducing borrowing in the public sector and limiting it in the private sector, increasing the cost of public services and raising interest rates. In addition, the peseta was to be devalued and a stop put to multiple exchange rates. Finally, measures would be put in place to liberalize foreign investment and trade (Salmon 1995: 4). However, while the Plan had as its principal aim the creation of economic stability, coinciding as it did with a period of dynamic growth in all Western economies, its effect was actually to stimulate rapid growth (Salmon 1995: 4). This growth would be generated principally by two factors which were dependent on the external economy. One was tourism and the other migrant Spanish workers in Europe. Both of these were sources of much needed foreign currency within Spain. As ever, change and progress in Spain were intimately linked to external factors.

For this reason, the nature of the technocrats' role is often questioned. A recent study stresses the fact that Spain's economic miracle was part of a larger miracle occurring at a European level (Martín Aceña and Martínez Ruiz 2007: 46). At that time, the rest of Europe had been experiencing since the early 1950s a period of unprecedented prosperity, what Tony Judt called 'the age of affluence'. He cites how between 1950 and 1973, 'historically poor countries saw their economic performance improve spectacularly: ... in Spain from $2,397 to $8,739' per capita GDP and, since this was fuelled by a massive increase in overseas trade, 'merely by removing impediments to international commerce, the governments of the post-war West went a long way towards overcoming the stagnation' (2007: 324–6). This expansion, along with the decline in availability of skilled men to operate the factories, led to mass migrations. Starting with internal migrations from countryside to town, eventually it led to emigration to Northern Europe. A related aspect of this economic expansion and prosperity was the growth in mass tourism, and Spain would quickly become the beneficiary as its newly developed resorts offered alternatives to the more traditional destinations in France and Italy. Between

1959 and 1973 visitors to Spain increased from 3 million to over 30 million. As Judt remarks, 'in parts of the north-east and Spain's Mediterranean littoral, the transition from a pre-industrial economy to the age of the credit-card was accomplished in half a generation' (2007: 343).

1.16 Conclusion

By the end of the 1950s, the regime could start to relax a little as Franco had managed his early objectives of securing his position in power, neutralizing his rivals, eliminating his enemies and weathering the economic crisis. The emphasis of the regime's propaganda would shift away from the victory in war towards the assurance of peace and stability in an increasingly uncertain international context. Much capital would be made of the myth of Franco's securing of neutrality for Spain in the Second World War to shore up this image of him as the avuncular architect of a peaceful nation. The seal on this process was given by the economic progress seemingly engineered, more realistically 'facilitated', by the new breed of technocrats.

The impact and modernizing style of this new generation of politician was undeniable. They did much to counter the negative images and stereotypes of Spanish inefficiency and shady dealing abroad. Also, the opening of the borders allowing Spaniards to travel for work or leisure opened their eyes to the reality hidden behind the regime's propaganda: 'the outside world was not hostile to *Spain* but *was* hostile to Franco and his regime' (Blaye 1976: 197–8). Likewise, tourism would be seen as a way of combating the Black Legend of anti-Spanish feeling and preconceptions of its 'starchy traditionalism, ethnic inferiority and antimodernism' by showing tourists a 'modern people, open to all initiatives and receptive to all suggestions' (Pack 2006: 67).

Eisenhower's visit came in the same year, 1959, as the inauguration of the vast megalomaniac monument of the Valley of the Fallen, on a hill in the Guadarrama Mountains looking down on Madrid. Started in 1940 and built with the effort of Republican prisoners, 'labour batallions', as they were called, it was the ultimate monument to Franco's victory and appropriately close to the Palace of the Escorial, that monument to Philip II, an absolute monarch acclaimed by the regime. Franco's inaugural speech was both 'triumphant and vengeful' (Preston 1995a: 679).

Both events, the visit of Eisenhower and the opening of the Valley of the Fallen, came at the high point of Franco's regime. According to Payne, at 'no other point would he command greater acceptance or recognition' (Payne 1987: 459). Following the President's visit the *New York Times* wrote of it 'adding momentum to the gradual reincorporation of Spain into the Western family of nations' (Blaye 1976: 205). However, as the next decade and the story of Spain's uneasy relationship with its European neighbours would show, this would not involve, intentionally at least, political liberalization of any but the most cosmetic form. Rather it seemed that once again, Franco was merely further confirmed in his view that Spain could achieve all it wanted in terms of material prosperity without any significant changes to its political structures. Indeed, the risk of losing these material benefits was used to justify a continuation of the political status quo (Ellwood 1994: 184). As we will see in the next chapter, this strategy of 'political anaesthetization' (Vincent 2007: 180) would work up to a point, but the benefits of the improvements in social conditions actively pursued by the regime, such as the expansion in the education system, would sow the seeds of its destruction.

2

THE SPAIN OF *DESARROLLISMO*, 1960–75

2.1 Introduction

While the Civil War and the democratic Transition are the most studied periods of Spain's history in the twentieth century, the period of the 1960s and early 1970s was also one of momentous change and significance. A relative economic backwater emerged as the ninth most industrialized country in the world. It was a time of such deep transformation that it is now commonly acknowledged that it paved the way for the success of the democratic Transition of the 1970s. Edward Malefakis, speaking of the two decades that preceded Franco's death, has referred to a period of 'protodemocratization' (Palomares 2004: 3). There were two distinct narratives as to why this actually happened. One was the 'triumphalist' version presented unrelentingly by the spokesmen for the regime, including Franco himself, according to which the regime had steered Spain for 25 years through a turbulent international context, had solved economic difficulties with the Stabilization plan and, through its Development Plans, was the architect of what became known as the 'economic miracle', or developmentalism (*desarrollismo*). An extension of this argument are the claims made relatively recently by some of those who were ministers in the early 1960s that their reforms were, more than any moves made by Suárez, responsible for democracy (Juliá 2005: 70). The other narrative was that of the frustrated opponents at the time, aware that economic success was putting paid to any hope of deposing the

dictator, according to which Spain was yet again the lucky beneficiary of a fortunate series of events, most of them external to
its borders and outside its control (Carr and Fusi 1981: 59). As a
recent study notes, this is still 'an object of heated historiographical debate' (Martín Aceña and Martínez Ruiz 2007: 45).
Spain's success in the 1960s was due to a more general international bonanza, and it was also the case that thanks to certain
key figures within the regime and the changes they instituted or
facilitated, Spain was able to capitalize on that situation. Carr
refers to the work done by the Opus Dei technocrats from 1957
as the 'one decisive governmental decision in the realm of
domestic affairs', a 'Copernican revolution in economic policy'
(1995: 8) Nonetheless, it is no less true that, much as had
happened in the aftermath of the Civil War, the regime's inter-
ested management of the situation, particularly on the part of
the Opus Dei technocrats, actually ensured that progress was
not as good as it could have been (Preston 1986: 20).

Aside from the debate over the responsibility for the changes
wrought in Spain in the 1960s, what is undeniable is that they
were monumental and irreversible. They ensured that, barring
a minority of hardline 'continuists' or 'immobilists' (*inmovilistas*),
whatever side Spaniards were on, by the end of the decade their
satisfaction with the regime was reaching an end.

2.2   Peace through Prosperity

The evolution of Spanish society and the regime in the 1960s
can be summed up in an arc that spanned the two extremes of
'conformism' and 'confrontation' (Carr and Fusi 1981: 134). It
was the view of the regime that economic stability and prosperity would in themselves act as a solution to its constant quest for
political stability. What had previously been established by
force it was thought would now happen naturally, or 'organi-
cally', to employ the phraseology of the rhetoricians of the
regime. This, of course, was the philosophy of the dominant
group Opus Dei. Their principles sought to combine Christian

values and capitalist practice, believing that 'a minimum of comfort is needed for virtue and that individual asceticism must not degenerate into collective misery' (Blaye 1976: 262). This offered the possibility of justifying the much needed change of economic tack towards a free-market economy, or as close to it as the vestigial autarchy of the Franco regime would permit, without sacrificing the Catholic values that lay at the base of what was probably still one of the most traditional societies in Europe after Ireland. Indeed, the idea that social and political stability would come with the attainment of a particular level of per capita income was written into the 1971 Development Plan, which predicted that on reaching an average per capita income of $2000 in 1980 life in Spain 'will be more pleasant and the degree of social cohesion greater' (Carr and Fusi 1981: 95).

Such a simplistic connection between material comfort and political acceptance was totally misplaced. While Spaniards undoubtedly experienced the 'apathy of contentment' in the early years of the decade, it soon gave way, as expectations rose, to a mood of dissatisfaction and often the need to protest. A rising standard of living did not dampen working-class militancy but rather fed a growing demand for greater political freedoms and improved working conditions. Increased prosperity forced Spain to look outwards as 'economic development dissolved the closed space of autarky: in both a rhetorical and a real sense, Spain was now recognised as part of Europe' (Vincent 2007: 183).

The general improvement in the European economy in the 1960s was to have an enormous effect on Spain. This was largely a result of the establishment of the Common Market in the late 1950s. Bolstered by projects such as the Marshall Plan, Europe was by the 1950s starting to recover from the ravages of the Second World War. Germany in particular had become a driving economic force. The creation of the Common Market meant that these improvements became harnessed to tremendous effect.

This influenced Spain in two ways. First, its fledgling tourist industry profited from the greater prosperity of other

Europeans. Second, the aim of joining Europe would encourage Spain to introduce reform with a view to improving the image it projected to its European neighbours. While the regime was determined to limit liberalization's impact to the economic sphere, the cosmetic political changes, although signifying little in practice, did have an enormous psychological effect on Spaniards, convincing them that change was afoot and thus contributing to a gradual change in expectations. Likewise, the social impact of tourism was to alter the Spanish mentality for good and, in many ways, prepare the country for the eventual post-Franco era (Pack 2006).

2.3 Tourism and Emigration

It was once observed that Spain's development in the 1960s was the result of an exchange of sweat: the sweat of the European tourists who came to lounge on Spain's beaches and the sweat of the Spanish emigrants who left to work in Europe's factories. These two phenomena can in large part be viewed as the most significant factors underpinning Spain's economic miracle. Surpassing any supposed benefit of the Francoist developmentalism, the mere loosening of border controls to allow the massive influx of more prosperous European neighbours and the outflow of the Spaniards fleeing from the poverty of the countryside and, in many cases, eager to experience life outside the restricting confines of Spain, had an enormous effect on the economy first and the national psyche next. Opening the borders in 1959 saw over half a million Spaniards leave in search of work and, as a result, unemployment was slashed, especially its most intractable form, agricultural unemployment. Over the period of the boom, from 1960 to 1973, it is calculated that over one and a half million emigrants from Spain sought work in the flourishing economy of Europe, cutting unemployment figures to under 2 per cent by the early 1970s (Palomares 2004: 16). Foreign currency poured in both from tourist spending and from emigrants' remittances. Spain's balance of payments deficit was obliterated at a stroke. Good though this was, it also revealed the weakness of the Spanish economy, as its 'economic modernization was largely a by-product of other nations' prosperity' (Judt 2007: 517). Development was uneven and there were many areas that retained that third-world air about them. 'Even in 1973, per capita income in the country was still lower than that of Ireland and less than half the EEC average' (Judt 2007: 517).

In addition to the economic benefits, tourism encouraged institutional changes and social improvements among those conservative sectors of the regime who wished to see Spain become more accepted by the international community. It was not the conservative Opus Dei technocrats for whom a modern-ized industrial sector was the key to prosperity but rather future reformers such as Manuel Fraga, who saw the benefits of the tourist phenomenon (Pack 2007: 56).

2.4 Social Change

While the growth in the economy changed Spain's demo-graphic map as the population abandoned the countryside and sought work and a better life on the coast or in some cases in Madrid, potentially more significant was the psychological voyage undertaken by its inhabitants, as Spaniards came into contact with other Europeans whose mindset had not been shaped by nearly a quarter-century of politically and morally repressive dictatorship. Sasha Pack calls these European tourists 'naïve ambassadors' who acted as 'emissaries of an incipient and irresistible European empire marked by consumerism, effi-ciency, mobility, and permissiveness' (2007: 48). What was unusual about the social changes in Spain was the speed. As Carr and Fusi note, a 'process which had taken half a century in France or Britain, was telescoped into two decades'. The result was a case of 'superficial modernisation' where pre-industrial attitudes survive into a capitalist economic environment (1981: 79).

This clash of cultures and *mores* was well charted in the cinema with films depicting, from a variety of political perspectives, the consequences of the seismic cultural shifts that were rocking the country. Two were readily identifiable. One was the clash between rural and urban values. Even in the 1960s, modernity and urban progress were still viewed rather reluctantly by the authorities as necessary evils, undermining true Spanish values. Spanish cinema often depicted a good-natured village-dweller or a child charged with confronting the social ills that modernity had caused, in a desperate and usually successful bid to reassert traditional family values (Richardson, 2002). Another common scenario was the socio-moral clash between a traditional, and usually sexually repressed Spain, and its more liberated, indeed promiscuous, European neighbours. The traditional Spanish sex comedy of the 1960s explored this in a variety of ways, though inevitably the conclusion reflected a return to a relieved acceptance of an implicitly superior Spanish status quo (Hopewell 1986: 81). The rural–urban clash was often merely a variation on a different scale of the Spain–Europe divide, but both came under pressure from 1960.

The status quo did not remain unaffected by the contact with another set of values and, as a result of this social and cultural dialectic, by the end of the 1960s Spaniards' satisfaction with the restrictions of the regime, fragile at the best of times but certainly bolstered temporarily by the pleasures of consumerism and material comfort, had worn thin.

There was a rise throughout the 1960s of a new middle class of third-sector employees who were increasingly radical in their views, especially with regard to wage levels, and out of step ideologically with the regime. Economic growth was putting pressure on traditional Catholic values where it concerned the family and the role of women. Increasingly women were going out to work and finding ways of obtaining the contraceptive pill. While these changes mainly affected the urban areas, these were expanding as more and more young people abandoned the villages to seek work in the city or in Europe. The gap between rich and poor widened, but at the lower level, Spaniards were

initially happy with their new-found consumerism. The introduction of the tiny SEAT 600 in 1957 gave even modest, and
often inappropriately large, families the physical mobility to
match their social mobility. Car ownership rose to nearly 40 per
cent by the early 1970s. Nonetheless, by the end of the decade
economic progress in the form of a transformation of
Spaniards' standard of living was a fact, most often represented
by the increase in the number of cars, televisions and fridges in
their homes (Fusi 1985a: 163).

The economic transformation of Spain in the 1960s had a
significant impact on the situation of women and on the
discourse of the regime. The expansion of the industrial and
service sectors led to a greater incorporation of women into the
labour market (Harrison and Corkill 2004: 28). Up to 1969
women's presence in the workplace grew, though at half the
pace of men. From 1969 onwards the trend was reversed, as
women found employment in the tourist industry and service
sector as well as carrying out routine factory work (Brooksbank
Jones 1997: 78). A 1961 law on Women's Political, Professional
and Employment Rights recognized this trend and sought to
provide regulation and protection. However, women were still
excluded from certain professions such as the armed forces and
very much dependent on their husband's permission
(Brooksbank Jones 1997: 77). Though never challenging the
prevailing Francoist ideology, the *Sección Femenina* played a significant role in defending women's rights and showed some signs of
moving with the times. In its publications aimed at a young
female readership from the mid-1950s, there were even signs of
a new image of the modern woman coming to the fore, one who
'drives a Vespa, speaks a little bit of English, smokes and swims'.
The role model was the successful career woman, educated,
able to survive in a male world, albeit still obliged to retain her
feminine charm and with the priority on eventually assuming
the traditional role of wife and mother (Coca Hernando 1998).

As in other aspects of culture, the 1960s saw a greater availability of feminist literature both from the USA and home-
produced in the writings of the Catalan lawyer, Lidia Falcón.

Feminism, like Communism, could only exist under the cover of more general social movements or within tolerated organizations such as Housewives Association (*Asociación de Amas de Casa*) (Brooksbank Jones 1997: 3–5). However, the trends in the economy and education certainly created the context in which feminism could develop and fully emerge at the start of the 1970s, although its cause tended to be submerged by the more dramatic political battle of the Transition.

2.5   Economic Miracle

At the root of Spain's change in the 1960s was the economic 'take-off' (*despegue*), and it must be borne in mind that Spain's 'economic miracle' was 'part of a common "miracle" shared by the whole continent' (Martín Aceña and Martínez Ruiz 2007: 46). The merit of the technocrats was their clear vision that Spain's future lay in free trade and international cooperation, which allowed Spain to benefit from the circumstances. They collaborated with the international financial bodies, the IMF, the World Bank and the OEEC, to ensure Spain complied with the requirements laid down. Franco bowed to the inevitable, albeit reluctantly, and no doubt consoling himself that economic liberalization could be achieved without ceding an iota of control over the helm of state (Fusi 1985a: 171). Later, the economic success of the 1960s would lend support to his conviction that political change was unnecessary (Fusi 1985a: 159).

After a slow start, when unemployment rose to nearly 35 per cent, economic growth in the first years of the decade then reached an unprecedented 8.7 per cent, inflation grew at under 9 per cent on average and salaries rose between 8 and 11 per cent. Over the period 1960–73, average Spanish incomes trebled (Barton 2004: 240). Production of electricity almost doubled, as did that of steel (from 1.9 million tons in 1960 to 3.5 million in 1965). Car production rose from just under 40,000 in 1960 to over 100,000 in 1964. Imports tripled and exports doubled. In 1965 income from tourism exceeded $1,000 million and Spain welcomed a record 14 million tourists (Fusi 1985: 160–1), rising to 30 million by the end of the 1960s. By the early 1970s only 20 per cent of the workforce was on the land and Spain had crossed the UN's criteria for a developed nation by the middle of the 1960s (Judt 2007: 517).

Between 1966 and 1971 the economy grew by 5.6 per cent, electrical production in 1970 reached 56,484 million kilowatts per hour; steel production exceeded 7 million tons that year, and car production was 450,000. There were 21 million tourists, salaries rose by about 8 per cent and per capita income was $900 in 1970 and climbed to $1,239 in 1972 (Fusi 1985a: 161–2).

While the success of the boom was usually laid at the door of the technocrats, especially by the regime itself, their management was both partial and incompetent. A series of three Development Plans was drawn up, each of four years' duration. The first was in 1964, the second in 1968 and the third in 1972. Despite their names, economic growth frequently lacked planning and consisted principally of crisis management, 'stop-go policies which aimed no higher than the control of inflation and balance of payments deficits' (Preston 1986: 20). In fact the growth was the inevitable result of the emigrants' remittances, the tourists' foreign currency and the foreign investment that flowed into the country from 1960 onwards, giving Spain a healthy balance of payments surplus.

As Fusi points out, given Spain's undeniable economic progress from 1960, a progress that by 1964 was reasonably well consolidated, the Development Plans were, in economic terms, strictly speaking unnecessary. Moreover, in the main they were a failure, especially the regionalist policy of development poles and industrial complexes. There were isolated successes, such as Valladolid, but, aside from the corruption which was rife in a system that was still largely autarchical, Spain's industrial map was largely unaltered (Martín Aceña and Martínez Ruiz 2007: 44). Fusi quotes the philosopher Julián Marías to the effect that Spain was a 'developed country but badly developed' and from

1965 onwards, although the economy continued to grow, it did so in an uneven fashion, alternating periods of growth with inflation and periods of economic crisis. Lack of structural reform from 1964 meant that expansion and recession alternated practically on a two-year cycle (Fusi 1985a: 162). In fact, according to Fusi, the motivation behind the Plans was primarily propagandistic and he cites three ways: one, they were intended to have a psychological effect, inspiring confidence in the regime's projects, both at home and abroad; two, they formed part of the post-Franco strategy, presenting a future Spain as a technocratic and authoritarian monarchy based on development; and third, they gave their architect López Rodó a convincing blueprint to take to the EC to persuade them of Spain's suitability for membership (Fusi 1985b: 11).

2.6   The Goal of Europe

The Franco government applied first to the Common Market in 1962 for associate status along the lines of Greece and Turkey. This was rejected on the principle of there being 'an explicit link between democratization and accession' (Closa and Heywood 2004: 10). Franco himself was not keen on the European ideal and only agreed when it seemed clear that the 1963 Common Agricultural Policy would have damaging effects for Spain (Payne 1987: 528). Franco was determined that any economic liberalization would not bring in its wake similar political change. This might explain why one year after Spain's unsuccessful bid to join Europe the regime had no compunctions over trying and executing the captured Communist leader, Julián Grimau, in the face of international uproar and clamour for clemency. In August two anarchists who placed bombs in Madrid were subjected to death by garrotte, further evidence of Franco's well-known preference for 'public order to international goodwill' (Preston 1986: 20). Justification for Franco's lack of concern for the reputational damage of such incidents might be found in the USA's willingness later that year to renew its military pact with Spain for another ten years, although it may have weakened Spain's negotiating hand (Payne 1987: 530).

2.7 Regime Change

Still, the regime was keen to improve its international image. To this end it introduced two high-profile reforms to its legislation aimed at showing a greater move to democratic principles. One was the Press Act in 1966 and the other was the Religious Freedom Act in 1967. The former did away with prior censorship, which was its major claim to liberalization. It was the work of Manuel Fraga, who had replaced the reactionary Arias Salgado in 1962 as Minister of Information and Tourism. As usual, however, an examination of the small print revealed the limitations of the step. According to its infamous Article 2, publication was severely restricted to those items which conformed to a list of conditions, the overall import of which was obedience to the regime. Writers were free as long as they showed 'respect for truth and morality; obedience to the principles of the *Movimiento Nacional* and other fundamental laws; the needs of national defence, state security, the maintenance of law and order, and external peace; the respect due to institutions and persons in expressing criticism of public and administrative action' (Gilmour 1985: 64). Failure to comply meant that any subversive publication could be confiscated following printing and destroyed, which was a 'Damoclean sword held over editors and journalists' (Carr and Fusi 1981: 46). This was a much harsher threat to publishers than the original system of prior censorship, as it entailed an evident financial loss. That said, although the law did not in fact rid Spain of censorship and indeed in a way made things worse, there is no doubt that psychologically it had an effect. Something had undoubtedly changed and people sensed it, 'a uniform and monotonous press gradually became varied and plural, within clear limits. Previously taboo subjects began to find their way onto the page' (Barrera 1995: 95).

The other law concerning religion was long overdue and showed the regime reluctantly bowing to the influence of the changes emanating from Vatican II. Pope John XXIII's encyclical *Mater et magistra* in 1961 had advocated 'human rights such as the right of association and freedom of worship' (Lannon 1995: 278), and while the regime could not countenance the former it did reluctantly accede to the latter. Since the Spaniards' Charter (Fuero de los Españoles) of 1945, Catholicism was the state religion. Its original Article 6 made no mention of other religions but was modified to introduce the principle of tolerance with the insertion of the sentence: 'No one will be persecuted for their religious beliefs nor the private exercise of their religion.' The Law of Religious Freedom (*Ley de Libertad Religiosa*) of 21 July 1967 effectively decriminalized other religions but there remained strict limitations on their ability to practise. However, it did permit civil marriage among non-Catholics and in 1968 the first synagogue was opened in Madrid (Sánchez Marroyo 2003: 419).

The Religious Freedom law had not been warmly welcomed by the Church in Spain which saw it, naturally, as a threat to its monopoly, but the changes in the Catholic Church in general added to the pressure exerted on the regime by the other factors such as its European ambitions and the sociological changes that increased prosperity brought. Indeed, the Catholic Church from the 1960s on 'became, to the astonishment of many observers, a force for political change' (Lannon 1987: 276). Other groups such as workers and students were to add their voice to the calls for change. Even the sturdiest pillar of the regime, the Army, spawned in the last years of the regime a movement known as the Democratic Military Union (UMD) (Preston 1986: 69).

2.8 Movements of Protest

The decade of the 1960s saw what Juan Pablo Fusi has called 'the reappearance of conflict' centred on four areas: the university, the factories, the Church and the regions (Radcliff 2007: 142). On the campuses, what started off as discontent with the official student union spread to demands for democratic reform (Fusi 1985: 165). From 1965 to 1969, when the government declared a state of emergency, campus disturbances and protests were the order of the day. During most of the 1960s students were mainly protesting about their own academic freedoms and in protest at the imposition of a state student union, the SEU. As a result, in 1965 this was disbanded but students, fired by their readings of clandestinely distributed Marxist literature and influence from the other European student protests in the late 1960s, continued to ensure that university campuses were an almost permanent site of revolt and confrontation with the police. The early 1970s saw a greater radicalization of the student movement as it succumbed to more extreme, anarchistic tendencies which were less to do with anti-Franco protest than general anti-bourgeois rebelliousness. However, the effects of the movement had a profound indirect impact on the regime. By the early 1970s the student body had grown to the extent that that the government could not contain its activities to discreet levels. Spanish society was forced to take notice of their protests and in many ways they were giving Spanish society a lesson in the principles of democratic protest (Carr and Fusi 1981: 149). This phenomenon would be bolstered by the growth of legal associations in Spain centred on family and neighbourhood groups in the wake of a 1964 Law of Associations by which the Regime tried to channel a safe form of political pluralism (Radcliff 2007).

The regions of the periphery also became significant additions to the protest movement. In Catalonia a strong cultural movement developed throughout the 1960s based on the *nova cançó* group of singers such as Lluis Llach and Raimon, whose defence of their language and culture went hand in hand with a critique of the repressiveness of the regime. It even extended to the football club, Barcelona FC, or *Barça*, as it is known to its fans. Jimmy Burns tells of how the club always managed to thwart Franco's manipulation of football as a 'political sedative' and cites the example of the first organized protest of the regime that took place in Barcelona in 1951 over the rise in price of the public trams. It led to 'a mass boycott of this form of transport, student demonstrations and some worker unrest', and while the club went ahead with a match, 'hundreds of leaflets backing the boycott were distributed round the terraces, and when the match was over many fans ignored the empty trams that the regime had placed near the stadium, choosing to walk home instead as a mark of solidarity' (Burns 1999: 150–1).

As well as sport and culture, the Church in Catalonia and the Basque Country tended to adopt a more critical stance towards the regime. The Abbot of Montserrat, Aureli Escarré, was expelled from Spain for comments critical of the regime made to *Le Monde*. The Basque Bishop of Bilbao, Mgr Cirarda, defied the authorities by criticising the regime and asking for clemency towards the accused in the 1970 Burgos trial and his successor, Mgr Añoveros, was arrested for condemning the 1975 executions.

The Basque Church became one of the principal refuges for the Basque culture, including the early members of ETA (Sullivan 1988: 34). ETA was founded in 1959, on St Ignatius's Day, 31 July, as a radical offshoot of a student movement, Ekin, and underwent a progressive radicalization throughout the following decade, starting with the derailing of a train carrying Civil War veterans in 1961 (Sullivan 1988: 36). Between its first assassinations in 1968 and Franco's death, ETA would claim 47 victims and suffer 27 losses of its own (Fusi 1985: 166). The appearance of ETA itself was a result of the greater consolidation of the regime in the 1950s which meant that 'many Basques, even traditional PNV supporters, were prospering under Franco. Such people retained a cultural identification with the nationalist movement, although they had long since abandoned any kind of struggle against the Franco regime' (Sullivan 1988: 28). ETA also benefited from a 'moral identification' on the part of the democratic opposition as it was the only armed struggle against Francoism, despite the fact that its objectives were quite different (Aguilar 1999: 12).

2.9   Change in the Church

The importance of the Catholic Church to the Franco regime has been emphasized above. Prior to the 1960s, the leading force was the hierarchy which, for better or worse, had supported Franco not only in recognition of his role as defender during the Civil War when the Church was under threat from radical Republicans (see **1.2**) and subsequently as a bulwark against the Communist menace, but also as a defence against modernist trends in the ecclesiastical movement itself. The highly conservative values of the regime were pleasing to the majority of the hierarchy. The only dissenting voices came from those more radical factions within the younger clergy and especially in regions such as Catalonia and the Basque country, where there was a history of anti-Francoist, pro-Republican sentiment, even in the case of the Basque priests' evidence of support for ETA (Sullivan 1988: 84; Preston 1986: 19). In 1960, 339 Basque priests had signed a letter denouncing lack of freedoms among its own clergy in the region and 1963 saw the Catalan Abbot of Montserrat make his anti-Franco statements to *Le Monde* (Payne 1987: 500; Fusi 1985a: 166–7).

Now, however, all that would change. The reforms led by the new Pope John XXIII and which would coalesce in the Second Vatican Council (1962–5) would send shock waves through the international Catholic community and Spain would not be immune to its impact. The Council's requirement on bishops to retire at 75 meant that by the end of the 1960s Spain's hierarchy was starting to change. One of the most significant developments was Pope Paul VI's appointment of the reformist Cardinal Vicente Enrique y Tarancón as primate of Spain in 1969. Tarancón was to be 'the instrument whereby Pope Paul VI was to express his distaste for the Franco regime' (Preston 1986: 19), and eventually became such a thorn in the side of the regime that one of the commonest graffiti on Spanish walls was 'Tarancón al paredón' – 'Tarancón for the firing squad'. Subsequent progress would be steady and culminated in the astonishing occurrence of an Episcopal Conference in 1971 actually asking publicly for forgiveness for the Church's stance in the Spanish Civil War, and a Joint Assembly of Bishops and Priests in September 1971 made a declaration rejecting the regime's division of Spanish society into victors and vanquished (Preston 1995a: 755). In 1973 Spanish bishops published a document entitled *On the Church and the Political Community*, advocating separation of Church and State (Lannon 1995: 279). Tarancón described such events as an 'authentic bomb' for the regime (Callahan 2007: 190).

Such developments caused problems for the Church as well. The mood of change and dissatisfaction with the Church's record meant a decline in religious values themselves. If Spain 'could boast 8000 seminarists at the start of the Sixties, there were less than 2000 twelve years later. Between 1966 and 1975 one third of all Spain's Jesuits left the Order' (Judt 2007: 518). Equally the important activism carried out by the Catholic trade unions, the HOAC and the JOC, often serving as covers for the clandestine communist trade union, Workers' Commissions (*Comisiones Obreras*, CC OO), led to a clash between spiritual and political values which the Church found difficult to contain (Lannon 1995: 279).

2.10   Internal Opposition

The economic progress of the 1960s had the contradictory effect of, on the one hand, attracting adepts to the regime on the basis of the positive successes and prosperity its policies seemed to produce, but at the same time encouraging the development of oppositional groups that would ultimately threaten the system (Fusi 1985a: 164). The Opus Dei technocrats had subordinated 'politics to economic imperatives'; individual freedoms were made to wait until the achievement of material comforts. López Rodó was quoted as saying, 'We shall start thinking about democracy when actual income per head of the population exceeds $1000', a claim which must be viewed in the context of it taking ten years for the regime to raise income from $282 to $743 in 1969 (Blaye 1976: 262).

Internal opposition to the regime was distributed between those who operated as an illegal opposition, others who comprised a 'tolerated' opposition, and finally those figures within the regime's own ranks in favour of an opening (*apertura*) out of the system. There was considerable overlap between these last two categories.

In terms of an illegal opposition, the Communist Party, often operating under the cover of the tolerated Catholic trade unions, was the most prominent within Spain. Its experience supporting the guerrilla resistance in the 1940s showed it 'grasped the importance of action within Spain' (Carr and Fusi 1981: 161). It mobilized protest strikes from as early as 1962, mainly in the northern region of Asturias and with the aim of achieving renewal of the contracts for collective bargaining. The 1958 Collective Bargaining Act had brought about increased militancy among the working class as unions became more confident about taking on the employers. In 1962 there were strikes for higher pay in the Basque Country, Asturias and Catalonia which not only escaped serious repression, but were reported in the press and, moreover, achieved their aim of wage increases. Bearing in mind that strikes were illegal and would remain so until 1975, there were official records of 777 'labour disputes' in 1963 and 484 in 1965, reaching over 1500 in 1970 (Fusi 1985a: 164). As Fusi points out, while at the start the strikes were in typical areas and sectors such as mining in Asturias or the metal industry in the Basque country, they eventually spread to other sectors and regions and even crossed the class divide affecting middle-class professions such as teachers, bank workers and doctors (165). The nature of the protests evolved also. From the early wage-related action, strikes in the latter part of the decade were more often solidarity strikes, 'a clear indication of the growing radicalisation and politicisation of the workers' movement' (Carr and Fusi 1981: 141). By the 1960s the Spanish Communist Party (*Partido Comunista Español*, PCE) had left behind most of its Stalinist trappings and embraced the idea of democracy and national conciliation, a decision that their leader, Santiago Carrillo, dates from 1956 (Carrillo 2000: 53).

If, from the 1960s on, the Communists waged a heroic clandestine activity within the country, often shielded by the Catholic unions mentioned, making them 'the most visible and resolute opponent of the regime' (Carr and Fusi 1981: 164) by way of contrast, the Socialists had suffered a more tortured experience during their 40-year opposition in exile. Based in Toulouse since 1947, they were increasingly isolated and ineffective by the 1960s. Although things improved when young radicals emerged in the early 1970s, led by Felipe González, and adopted more revolutionary Marxist principles to challenge the PCE, the party could not match their rivals' heroic record of anti-Francoist militancy (Heywood 1995: 193–4). This had led to their 1979 centenary celebrations' slogan '100 years of honesty' often being qualified in the streets with a humbling graffito, attributed to Marcelino Camacho, 'and 40 years of holidays' (Vázquez Montalbán 2005: 199).

The 'tolerated' opposition was an internal reformist movement, largely Christian Democrat in persuasion, which was trying to steer Spain in the direction of democracy. This new opposition had gradually replaced what Carr and Fusi call the 'historic opposition' of the exiled Republicans, and was made up of Christian Democrats, Social Democrats and liberal monarchists (1981: 163). Many were linked with the journal *Cuadernos para el Diálogo* founded by Joaquín Ruiz Giménez. More extreme members of this faction were led by José María Gil Robles, a close supporter of Don Juan who, after a period in exile, was allowed to return to Spain in 1957. He became involved in the Munich incident in 1962 when a group of opponents of the regime, from inside and outside Spain, including the exiled Socialist leader Rodolfo Llopís and the disillusioned Falangist Dionesio Ridruejo, attended the Fourth Congress of the European Movement. They issued a statement calling for change in Spain which, given its timing to coincide with Spain's first overtures to the EC, incurred the wrath of the Spanish authorities. On their arrival back in Spain Ridruejo and Gil

Robles were arrested and sent into exile (Preston 1995a: 702–3). As the American journalist Benjamin Welles wrote back in 1965, 'the anti-Franco resolution was mild by any standards but to Franco it was a public affront from Spaniards who had travelled on passports granted by the regime and who were "washing Spain's dirty linen" before all the world' (Welles 1965: 224). The tolerated opposition also included the Catholic trade unions, the HOAC and the JOC, as well as certain sectors of the press such as the newspaper *Madrid*, and the magazines *Triunfo* and *Cambio16*.

Finally, throughout the 1960s, there emerged a generation of its supporters, who favoured *apertura* ('opening'), 'a tightly-controlled liberalization of the regime in order to meet popular demands for political modernization, and … as the best way to guarantee their political survival' (Palomares 2004: 5). One group were the Christian Democrats who, towards the end of the regime, advocated democracy in a series of articles published in newspapers such as the Church-backed *Ya* under the collective signature 'Tácito'. Many of these figures, such as Leopoldo Calvo Sotelo, Landelino Lavilla, Marcelino Oreja and others would subsequently play important roles in the Transition as members of the Union of the Democratic Centre (*Unión de Centro Democrático*, UCD).

2.11 The Issue of the Succession

The 1960s saw the further diminishing of Franco's control on the state and its delegation to trusted colleagues. By 1962 he was 70 and had had a shooting accident in the previous year. The incident gave the regime supporters a fright and measures were taken over the coming years to deal with a more long-term absence of the Caudillo. In that year's reshuffle the post of Deputy Prime Minister was reintroduced and given to the loyal Falangist general, Agustín Muñoz Grandes, thus seeming to point to a *continuista* future for the regime.

By 1965 the burning question in Spain at the time was

summed up in the title of a pamphlet written by the leader of the Spanish Communist Party, Santiago Carrillo, 'After Franco, what?' A cabinet reshuffle in 1965 led to work being done on a new law, the Organic Law of State, passed in 1966. Part of its aim was to clean up Spain's image vis-à-vis Europe by toning down most of the remaining fascist rhetoric and allowing for a limited amount of elected representation, such as the 108 members of the expanded Cortes who would be elected by family representatives (Payne 1987: 513–14). It laid down the separation of Head of State and Head of Government, though this did not actually come about in practice until 1973, when Carrero Blanco was appointed Prime Minister. Rather than an additional Fundamental Law, the real aim of the Ley Orgánica del Estado was to synthesize and harmonize all existing legislation, acting as the final phase of the process of institutionalization and, as such, it was a disappointment to those *aperturistas* like Fraga who had hoped it would lead to some opening up of the regime to reform (Palomares 2004: 56).

On 14 December 1966 the law was put to a referendum and almost unanimously supported. The latter was a clever piece of political propaganda, since the law did not plan to change much and so voting one way or the other had little real significance. However, the mere fact of holding a vote gave the impression of democratic consultation and the illusion of an evolving political system, something which Franco had been keen to stress in his speech to parliament when presenting the law, eager as he was to dispel the accusation that the regime was against progress. 'In politics there is no room for immobilism', he had declared to the Cortes. Ironically, the most contentious issue at the time concerned the monarchical succession to Franco and yet that was one issue the Law did not address.

Franco was opposed to the cause of Don Juan from the beginning, but the final straw had been the Lausanne Manifesto in 1945. Don Juan never accepted the terms of the Law of Succession and pressed his case throughout the 1960s, supported by distinguished figures like José María de Areilza, ex-ambassador of Franco, who argued the need for the return of a democratic, pluralist state under the monarchy of Don Juan. Juan Carlos's case was promoted by Carrero Blanco and the *opusdeístas* and the former's appointment in 1967 to the vice-presidency strengthened the cause. Throughout the 1960s, Carrero Blanco would assume increasing responsibilities, and this represented a serious block to reformers such as Fraga. Carrero was a deeply religious man and totally opposed to any kind of liberalization other than the economic sort proposed by his Opus Dei colleagues, and the Monarchy was the preferred solution.

This was given its final impetus in 1968 when Carrero Blanco sent a document to Franco arguing the case for Juan Carlos and discounting the other pretenders, Don Juan, his nephew Prince Alfonso and the Carlist pretender Carlos-Hugo. Thus the question was resolved. Juan Carlos appeared to ensure the only kind of monarchy which Franco's 1947 law dictated, that is, one based on the principles of the Nationalist movement, not the traditional liberal monarchy that was promised by the prince's father. Franco liked to refer to this as an installation (*instauración*) of the monarchy rather than a restoration (*restauración*). Early in 1969, Juan Carlos, at Fraga's prompting, made declarations to the press that he accepted the principles of the regime and was prepared to respect them. This gave Franco the assurance he needed and the decision was announced in the Cortes on 22 July 1969. Juan Carlos rewarded Franco by stating early in his speech, 'First, I wish to state that I receive from His Excellency the Head of State, Generalissimo Franco, the political legitimacy which rose from 18 July 1936', thus confirming the worst fears of the opponents of the regime that the prince was Franco's stooge (Preston 2004: 244).

2.12 Rightward Lurch

If some *aperturistas* still held out the hope that the 1967 Organic Law of the State might be the 'platform for the introduction of at least some reforms: greater popular participation in national affairs, and the acceptance of a "legal opposition" … within the boundaries of the Movement' (Palomares 2004: 57), they were sadly disappointed by the direction the regime was to take after the last shuffle of the decade.

The year 1969 in many ways marks the beginning of the final phase of the Franco regime. The year began with a state of emergency in response to worker and student unrest. The naming of Juan Carlos as successor had been 'met with the greatest calm, even with total indifference, by the man in the street' (Blaye 1976: 259), and while towards the end 'Franco's regime … depended not on open and violent repression but rather upon a sort of enforced passive acceptance, a decades-long de-politicization of the culture' (Judt 2007: 517), increased pressure was being applied from specific sectors of society. In response, there was a return to a hard line from 1966 onwards.

Much of this was due to the enhanced influence of Carrero Blanco, who became vice-president in 1967, taking over from the former leader of the Blue Division, General Múñoz Grandes, thus allowing an ageing and infirm Franco to take a back seat and spend more time on his leisure pursuits. Throughout the 1960s, Carrero was the key figure in promoting the continuance of the regime at whatever cost. In this he was abetted by Opus Dei. The culmination of their influence was the cabinet reshuffle of October 1969, when Carrero engineered an Opus-dominated, 'monotone' cabinet, 'the most homogeneous cabinet in the history of the regime' (Ellwood 1994: 208). It reflected Carrero's perspective, which held that unity of government was more important than accommodating the various competing forces, as Franco had tended to do. In part, too, it was a response to the MATESA scandal which had occurred earlier in the year and revealed once again the tensions in the government between the Opus Dei technocrats and the Falange.

MATESA was a textile company run by a leading *opusdeista* and close friend of López Rodó, which, over a period of ten years, had received government loans, purported to be up to ten billion pesetas (£80 million) (Ellwood 1994: 207) to finance exports of looms. Unfortunately these exports were never made. In fact the money had been used for private investment abroad (Carr and Fusi 1981: 189). The scale of the fraud was astounding and can only be explained by the economic mindset of the time which was so favourably disposed towards exporting that the detail was overlooked.

The close connections between the company's owner, Juan Vilá Reyes, and the Opus Dei organization and its representatives in government led those in the Falangist camp, especially reformists like Fraga, hostile to the lay organization, to attempt to exploit the scandal for maximum damage. In the end, it was the moderate Falangists like Fraga who lost as Carrero took exception to the Falange's jeopardization of the planned monarchical succession, engineered by Carrero with the backing of Opus (Preston 1986: 23). In a display of hypocrisy that characterized the regime, it was decided that the financial fraud was less damaging than the publicity which Fraga had given it. In the 1969 reshuffle Fraga and his fellow Falangist José Solís were dismissed, as were the two Opus ministers implicated in the MATESA scandal. The scandal was important in that, for the first time, it publicly revealed the divisions in the Francoist regime and 'the scandalous incompetence of the bureaucratic system that guided the developmental policy' (Cabrera and Del Rey 2007: 119).

The move to the right crystallized in the 1969 reshuffle had really begun earlier with the introduction of the Organic Law of the State in 1966. The aim of this law was not so much to promote change as 'to adapt to changing external circumstances in such a way as to preserve intact the values which had always been the pillars of Francoism' (Ellwood 1994: 203). The referendum made it clear it was principally a 'plebiscite for Franco's personal rule' (Ellwood 1994: 204). Campaigning for a 'no' vote was prohibited, and in the end it was claimed that 95 per cent had voted 'yes' in a turnout of 88 per cent and the law was passed on 10 January 1967.

The Law and the change of government were responses to the changes, or expectation of change, aroused by the early

1960s. Where in the early part of the decade there had been some attempt to move the regime closer to its European neighbours, this was, if not quite reversed, certainly resisted by a new government run by arch-conservatives whose sole aim was perpetuating Francoism at all costs. As Ellwood noted, the 'second half of the decade saw the regime on a continual see-saw between gestures which appeared to concede greater freedom of movement in social, political and cultural matters, and knee-jerk repressive reaction to pressure for those appearances to become reality' (1994: 201). Carrero was not at all happy about the way the press had evolved since 1966 and contemplated a retrograde reform. He was as obsessed as his master by the threats of Communism, atheism and Freemasonry.

This move to the right by the government had the effect of strengthening the existing pressures for change. These were coming from three main areas: the workers, the students and the regionalists, in particular, the Basque group ETA which, in August 1968, had carried out the first assassination of a police chief and reputed torturer, Melitón Manzanas. Continued social unrest throughout the early 1970s and, in particular, the political fallout from the Burgos trial of Manzanas' killers, would push Carrero's government even further to the right in an attempt to impose control and mollify the ultra-right.

2.13   ETA and the Burgos Trial

Franco had considered the continuance of the regime assured; everything was 'atado y bien atado', well tied-down by the institutionalization process. The refrain was 'después de Franco, las instituciones' ('after Franco, the institutions'), and these were felt capable of withstanding any pressures for radical change. 'In fact', writes Ellwood, 'the last five years of his life were to show how futile had been his efforts indefinitely and totally to control the course of Spanish history' (1994: 206). The early 1970s were one of the most turbulent periods for the regime. ETA activity intensified, there was serious labour unrest and most universities were closed. Terrorism also took a new form, with the appearance of a hard-line left-wing group, the FRAP, which killed a Madrid policeman in May 1973. Carrero's government's response was fiercer repression and restriction of freedoms. The press was shackled, and one newspaper, *Madrid*, was closed down in 1971. Other publications were fined but the press persevered in its attacks on the regime and became 'a "paper parliament", a true Fourth Estate, where almost every opinion could find a place' (Carr and Fusi 1981: 193).

The regime continued to clamp down on terrorists, though now with more of an eye to international opinion. Spain's image abroad, however, was dealt a severe blow with the Burgos trial in December 1970 against 16 ETA militants. The regime's prosecutors made the mistake of thinking that a show trial would discourage unrest and so merged a number of cases that could have been dealt with separately (and even *in camera*, as two of the accused were priests). As Sullivan pointed out, the trial had the effect 'of bringing the ideas of ETA-VI before the entire population of the Basque country, and indeed of the world' (Sullivan 1988: 92).

ETA's brand of extreme nationalism had grown out of the original movement, centred on the moderate Basque Nationalist Party (PNV, *Partido Nacionalista Vasco*). Basque nationalism at a cultural level was simmering throughout the nineteenth century and was stirred by resentment at the loss of ancient privileges (*fueros*) after the Carlist Wars which ended in 1876. Sabino Arana's PNV was a response to the changes produced in Basque society towards the end of that century as a result of industrialization. The influx of immigrants from the rest of Spain to work in the steel and shipbuilding industries led sectors of the rural middle class to see their centuries-old culture and identity in jeopardy. The Basque oligarchy supported the immigration on which its factories and businesses relied for labour but, as in Catalonia, a sector of the bourgeoisie saw self-rule as synonymous with protecting their own interests and gave support to the incipient nationalist movement (Conversi 1997). The second factor influencing ETA's appearance was the

Franco regime's persecution of Basque culture and the younger generation's disenchantment with the PNV's passivity. A university movement, *Ekin* (from the Basque for 'to do'), soon gave birth to a more radical, leftist movement, *Euskadi ta Askatasuna*, Basque Homeland and Freedom (ETA), in 1959. Violence in the early stages was limited to the planting of some bombs, robbing banks and, famously, derailing a train carrying Falangist veterans to San Sebastián for an 18 July commemoration ceremony in 1961. The assassination campaign effectively started by accident in 1968 when ETA militants stopped at a roadblock shot and killed a Civil Guard to avoid arrest and one was subsequently killed by Guards. His death provoked the first planned retaliation, the shooting of a reputedly brutal police chief, Melitón Manzanas, in 1968 (Sullivan 1988: 72). Thus the cycle began. Manzanas' assassination would be one of the charges levelled at the Burgos trial.

When sentences between 12 and 90 years were imposed on 9 of the defendants and 6 were sentenced to death, the regime was subjected to a massive international campaign for clemency as well as pressure from within, and two days later Franco commuted the 6 death sentences. He may have been influenced by the Preferential Agreement Spain had signed with the EC in June 1970 and the financial aid it was receiving from the World Bank and the Federal Republic of Germany, whose honorary consul in San Sebastián was being held hostage by another ETA faction. Nevertheless, the incident and the campaign in favour of democracy that it generated dealt a huge propaganda blow to the regime and to Carrero's monarchist continuist strategy. It aggravated the enmities between the hard right and the Opus Dei monarchists, made reformers within the regime despair of change and provided a fillip for the opposition, including Basque nationalists.

2.14 Regime in Crisis

ETA's spectacular assassination of Carrero almost exactly three years later, on the 20 December 1973, as he returned from daily mass, was partly a result of the boost the organization received at Burgos. The regime had angered the Basque people by making them feel the trial was directed at them as a whole and this gave ETA the environment it needed to grow, as had the repression that followed (Sullivan 1988: 113). Carrero had been, without a doubt, the best candidate to be Franco's successor and had all the credentials for doing so successfully, as his unswerving loyalty to Francoism and his support for the modernizing project of the Opus Dei technocrats meant that he had some appeal for both the 'immobilist' and the reformist elements of the regime. His brand of 'post-Franco Francoism' would be built 'not of political liberalization but of continued prosperity' (Preston 1986: 24). ETA, certainly in its communiqué issued after the assassination, portrayed its action as extending beyond the confines of the Basque situation and in the interest of 'all those who are exploited and oppressed within the Spanish state' (Preston 1986: 49).

The assassination produced the expected threat of an ultra-right-wing backlash, but this was kept in check by a provisional governing team, including the Interior Minister, Carlos Arias Navarro, who eventually succeeded Carrero as Prime Minister. He was a loyal Francoist whose former roles had been as wartime military prosecutor, director-general of security and mayor of Madrid. His appointment under Carrero was itself a feature of that government's attempt to appease the extreme right and by choosing him as Carrero's successor a by now ailing and virtually senile Franco hoped to do the same. Still, he surprised observers in his first government on 3 January 1974 by balancing the hardliners with the presence of some liberal ministers. His challenge was the same as that which had faced Carrero, the 'resolution of the contradictions between a developing society and a retrograde polity' (Preston 1986: 53), and in his first public pronouncement of his political project on 12 February, he appeared to be moving in that direction.

The social circumstances were very grave. Spain was experiencing the consequences of the end of the European boom. An international oil crisis in 1973 did not immediately affect the economy as the government rather foolhardily chose to cope internally, keeping oil prices under the average for Europe through subsidies and tax deductions, though it did impact on the inflation rate, which rose to over 25 per cent in 1974 (Preston 1986: 54), but the indirect effect of the crisis was considerable. Revenue from tourism dropped as Spain's neighbours tightened their belts and as economies abroad shrank, many of the emigrants returned, with the result that the flow of remittances slowed and the unemployment rate rose. With an ailing Head of State and a turbulent society, to crown it all Spain was heading for a severe economic recession.

2.15   The Spirit of 12 February

It is clear that whatever his hardline credentials, even Arias was aware that some concession to change was necessary. He had introduced a modernizer as Deputy Prime Minister in charge of Labour and others who were close to the reformist views of Fraga. In addition, the civil service came under the control of a number of leading Christian democrats closely linked to the democratically inclined *Tácito* movement. Following their lead, rather than his own more hardline instincts Arias made public his government's intended direction in a speech delivered in February 1974, subsequently dubbed 'the Spirit of 12 February'. Essentially it promised timid moves towards greater political freedom, increasing the numbers of elected representatives in the Francoist parliament or Cortes. Political associations but not parties were promised at some point in the future and more elections rather than appointments for local government posts.

Nonetheless, the programme failed its first test in the Añoveros case later that month. A Bilbao bishop, Antonio Añoveros, was denounced in the press for interpreting the words of Pope John XXIII's encyclical *Mater et magister* as a defence of Basques' right to exercise their cultural differences. Arias refused to defend the Bishop, who was first placed under house arrest and then threatened with exile until Franco stepped in to calm matters (Payne 1987: 595–6). The execution on 2 March by garrotte of a Catalan anarchist, Salvador Puig Antich, amid a massive clampdown on working-class groups, and terrorist organizations such as ETA and the left-wing FRAP, was further evidence of the negligible influence of Arias's promises of reform. Caught between pressure to reform and the regime hardliners who accused him of complicity with the enemies of Spain, Arias increasingly sided with the hardliners.

International pressures were building, as well, in the form of condemnation and also example-setting. Spain had been roundly condemned by the European Community for the Añoveros and Puig affairs. In April 1974 Spaniards heard reports from across the border (the television images of celebrations in Portuguese streets having been censored in Spain) of how the military could peacefully dismantle a dictatorship. While there was no chance of a similar military revolt in Spain, the opposition was given a much-needed fillip. Arias did manage to defuse a counter-plot to seize power by hardline Francoists, but his attempts to introduce limited political association satisfied no one, and at a speech in Barcelona in June 1974 he effectively closed the door on reform (Prego 1995: 140).

2.16   The Third Way

The boost that ETA had received as a result of the Burgos trials and with their removal of Carrero merely confirmed the organization in its action–repression–action strategy, which by inflaming the hard right complicated any moves towards an opening out of the regime (*aperturismo*) towards, if not democracy, then political pluralism. The latter half of the 1960s had seen a debate within the regime as to how to introduce political associations, by which was meant expression of political opinions short of forming actual parties. The debate was paralyzed by the militancy of the opposition towards the end of the decade as Carrero's government could only respond with increased repression. The appearance of neo-fascist direct-action groups such as Fuerza Nueva and Guerrilleros de Cristo Rey which, with seeming official impunity, carried out attacks on progressive groups – students, clergy and intellectuals – in addition to creating a climate of fear, intensified this social polarization (Payne 1987: 585).

The powerlessness of the government and the inspiring effect of the Portuguese revolution had had the effect at least of galvanizing the communist and socialist opposition into some kind of joint action. The Communists and a range of allies had set up the Junta Democrática de España in July 1974. This was an extremely broad grouping of communists, socialists, monarchists and regionalist socialists. Overtures had even been made to Don Juan to grant his support. Its programme was not unlike what would eventually be implemented in the Transition, but its aim was to do so immediately, what was known as *ruptura democrática*, a definite democratic break with the preceding authoritarian system. The Socialists, boosted by the election of the dynamic young Felipe González as their leader in 1974, set up their parallel Plataforma de Convergencia Democrática the following year, uniting Socialists, leftist Christian Democrats and the moderate Basque nationalist PNV.

The two options that were coalescing at this point as alternatives to the 'immobilism' or continuism of the hard right were, on the one hand, that of *ruptura* favoured by the Communists and Socialists, change without concessions and, on the other, reform or *apertura* (opening) also referred to as *ruptura pactada* (negotiated change). The latter was favoured by the internal opposition, sometimes referred to as the 'civilized right' of monarchists, liberals and Christian Democrats (Soto 1997: 81). It would be this group that would eventually constitute a 'third way' solution to the post-Franco period by advocating a peaceful internal evolution of the regime towards democracy with the cooperation of the prince, Juan Carlos (Pérez Serrano 2007: 64).

2.17   Death of a Dictator

Franco was hospitalized in the summer of 1975 with phlebitis in his right leg. He suffered a relapse in July, and on this occasion Prince Juan Carlos reluctantly took charge of the country. Resilient as ever, Franco recovered the reins of power in September and was well enough to dismiss the Minister of Information, Pío Cabanillas, in October on account of what Franco perceived as a overly outspoken press (Ellwood 1994: 213). More dramatically, he was well enough to approve the execution on 27 September 1975 of two ETA and three FRAP terrorists under a new, draconian anti-terrorist law which made the death penalty mandatory and retroactively applicable for murder of a member of the security forces. Unlike in 1970, Franco was indifferent to the pleas from the Vatican (twice), the United Nations and even from Don Juan and Prince Juan Carlos (Preston 2004: 308). This may have been owing to the extreme pressures the regime was under that year, one of the most violent in its history, with eight policemen killed in as many months. Their funerals were turned into mass demonstrations by ultra-right sympathizers, and attacks against progressives, the opposition and, even in some cases, ministers in their cars, were the order of the day (Payne 1994: 248).

In his last public appearance on the balcony of the Plaza de Oriente, Franco's supporters acclaimed him on the 39th anniversary of his appointment as Head of State and he still found the strength to blame the international protests on 'a political leftist–masonic conspiracy in cahoots with a social communist–terrorist subversion' against Spain which, he claimed, merely enhanced Spaniards' sense of pride. 'Clearly', he added somewhat enigmatically, 'being Spanish is once again a serious matter in the world.' Proof of both the futility of the regime's intransigence and its weakness was that that same day, a radical left-wing organization, GRAPO, killed four policemen in separate incidents in Madrid (Payne 1994: 249–50). Fifteen days later Franco suffered a heart attack and three more five days later. Juan Carlos took control of the country on 30

October 1975. On 5 November Franco was admitted to hospital for the final time and died in the early hours of 20 November. There is no doubt that in the preceding weeks he had endured great suffering, and it is ironic that someone who approved executions of opponents with such ease was quoted in his last days as saying, 'Lord, how difficult it is to die' (Payne 1994: 252).

2.18   Conclusion

The fact that Franco died in his bed, albeit a hospital bed, might be seen by some as an affront to the victims of his regime. That it was a long and painful passing might satisfy some of his remaining enemies, but the slow and gradual decline of the dictator was ultimately good for Spain. It allowed his successor not only to have several practice sessions in the seat of power during Franco's illnesses, but more importantly to carry on as he was assiduously doing in liaising with the liberal reformist members of the regime and conducting cloak-and-dagger meetings with the representatives of the still illegal opposition in order to send out the 'message to all … that there was going to be significant political change and that the takeover should not be undermined' (Preston 2004: 320). As a result, by the time Carlos Arias Navarro appeared on Spanish television screens to tearfully announce his leader's demise, after over a decade of social change both Spanish society and the apparatus of succession were primed and ready to go into action.

There is no doubting the economic success of the period since 1960. Spain in 1975 had definitively joined the first world as its ninth most powerful economy with a per capita income of over $2000. Nevertheless, the Spain emerging from the shadow of the dictator, while vastly transformed over the preceding 30 years, was undoubtedly scarred and traumatized by an experience which it could so readily have done without. While Malefakis can hypothesize the 'sad truth' that 'Spain in 1975, when Franco died, was at approximately the same level of socio-economic development as it would have been had he never lived', and that at least by permitting the changes from 1960 onwards the regime ensured that it was 'only a parenthesis, however awful, in Spain's history' (Malefakis 2007: 253), there is no escaping the damage that had been done nor the way it would colour the country's subsequent history and the lives of its people. The success of the Transition would be attributable less to the deliberate initiatives of the regime than to the often heroic achievements of its people and politicians against the odds. One example is the gradual development of a civil society through legal associations and citizens' groups in the face of the regime's determination to block associationism. The importance of these groups, often eclipsed by the emphasis on the actions of the politicians during the Transition, was to create 'a broader democratic culture [which] had to be in place before the elites could even imagine making certain choices' (Radcliff 2007: 141).

That Franco's funeral was attended by few foreign representatives, among whom, significantly, were Augusto Pinochet and Imelda Marcos, whereas Juan Carlos's coronation mass attracted the presence of the presidents of France and Germany, as well as the German prime minister, Willy Brandt, and from Britain, the Duke of Edinburgh, underlined the climate of good will that greeted the new monarchy and passed a damning verdict on the preceding regime. Juan Carlos rewarded this show of confidence when, on his first foreign trip, to the USA in June 1976, he made an unequivocal statement of commitment to democracy before a joint session of the Congress and the Senate, which 'had an electrifying impact in Spain' (Preston 2004: 349) and confirmed Juan Carlos's resolution to initiate immediately Spain's transition to democracy.

3

THE TRANSITION, 1975–82

3.1 Introduction

The death of Franco marked the beginning of a period which became known simply as the Transition. It is considered to end with the victory of the Socialists in the general elections of October 1982. The political maturity and democratic stability that allowed a peaceful accession to power by means of free elections of a left-wing party so relatively soon after the end of a prolonged right-wing authoritarian regime was seen as a sign that democracy was truly installed. Of course, this situation was not limited to Spain. Similar transitions and comparable successes by the local Socialist party were a characteristic of Greece and Portugal (Judt 2007: 523). Some might argue that the Transition ended with the entry into effect of the Constitution in December 1978, or even with the first truly free democratic elections held in 1977. One influential documentary by the journalist Victoria Prego begins with the assassination of Carrero and ends with the first democratic elections of 1977. Prego justifies her decision for the start date, not with the idea that the elimination of Carrero put an end to the continuance of the regime, but rather that it was a brutal psychological blow to the regime showing its leaders were vulnerable (Prego 1995–6: 159). Hence it marked a watershed.

It has been noted that the historiography of the Transition has been dominated by three basic accounts of its success. One stresses almost deterministically the economic and social changes in Spain over the 1960s and 1970s which made the Transition 'inevitable'. Another approach, which Radcliff sees as more characteristic of transition theorists, or 'transitologists', as they are increasingly known, stresses the 'agency of elite protagonists' whose decisions and pacts, regardless of the socio-economic conditions, sealed the process (2007: 141). Yet another highlights the role of social groups such as trade unions, neighbourhood associations and student organizations (Díaz 1999: 36). Most commentators would agree that any interpreta-tion must attempt to take all three aspects into account (Quirosa-Cheyrouze y Muñoz 2007: 17), and even proponents of one or the other interpretation recognize the 'multidimen-sionality and complexity' of the topic (Gunther, Montero and Botella 2004: 83).

Spain's Transition benefited from the presence within the regime of certain reformist figures who had attained a position of influence. A second factor was undoubtedly the pragmatism of the main opposition groups, especially the Communists, which ensured that they could be accepted by the political estab-lishment and Spanish society. Finally, the significant economic and social transformation Spanish society had undergone as a result of the economic miracle of the 1960s meant that as a nation Spain was ready, not to say impatient for change.

An unquestionably vital factor was the presence of certain key figures such as the King Juan Carlos and his chosen premier, Adolfo Suárez. Recent revelations by Suárez's son suggest their strategy was hatched as early as 1968 (Palomares 2007: 132). Juan Carlos had the further benefit of having learned lessons from his brother-in-law, ex-King Constantine of Greece (Preston 2004: 211). Suárez was skilled in guiding the country through the political minefield at the time, abetted by the good sense and maturity of the political elite in general, learning no doubt from the errors made by Portugal the previ-ous year, to make the correct compromises to ensure the process remained in the hands of politicians and not the military (Magone 2004: 16). Even more significant, perhaps, than the example of contemporary events in other countries was the ever-present memory of Spain's relatively recent past. Paloma Aguilar has stressed the importance of the traumatic memory of the Civil War on Spain's political elite during their decision-making, thus ensuring that past mistakes were not repeated. This was helped by the prevailing attitude by the end of the regime that in the Civil War 'two warring sides were equally responsible', thus it was best forgotten (Aguilar 1999: 7). This paved the way for the policy of consensus that underpinned the first half of the Transition period.

Nevertheless, while most accounts remark on the speed and success of the transition owing to a felicitous combination of historical circumstance and key players, it is worth remembering the precariousness of the situation which meant that the 'Spanish democratic transition was neither "natural" or "inevitable" ... almost all of the problems that had resulted in democratic breakdown in Spain previously, were still in existence in the 1970s' (Edles 1998: 7).

3.2   Weighing up the Options

As we have seen (**2.16**), the options available at the time ranged from preservation of the status quo (*continuismo*), favoured by the Francoist hardliners, to the favoured option of the opposition, that of a total overthrow of the regime and installation of a democratic government of national reconciliation (*ruptura*). Well before the dictator's death a third option, that of reform (*reforma* or *ruptura pactada* – negotiated change) started to gain ground. The new monarchical regime with Juan Carlos at its head began with a very *continuista* look to it. The King's first move, to widespread disappointment, was to keep the standing prime minister, Arias Navarro, in charge of his first government. Another former Franco minister, Manuel Fraga, was brought into the cabinet in charge of public order (*Ministerio de Gobernación*) and the aristocratic José María de Areilza was charged with improving Spain's image abroad. While the latter two had reputations as modernizers, Arias was essentially an unreconstructed Francoist. Though he attempted reform, his heart was clearly not in it and he quickly proved himself unable to control events. Between 1975 and 1976 Spain experienced spectacular bouts of worker unrest, including one strike at a metal company in the Basque Country during which five people were killed in clashes with the police. In Fraga's absence the acting Interior Minister, Adolfo Suárez, efficiently dealt with the crisis (Palomares 2004: 156). As a result of such social tension, the Socialists and Communists saw the sense of joining forces and merging their separate groups, the Junta and the Plataforma, into a unified entity called popularly the *Platajunta* on 17 March 1976.

There were signs at the time of the opposition, particularly from the socialist side, favouring negotiated reform rather than outright overthrow, and Arias's government did foster this slightly by a greater tolerance of socialist activity, such as permitting the holding of the 30th Congress of the UGT in Madrid while at the same time his Interior Minister, Fraga, who under Franco had been a centrist but became increasingly right-wing (Palomares 2007: 133), insisted on clamping down on communist militants such as Marcelino Camacho, the leader of the Workers' Commissions (CC OO) trade union, who was arrested as he left a meeting about the Platajunta merger in Madrid (Prego 1995: 426–7).

Arias's inability to push through even moderate reform, such as decriminalizing all parties except the Communist Party (PCE) and separatist groups, led the King to look elsewhere for a replacement and, since constitutionally it would be difficult to sack him, he chose to undermine his position by allowing a report in *Newsweek* according to which he referred to Arias as an 'unmitigated disaster' and as the 'standard-bearer of the *búnker*' to go unchallenged (Prego 1995: 445). This was one of several significant interventions that Juan Carlos would make in the Transition period and led to him being dubbed the 'engine' or the 'pilot' of the process of change in Spain. What Juan Carlos and those around him quickly realized was that change would only be successful if it was freely entered into by the regime itself. Rather than overthrowing the system, it would have to be reformed from within. For this to happen it was essential to find a replacement for Arias from among the Francoist ranks and that person was Adolfo Suárez, a protégé of the *éminence grise* of the Transition, Torcuato Fernández Miranda.

3.3   The Dream Team: Juan Carlos and Suárez

It is hard to overestimate the achievement of Juan Carlos in very difficult circumstances. Not only did he have to fend off the pressures from the extreme right of the Francoist hardliners or *búnker*, as they were known, led by José Antonio Girón de Velasco, who wished him to be, at most, a symbolic head of an essentially Francoist regime, but he also had to placate the opposition who wished to see an immediate installation of a democratic system (*ruptura democrática*). He also had to put up with the respected Communist leader, Santiago Carrillo, assuring everyone he was a puppet who would last only a few months as King (Prego 1995: 302). He did this with great skill, using close collaborators like Manuel Prado de Carvajal, who acted as a roving ambassador to enlist the support of international figures such as Giscard d'Estaing, Gerald Ford and Henry Kissinger to support his coronation, meetings with prominent socialists such as Luis Solana to convey the message to Felipe González, the PSOE leader, of his intention to progress towards democracy, and delicate diplomacy with both the reformists and the hardliners within the regime to ensure their support for his creation of a government conducive to the changes he planned (Prego 1995: 444). As Juan Linz noted, the case of Juan Carlos was 'clearly one in which leadership emerges in response to a situation, a task, rather than through a slow process of selection before the events, and certainly not on the basis of broad popular appeal pushing the leaders in their position' (Bernecker, 1998: 65).

One of the greatest cards that Juan Carlos held and which he managed always to play magisterially was his role as head of the armed forces. This, as well as his surprising skill at diplomacy and ability to call on political favours (in this case with

Henry Kissinger), was powerfully illustrated in his success in defusing the crisis with Morocco in 1975 when King Hassan planned a 'green march' against Spanish garrisons in the Western Sahara (Preston 2004: 314–15). In the Transition it was this role that was to save the Transition from the menace of *golpismo* that, until well into the 1980s, threatened to undo the progress made.

The King's astuteness was shown when he succeeded in persuading the Francoist, Rodríguez Valcárcel, not to stand for reappointment to the Presidency of the Cortes, thus ensuring that Torcuato Fernández Miranda's name figured on the *terna*, the trio of candidates' names from which he as King, following the regime's procedure, would have to choose. Fernández Miranda, while a loyal Francoist, had been the King's former tutor and was someone he could trust. In addition, he was 'a "behind-the-scenes" figure with a fine legal mind and a somewhat Machiavellian reputation' who 'understood the institutions as well as anyone, and he was the ideal person to plan their dismantlement' (Gilmour 1985:139). Remarkably, given the tensions in their relationship, Juan Carlos was able to persuade Girón and Arias to neutralize the diehards and accept Fernández-Miranda's inclusion. Once in place, the latter was able to assist in manoeuvring Adolfo Suárez into position to substitute the ineffectual Arias after a diplomatic lapse of time.

3.4   Dismantling the Regime

That Suárez was a man picked to do a political job (which he did) rather than a politician pursuing his own democratic convictions is illustrated by the fact that as late as the previous year, he was still involved in an association, the Unión del Pueblo Español, which sought no more than moderate *continuista* reform of the regime (Preston 1986: 72). Once in post, however, in July 1976, Suárez rose to the more ambitious task of moving Spain in the direction of democracy. He championed a

Political Reform Law, a text of less than one thousand words in length, which set out the principles for a democratic system based on universal suffrage for the election of a two-chamber parliament. The law was actually the brainchild of Fernández-Miranda, but he generously allowed Suárez to assume paternity over it (Prego 2000: 37). It was overwhelmingly approved (94 per cent) by the Spanish people in a referendum on 15 December 1976. Suárez's greatest triumph was 'bringing the opposition to collaborate in a process of democratization within Francoist "legality"' (Preston 1986: 94).

In spite of the dissatisfaction of the Communist Party, which still found itself officially unaccepted, most of the democratic opposition were gradually won over by the moves made by Suárez. In particular, Santiago Carrillo proved to be a very willing collaborator as he was eager that the Communists would not be left out in the cold, and he was acutely aware of the danger of provoking the right-wing bunker. González, too, was won over to Suárez after the latter's first Cabinet Meeting on 17 July when he announced free elections for June 1977, and the first wave of amnesties took place a few days later (Sánchez Cervelló and Tubau 2004: 72). The introduction of the Law of Political Reform and the promise of free elections tempered their demands. Suárez used considerable back-room skills to ensure that the Political Reform Law was passed by the Cortes in November 1976, an event which Preston described as the Francoist system committing 'collective suicide' (1986: 101). Suárez, too, cleverly used the pressure from the military bunker to argue against a rash decision on PCE legalization. In addition, by permitting the mobilization of alternative socialist groups within the country, such as the Partido Socialista Popular of the very popular Enrique Tierno Galván and the PSOE-Histórico, representing the exiled socialist leaders ousted by Felipe at the PSOE's Suresnes Congress in 1974, Suárez put pressure on González's PSOE to commit to the future electoral process.

3.5 Challenges to Democracy: *Golpismo* and Terrorism

The year 1976 saw constant pressure from the military. Juan Carlos was unsuccessful in promoting his preferred choice, Gutiérrez Mellado, a moderate general who had sympathy with the democratically inclined sector of the military, to the position of Defence Minister and instead had to accept the more right-wing Fernando de Santiago y Díaz de Mendívil. Gutiérrez Mellado was, however, made Chief of the General Staff. Under intense pressure from representatives of the hard right, Suárez met with senior military figures in September 1976 and persuaded them to accept his plans for political reform, which at this stage excluded legalization of the PCE, something which Suárez did intend to do once he could persuade the communists to amend their statutes to make them more acceptable (Preston 1986: 97–8). The subsequent destitution of Santiago y Díaz for his outrage at a proposal for trade union reform and the raising of Gutiérrez Mellado to the Defence ministry unleashed a wave of hostility towards the latter and Suárez and inaugurated an atmosphere of military conspiracy and planning of coups, known as *golpismo*, which was to endanger the success of the Transition until well into the 1980s (Preston 1995b: 39). It did not, however, prevent Gutiérrez Mellado carrying out the necessary reform of the army, principally through a policy of stategic promotions of younger, more democratically minded military men.

From September 1977 there were regular calls from the right for a government of national salvation and attacks on the person of Gutiérrez Mellado. One incident was a meeting of military officers with Gutiérrez Mellado, when a commander of the Guardia Civil, Juan Atarés, insulted him, calling him a traitor. He was ordered by the Minister to leave the room but he returned to add 'freemason, traitor, pig, coward and spy' to the list of insults (Preston 1986: 147). It was shortly after this when on 16 November a plot, code-named *Operación Galaxia*, to kidnap the President and his cabinet in the Moncloa Palace was uncovered and foiled. The subsequent soft treatment of both Atarés, acquitted by a military tribunal, and the plotters, Tejero and Saenz de Ynestrillas, condemned to a mere six months' detention, showed the government's reluctance to confront the Francoist bunker.

The Army's principal concern centred on the decentralization process (*proceso autonómico*), which it saw as a threat to Spanish unity. Since the passing of the Constitution, which itself had incurred the military's displeasure, the role of the armed forces had been reduced from defenders of public order to the more restricted one of guardians of national unity, a factor which in turn served to 'justify' *golpista* tendencies. An example was the 1981 coup attempt when 'the conspirators arrogantly claimed during their trial that they were acting in accordance with their constitutional duty to protect the integrity of the Spanish state against the threats represented by regional demands' (Heywood 1995: 53). This was an attitude that was to resurface as late as 2005 in the response of some officers to the reform of the Catalan Statute (see **6.7**).

Tusell notes that after the death of Franco, the proportion of GDP allocated to Defence was small in comparison to the number of the officer class (Tusell 1997: 76). This in itself was sufficient cause for military revolt, as seen in the Tejero incident of February 1981. However, military discontent was fuelled by the constant terrorist campaign waged by ETA, despite the apparent gains for the Basque nationalist cause in the Constitution, and the subsequent passing of the Statute of Guernica granting considerable self-government. Over the years from 1978 to 1980 the death toll wreaked by ETA was 66, 76 and 92, respectively (www.mir.es).

The weak link in Suárez's otherwise smooth handling of events was the situation in the Basque country. Alfonso Osorio, the Deputy Prime Minister, noted in his diary at the time that Suárez was unable to understand the Basques (Preston 1986: 104). Where Suárez managed to keep one step ahead of his adversaries elsewhere, with the Basque situation it was the opposite. He only acted when forced to do so by events on the street, though there were signs that he was conscious of the need to do something to ease the tension, 'otherwise the Basque Country will become our Belfast', he told a colleague in 1977 (Powell and Bonnin 2004: 126). In Catalonia a massive demonstration of over one million people on 11 September 1977 led the government to establish the provisional Generalitat or regional government on 29 September. The following month the exiled leader Josep Tarradellas was invited home to assume the presidency (Conversi 1997: 143). The Basque problem required a more deep-rooted and symbolic political response in order to win over the moderate majority and isolate the radicals. Suárez made the mistake of leaving it to his Interior Minister, Martín Villa, to carry out a purely police response. There was massive popular demand in the Basque country for amnesty, unabated with the partial amnesty of 30 July 1976, which did not include crimes of blood and left 145 ETA members in jail. The end of a voluntary ceasefire by ETA with the murder of a government representative in Guipúzcoa in October 1976 led to clandestine talks between the government and the terrorist organization. Suárez restored fiscal privileges to Vizcaya and Guipúzcoa (withdrawn by Franco) in October 1976, legalized the Basque flag in January 1977 and granted an amnesty in March, thus going a long way to appeasing Basque demands, but it always seemed too little too late.

Parallel to this, terrorism practised by the mysterious apparently radical left-wing organization GRAPO (Grupo Revolucionario Antifascista Primero de Octubre) was a constant threat to Suárez's reforms, designed as it was to provoke the already excitable bunker. One such action was the kidnap of the President of the Council of State, General Villaescusa Quilis. Many at the time, including Gutiérrez Mellado and possibly Suárez, believed that GRAPO might be right-wing-controlled and bent on destabilizing the transition process (Gilmour 1985: 160). The infamous murder of five people, including four communist labour lawyers, in their offices in Atocha, Madrid, by a right-wing gang was believed to be retaliation for Villaescusa's kidnap. Whether or not this was so, it had the opposite of the desired effect as the restrained reaction of the communists to the atrocity actually gained them much respect and made it easier in the long run for Suárez to push for their legalization (Preston 1986: 107).

Negotiations with ETA, which resumed in February 1977, led to some progress in terms of a truce in return for further amnesties. However, the demand for total amnesty remained with not only the threat to boycott the coming elections but a resumption of violence on the part of ETA. When Suárez granted the complete amnesty on 20 May it clearly seemed as a result of pressure rather than a positive initiative on his part (Gilmour 1985: 219).

3.6 A Leader in Search of a Party

Suárez's long-term hope was to consolidate a party of the centre-right which would fend off the strong challenge of the parties of the left. However, his project was scuppered by the rapid mobilization of the representatives of the liberal wing of the Francoist establishment, organized around the figure of Manuel Fraga, who established a right-wing party, Alianza Popular, to challenge Suárez's command of the centre ground. Suárez was still able to manoeuvre himself into a commanding position as the leader of a centrist coalition, but this could only be maintained in the mood of political consensus that characterized the early part of the Transition and which discouraged members of that centre coalition from gravitating towards their true ideological stamping ground further to the left or the right.

UCD was a rather messy coalition of parties from the broad centre of the political spectrum and included Christian Democrats, liberals, social democrats and even some ex-members of the Francoist *Movimiento*. Their union was based on political expediency in the light of imminent elections and was characterized as a 'ruthless quest for profitable alliances, which ... rode roughshod over ideological, personal or moral considerations' (Preston 1986: 111). Suárez, a sharp media performer, appeared on Spanish television on the night of 3 May 1977 to explain two things: one, his reasons for legalizing the Communist Party and two, his decision to fight the 15 June elections at the head of a new coalition, UCD (Prego 1995: 673).

3.7 Cutting the Gordian Knot: the Legalization of the PCE

Legalizing the Communist party was perhaps the principal political hurdle faced by Suárez. For the stalwarts of the Franco regime, saving Spain from communism was still seen as the major justification of the Civil War. Legalization would constitute a betrayal not only of the memory of Franco but of all those that had fought and died between 1936 and 1939. The way that the hurdle was negotiated displayed both the skill and the shortcomings of Suárez. One of Suárez's great phrases was 'Hay que convertir en real lo que ya es real a nivel de la calle' ('It is necessary to make real what is already real in the streets'). By March 1977 the opinion polls were telling Suárez that 40 per cent of Spaniards supported the legalization, a mood undoubtedly influenced by the brutal killing by right-wing extremists of five people, four of them communist labour lawyers, in January (Prego 2000: 58; Preston 1986: 107).

Suárez had met with the senior members of the military command in September 1976 to gain their support for legalization of parties and to assure them that this would stop short of the PCE. Meanwhile he engaged in prolonged negotiations with Santiago Carrillo, the veteran communist leader, to persuade him and his party to recognize the monarchy, the unity of the nation and the Spanish flag (Prego 1995: 664). Carrillo, ever the pragmatist, was accommodating and indeed his attitude throughout the Transition was a major factor in its success. Suárez then waited until the Easter break of 1977 when major figures in the armed forces were on holiday and off guard to announce the legalization. His subsequent attitude was that he had not betrayed a promise as the Communists had substantially changed their stance, and therefore his promise the previous September had been superseded by events. The military never saw it that way, despite Suárez going to the extreme of playing them a recording of their earlier meeting. He was never trusted by them again, although only the Navy minister, Admiral Pita da Veiga, a notorious hardliner, presented his resignation (Prego 2000: 61).

Nonetheless, the presence of Carrillo and the Communists within the political process was crucial not only to its legitimacy but also its success. The communists showed dignity and restraint, especially at the time of the Atocha murders (see **3.5**), and were welcoming in their response to the King's vision of a democratic future, which went a long way towards placating the left.

The results of the elections on 15 June 1977 (see Appendix 1) proved that Spaniards wanted to look to the future rather than the past. The parties of the extreme left and right, the Spanish Communist Party (*Partido Comunista de España*, PCE) and the Conservative Popular Alliance (*Alianza Popular*, AP) under Manuel Fraga, fared badly with only 9.4 per cent and 8.2 per cent of the vote, respectively. Suárez's UCD came top with 34.5 per cent and was followed by Felipe González's PSOE with 29.4 per cent. Suárez had used his control of the media to perfection and benefited from the new women's vote (over 60 per cent of UCD's vote was from women) (Vincent 2007: 216). The Popular Alliance, on the other hand, had revived memories of the regime by giving media prominence to Arias Navarro, who unashamedly reiterated his reverence and nostalgia for Franco. The communists suffered also from their old-fashioned image and their leaders' connections with the Civil War. The results were good for Suárez, as a more overwhelming victory might have recalled a previous era.

3.8 A Constitution for All

After the success of the elections the next challenge for the fledgling democracy was the creation of a successful constitutional framework to anchor the new system. Spain's constitutional history dated back to the early nineteenth century when on 19 March 1812 a liberal parliament meeting in Cádiz produced the country's first progressive charter. Thus, too, began a pendular process whereby with each change of regime from liberal to conservative and back again, there followed a constitutional change that reflected the ideology of the party in power (Gilmour 1985: 194). It has to be said that Suárez was originally of a mind to do the same and have a text drafted by UCD lawyers. In the end, he was persuaded of the benefits of a constitution that would receive the backing of a wide range of the populace and political classes. The task was assigned to a subcommittee of seven representatives, reflecting approximately the proportion of support for the parties. Hence, UCD was represented by three members, Miguel Herrero de Miñón, José Pedro Pérez Llorca and Gabriel Cisneros. The Socialists had one representative: Gregorio Peces Barba, a moderate Catholic human-rights expert. All nationalists shared as their representative the Catalan Miquel Roca, since both Basques and Catalans at the time formed part of the same parliamentary group, but he was rejected by the Basques of the PNV who withdrew from the larger, 36-strong parliamentary Constitutional Committee. Alianza Popular on the right was represented by its leader Manuel Fraga and the Communists by law professor Jordi Solé Tura, who belonged to the Catalan branch of the Partido Comunista which had been the most successful in the recent elections.

The 1978 Constitution was unusual in many respects. First, in terms of its drafting it was neither the product of a constitutional assembly nor a provisional government specially designated for that purpose. Secondly, while designed to usher in a new era, it was very much a 'continuist' document, in that it did not challenge the existing parliamentary system and monarchy, but rather confirmed them in a renovated format (Soto 2005: 104). It was, as one commentator put it, a 'triumph of political compromise' (Heywood 1995: 37). It was also a text 'based on a wilful amnesia', as it drew heavily on its 1931 precursor but could not refer to it so as not to offend the right since 'the Franco regime was built on the rejection of the democracy for which the Republican Constitution had stood' (Balfour and Quiroga 2007: 45). The detail is yet one more example of the process of forgetting which necessarily lay at the root of the Transition's success.

Much of the groundwork for the Constitution had been laid by the Political Reform Law (LRP) of September 1976 which converted the Cortes into a two-chamber parliament, Congress and Senate, with a system of universal suffrage to elect the former (the Senate would be by a mixture of election and appointment). The flexibility implied in the law allowed the Government and Suárez to design an electoral process that both suited them and the need of the country at the time for a process of stable change. In March 1977 the electoral rules were published. These included a version of the D'Hondt system and voting for party lists. This was a proportional representation system that favoured provinces (the electoral constituency according to the LRP) with small populations. These tended to be conservative and rural in outlook and therefore inclined towards the centre-right parties. This was reinforced by the choice of 21 as the legal voting age to avoid the influence of a supposedly more radical youth vote. The setting of a minimum number of MPs per province and a limit on the percentage of votes needed (3 per cent) to ensure representation, meant that effectively the proportional representationality of the electoral system was sacrificed for one that approximated more to the majority system and which favoured the large party formations. Thus it was designed to produce artificial majorities and stable governments where even if coalitions were required, they would be limited in number (Soto 2005: 85).

The committee produced two drafts of the constitution in April 1978 which were duly approved by a Committee of Constitutional Matters and Public Liberties on 1 July and subsequently, the Congress, the lower chamber of Parliament on 21 July. The upper chamber or Senate introduced some amendments before the final text was approved on 28 October 1978 and passed by the people in a referendum on 6 December, with 87.7 per cent of those casting their vote giving their approval with 7.9 per cent against.

The important and enduring flaw in the constitutional process was the absence of the Basque nationalists in the form of their majority party, the moderate PNV. According to Heywood, their exclusion from the *ponencia* (constitutional committee) was seen as a result of deliberate strategy on the part of UCD and the Socialists in the belief that they 'could marginalize nationalist forces in the Basque Country and divide control of the region's politics between themselves' (Heywood 1995: 45). González, however, has argued that while the Socialists conceded one of the places on the *ponencia* that they were proportionally due in order that the Catalans could have a place, this was not reciprocated by UCD, who refused to cede one of their three places to the Basques (Sánchez Cervelló and Tubau 2004: 76). As Heywood points out, the sidelining of the PNV extended to the rejection of all their suggested amendments to the constitutional text, leading eventually to their abandonment of the Constitutional Committee and, to this day, their ability to claim no involvement in or necessary allegiance to the document (Heywood 1995: 46). As a result, in the Basque Country there was a 55.3 per cent abstention rate, compared to 32.9 per cent overall for Spain. Of those that voted in the Basque region, 69.7 per cent voted in favour but, as Soto points out, the combined 'no' vote and abstentions total 65.9 per cent (2005: 125).

Roca's role was important in one detail: deciding the terminology for the different regions. This would be (and still is) a particularly intractable problem for Spain's decentralization process. The 'historic' regions insist on what is referred to as their 'differential quality' (*hecho diferencial* in Spanish or *fet diferencial*, a term dating from early twentieth-century Catalan nationalism, returning to vogue in the 1990s with the increasing threat of federalism). To reflect this, the Constitution, in the face of protest from Fraga and his supporters, adopted the term suggested by Roca of 'nationality' (*nacionalidad*) to refer to the three historic regions, reserving the word 'region' for the other fourteen and protecting the use of 'nation' solely for Spain. The 1978 Constitution had rejected the option of federalism (popularly known at the time as 'coffee for everyone' – *café para todos*) to propose a form of asymmetrical devolution, thus preserving Basque, Catalan and to a lesser degree Galician sensitivities, but inevitably storing up problems for the future (Balfour and Quiroga 2007: 61).

The resulting Constitution was a classic example of the consensus principle underlying the Transition. It was decided through a complex system of vote trading (Colomer 1999) in which the centre-right UCD secured the monarchy and a capitalist system and the left won social and individual rights. The conservatives and nationalists reached agreement on territorial issues whereby a unified Spain with its centralist administration via the provinces coexisted with three paths to self-government, one immediate for the historic regions, one fast and one slow.

3.9   From Consensus to Disenchantment: the 1979 Elections

The success of the Spanish Transition owed a great deal to the much vaunted concept of *consenso*, not to be disparaged in a country that had, for so many years under Franco and even centuries before, been ruined by the clash of 'two Spains', one progressive, the other reactionary (Aguilar 2002: 210–11). Nevertheless, as Preston makes clear, the success of the Transition owed, therefore, as much to the sacrifices made by the legitimate opposition to the Franco regime, the heirs of the legitimacy that Franco and his troops had so violently usurped in 1936, and that these sacrifices were not rewarded in terms of true social change for the sectors of society those on the left represented. Hence, 'while the Suárez reform was ample for the conservative middle classes, the great popular hunger for change went unsatisfied' (Preston 1986: 120–1). As Edles points out, Spain is a classic example of 'elite settlement', one in which these elites 'defined their goals not as the maximalisation of the interests of their respective clienteles, but rather the creation of a legitimate and stable regime within which their supporters' interests would merely be "satisfied"' (1998: 14–15). In other words, 'democracy' was defined as the goal, and while this was part of the success of the Transition, it was also a cause of disappointment.

For many Spaniards, the arrival of the Constitution and the consolidation of the democratic system (despite the threats of *golpismo* and terrorism) would lead soon to a dissatisfaction with the status quo, especially when it was clear that 'large numbers of the Francoist cadres remained in positions of power by means of a simple transfer from the *Movimiento* to UCD' (Preston 1986: 120). There was a sense that the new political regime was a product of a 'transaction between political elites' (Powell 2001a: 237). As a result, the high ideals that had greeted the arrival of democracy were replaced with a lowering of expectations faced with the reality, and a subsequent mood of *desencanto* (disillusionment) set in.

Certainly, faced with the new post-Constitution reality, all parties, institutions and sectors were obliged to revise their strategy. With democracy seemingly consolidated, parties had to set about redefining themselves. Hence, although not strictly necessary, Suárez decided to call new elections for 1 March 1979 in the hope that the success of the Constitution might carry him to an absolute majority. In the event, the results were much the same (see Appendix 2). UCD won 168 seats against 121 for the Socialists. It was said that among the Socialists there was a certain trepidation about the possibility that they might actually win, and some took this to explain González's rather lacklustre performance (Sánchez Cervelló and Tubau 2004: 76). Certainly, the result was disappointing, as not only had the party absorbed the PSP of Enrique Tierno Galván, which had won six seats at the previous election, but the Constitution had lowered the voting age to 18, leading some to expect a boost from young radical voters. The polls had shown a high number of undecided voters (40 per cent), and therefore UCD's control of the media was an undoubted advantage in swaying the waverers. In addition, Suárez's blatant scaremongering during the campaign regarding the consequences of a Socialist victory, in which he emphasized their 'Marxism', was seen as a sign of the end of consensus politics (Powell 2001a: 236).

The fortunes of the PCE rose slightly as it gained 23 seats, but there was also a worrying rise in support for the extreme right with Blas Piñar's party, *Fuerza Nueva* (registered as *Partido Unión Nacional*), gaining one seat with nearly 400,000 votes. While the main parties' positions remained largely unaffected, there were some casualties. Fraga had teamed up with more moderate groups to form the Democratic Coalition, but was still unable to challenge UCD for the centre ground and saw its vote fall to just over 6 per cent, dropping from 16 seats to 10 in Parliament. UCD's vote stayed stable, but far from the absolute majority Suárez had hoped. The main change was the growth in support for the smaller regional parties, such as *Herri Batasuna* (HB, People's Unity) in the Basque country. Formed just the previous year and close to ETA, it gained three MPs and one senator.

The 1979 elections were marked by *desencanto*, a general disenchantment with the democratic process which accounted for a turnout of 68 per cent, nearly 11 per cent down on 1977 (Prego 1995: 676). This had been the case, too, during the referendums for the Constitution and the Basque and Catalan autonomy statutes. In the March local elections the abstention rate rose to 40 per cent. The reasons were not hard to identify. Partly it was due to voter fatigue, a result of an intense period of politicking and plebiscites since 1976. Consensus politics also fostered the view among the electorate that deals were hatched among the politicians in back rooms and over meals in restaurants, regardless of voters' opinions. The continued presence of many of the same political figures as under the previous regime did little to suggest that democracy was any different from dictatorship. Finally, especially for the conservative sectors, the apparent threat to Spanish unity implicit in the decentralization process and the persistence of problems such as terrorism, as well as the emergence of seeming new ones, such as widespread promiscuity and crime, had managed to take the shine off the fledgling democracy. For that reason, *desencanto* was merely one sign that, as the veteran Monarchist José María Areilza observed, Spanish politics was reverting to normality (Fusi and Palafox Gámir 1999: 30). Nostalgic supporters of the regime started to fill Spanish walls with the slogan 'Con Franco vivíamos mejor' ('Things were better with Franco'), and the writer Manuel Vázquez Montalbán coined, but did not endorse, the phrase 'Contra Franco vivíamos mejor' ('Things were better against Franco') to sum up the disenchantment on the progressive left (2005: 190).

Suárez had been eager to call elections as soon as possible to seek a constitutional mandate and cease to be the King's appointed leader. While the outcome was almost identical to 1977, the results of the local elections held slightly over a month later showed that change was under way. Pacts between social-ists and communists led to victories in the principal cities of Madrid and Barcelona where the popular veteran socialist, Enrique Tierno Galván, and Narcís Serra, a future defence minister under Felipe González, respectively, were elected mayors. The communist and future leader of United Left, Julio Anguita, became mayor of Córdoba. Overall approximately three-quarters of the population were governed by local author-ities run by the left.

At a national level, Suárez's party was entering into crisis. UCD was now officially a party but still very much in thrall to the leaders of the parties which had gone to make the original coalition, the so-called *barones*. The internecine disputes of the parliamentary party and the barons' harrying of Suárez to clar-ify the party's ideological direction were not reflected nor appre-ciated at grass-roots level, where the recent battle in the local elections had forged a certain party solidarity and where there was still considerable support for their leader (Powell 2001a: 240–1). Suárez's position was not helped by an ailing economy. Inflation had hit almost 20 per cent in 1978 and was still just under 16 per cent in 1980. Unemployment hovered around 11 per cent in the same year.

Within the PSOE, the gains made through pragmatism up to 1979 had not been enough to deliver power (Powell 2001a: 233) but González, aided by his deputy and close friend, Alfonso Guerra, continued to push the party towards social democracy. Even prior to the 1979 elections González had argued against the effectiveness of having the term 'Marxist' included in the party statutes. The recent elections had added weight to this argument and so, when the party congress in May 1979 seemed to accept the resolution of the traditional wing of the party to maintain the 'Marxist' definition of the party, González resigned. An extraordinary Congress was called for September of the same year, in which Guerra was a prime mover, and González's vision of a non-Marxist party won the day (Gilmour 1985: 259–60). The ideological battle, important as it was, was secondary to the re-election of González and it was undoubtedly his popularity and charisma which were the key to the Socialists' success.

On the other side of the political spectrum, Fraga's Popular Alliance had its conference in December 1979 and decided to realign itself as a conservative party – something that would stand it in good stead in the event of the imminent demise of the centrist UCD. More relevant, perhaps, was the entry into the party of new blood, one of which, José María Aznar, would, almost exactly a decade later, be the architect of a reversal of the party's fortunes (Powell 2001a: 247).

3.10   The Decentralization Process

One of the principal challenges of the transition was to address the regional question, long suppressed by the Franco regime. In Spain the pressure for recognition of regional rights came mainly from the Basques and the Catalans. The other 'historic' region, i.e. one with a strong cultural identity, a sense of nationhood, was Galicia, which, because of its socio-economic history, lacked the strong autochthonous bourgeoisie that in the cases of Catalonia and the Basque Country had underpinned first the cultural then the political claims. The interruption of the process of granting these regions autonomy by the outbreak of war explains why there was general consensus regarding an addendum to the Constitution, the Second Transitory Disposition, which spoke of the right of those 'territories which in the past had voted in favour of autonomy' to accede *immediately* to full autonomy as laid down in Article 148 of the Constitution.

Satisfying Catalan demands was a priority. From as early as 1971 with the founding of the *Assemblea de Catalunya*, the Catalan opposition had been pressing not only for its own nationalist interests but also the democratic demands of the opposition in general. The first trip made by King Juan Carlos and Queen Sofia was to Cataluña. Suárez's decision to invite Josep Tarradellas, the leader of the Catalan regional government-in-exile, back to Spain was inspired as, although associated with the leftist Republicanism of the ERC (*Esquerra Republicana de Calalunya*, Republican Left of Catalonia) and from a different era, he was a symbol of Catalan resistance. Arias Navarro's government, in particular Manuel Fraga, his deputy PM, had sent a delegation to see Tarradellas in exile as far back as 1974 and again in 1976. However, the new Catalan nationalism bred under the regime had its roots in a more Christian Democratic tradition and its leader, Jordi Pujol, would eventually emerge as the dominant force.

The process for granting autonomy to the Basque region was more fraught as it was compounded by the terrorist pressure applied by ETA and the close attention paid by *golpista* generals to any sign of concessions to the radical Basque cause. A draft of a Basque statute was approved by local councillors in the region in December 1978. In addition to failing to satisfy the radicals of the pro-ETA party, HB, founded earlier that year, sections of it were considered to contravene the recently drafted Constitution. ETA tried to force the government's hand by launching a bombing campaign on the Spanish coast and attempting to kidnap one of the members of the Constitutional committee, Gabriel Cisneros. The situation was saved by the negotiating skills of Suárez who, in July 1979, reached an agreement over the statute with the provisional President (*lehendakari*) Carlos Garaicoetxea according to which the Basque region would have its own parliament, Basque and Spanish as co-official languages, substantial control over education, economy and social legislation, its own local police force, and the restoration of the historic *concierto económico* allowed the region (in fact, only the provinces of Vizcaya and Guipúzcoa, as Alava, loyal to Franco, had always retained its special status) to levy its own taxes and pay a lump sum to the central treasury. The issue of Navarre, central to ETA–HB's nationalist project, known as the KAS Alternative, was resolved by offering the region the opportunity to vote on its inclusion or not within the future Basque region (Carr and Fusi 1981: 250).

Both the Catalan and the Basque statutes were approved in referenda in October 1979. The Basque statute not only divided the extremes of Spanish society, with both HB and ETA and the Spanish right opposed to it, but it radically divided Basque society between the moderate nationalists and radicals (*abertzales*), but in the referendum over 60 per cent voted and over 80 per cent said 'Yes' (Preston 1986: 164–5).

The success of the Catalan and Basque statutes led to the fear that the desire for greater self-government might extend to other regions. In August 1979 local councils in Andalucía had voted overwhelmingly (97 per cent) in favour of acceding to regional autonomy via the fast route of Article 151 of the Constitution instead of the predicted slow route of Article 143. A referendum was held in February 1980 in which 8 of the 9 provinces (the exception being Almería) voted in favour. Legally, Andalucía lost the right to the fast route, but the closeness of the vote was such that it led the new UCD Prime Minister Calvo Sotelo and González to strike a deal and in July 1981 agree on a law, the *Organic Law for the Harmonisation of the Devolution Process* (LOAPA), which placed a check on the proliferation of requests for devolution. In return for the government allowing Andalucía, a socialist stronghold, to fast-track self-government, the Socialists agreed that no other exceptions should be made and the remaining 13 regions should proceed along the slow route as constitutionally ordained. Such cooperation between the major parties on the provocative issue of decentralization, although subsequently declared unconstitutional in 1983, was an example of how the attempted coup in February 1981 had caused a return of the spirit of consensus when the prize of democracy looked once again under threat.

3.11   The Break-up of UCD

Suárez's relative success in the high-profile issues of Transition politics was in stark contrast to his inability to cope with the more everyday aspects of political activity (Powell and Bonnin 2004: 172). His attempts to consolidate his leadership of the party after the 1979 elections ran into problems early on. One of his main weaknesses, for many, was, ironically, his inability to adapt to a more democratic style of leadership. In May 1980 the Socialist deputy leader, Alfonso Guerra, was quoted as saying: 'Suárez has reached the highest level of democracy he is capable of administering [… he] cannot stand any more democracy, and democracy cannot stand any more of Suárez' (Gilmour 1985: 250). An example of this was when at his investiture as President after the 1979 elections, he bounced Parliament into voting for him *before* a debate could take place (Powell and Bonnin 2004: 163). In his first cabinet after the elections he removed several of the powerful 'barons', leaders of factions within UCD, and while he tried to preserve the balance of power in government by spreading portfolios among these factions, it released those 'barons' to become a steady source of criticism.

Meanwhile, the party was to suffer a series of electoral blows from which it would not recover. The first was the referendum on the Andalusian statute on 28 February 1980. Given the high abstention rates in the Catalan and Basque referendums, Suárez and UCD calculated that the rate would be even higher in Andalucía. The party advocated abstention, denied media time to its opponents and initially tried to claim the result of the referendum, where only one province, Almería, narrowly failed to reach the 50 per cent affirmative vote, as a defeat for the 'Yes' campaign. Such behaviour not only lost both Suárez and UCD valuable support, but inevitably boosted the fortunes of the Socialists, who went on to triumph in the eventual elections held in May 1982, a precursor to their national victory five months later. As Gilmour wrote, 'With the benefit of hindsight, one can point to the Andalusian muddle as the first stage in the collapse of the UCD' (1985: 258). For Suárez's biographer, the man and the party who were key to the restoration of democracy had committed the 'serious strategic error' of asking Andalusians not to vote (Abella 2006: 358).

UCD continued to suffer electoral defeats in subsequent months. In the Basque elections on 9 March 1980, it came fifth after the PNV, HB, the PSOE and the Basque Country Left (*Euskadiko Ezkerra*, EE). In the Catalan elections on 20 March it came fourth after the Catalan centre-right coalition, Convergence and Union (*Convergència i Unió*, CiU), the *Partit Socialista de Catalunya* (PSC), linked to the PSOE, and the Communist *Partit dels Socialistes Unificat de Catalunya* (PSUC). In addition to the unpopularity at the polls, deep divisions were emerging in the party itself. The glue that had held together the different factions, originally parties within the UCD coalition, was becoming unstuck in the face of specific political issues that tested the ideological fabric of the party. These issues included educational reform, the proposed introduction of private television channels, a law on divorce and the management of the decentralization process.

In such circumstances, the PSOE pressed home its advantage and presented a censure motion in May 1980. The motion failed, but it enhanced González's image as a potential Prime Minister and underlined the weakness of Suárez's position (Tusell 1997: 74). Faced with pressure from the opposition, Suárez also had to come to terms with a party that was dividing along ideological lines. The rightist Christian Democrats were becoming a critical wing hostile to measures such as the projected divorce law introduced by the social democrat Minister for Justice, Fernández Ordóñez.

During this time, Suárez was gaining a reputation for aloofness and lack of interest in the day-to-day running of the government. He became victim to a condition subsequently referred to as the 'Moncloa syndrome' whereby Presidents become increasingly withdrawn. He seemed to rely heavily on his clique of advisers, known as the *fontaneros* (plumbers), and especially his friend and Deputy Prime Minister, Fernando Abril Martorell, in change of the economy, to shield him from problems (Powell and Bonnin 2004: 172; Preston 1986: 173). The latter, however, lacked the confidence of the social democrats in the cabinet and Suárez resigned on 29 January 1981.

3.12   The Triumph of the Monarchy: the 23-F

During the Transition one of the most enduring threats to the newly formed government had been that of *golpismo*, with as many as five separate coup plots discovered between 1978 and 1982 (Edles 1998: 144). The discontented ranks among the military saw with increasing frustration how their comrades were bearing the brunt of the terrorist offensive while the conservative elements in the army were being overlooked in the government's policy of promoting liberal-minded officers (Edles 1998: 143–4). In the days following Suárez's resignation the atmosphere was particularly charged. ETA had stepped up its offensive. In 1980 124 people died as a result of terrorism, 96 of them victims of ETA. A royal visit to the Basque country in early February had been disrupted by representatives of HB, who chanted the Basque anthem during Juan Carlos's speech at the historic Casa de Juntas (Meeting Place) in Guernica, traditional site of the Basque parliament. Overall, however, the visit was a success as the King handled the situation with great diplomatic skill and sensitivity and the gesture of the visit was appreciated by the majority of Basques. Nevertheless, some in the military were upset in the first place by the mere fact that the monarchy was willing to engage with the Basque region and its institutions in this way, and secondly, the affront by extreme nationalists to their King provoked outrage (Preston 2004: 460–1). On 6 February ETA brutally assassinated an engineer on the Lemóniz nuclear plant near Bilbao, José María Ryan, whom they had been holding hostage since 29 January in an attempt to force the government to destroy the plant. It provoked an intemperate outburst in the ultra-right-wing daily, *El Alcázar*, by a retired general, declaring the situation intolerable and interpreting recent trends of abstention at the polls as a sign of dissatisfaction with democracy and a desire for military intervention (Preston 1986: 192).

The conspiratorial mood was pervasive. The earliest serious indicator of this was the planning of Operación Galaxia in January 1979 in which Antonio Tejero was involved. The aim of Operación Galaxia was to kidnap the Prime Minister and his cabinet at the Moncloa Palace and effectively hold them ransom until demands were met. Luckily Suárez was tipped off a few days before and the plot was dismantled. Nonetheless, its existence was important not only for its demonstration of the extent of right-wing conspiracy but for its graphic illustration of the government's inability or unwillingness to punish the perpetrators as they deserved. Tejero's seven months' detention did nothing to inspire the moderate opposition that Suárez was serious about tackling the problem of *golpismo*.

As a result, when it came to Suárez's resignation, which took everyone by surprise, the plotters were forced to advance their strategy to take advantage of a moment of constitutional weakness. As the voting for the investiture of the new Prime Minister, the sober Calvo Sotelo, was taking place, the conspirators made their move. It seems that their intention, using the good relations that one of their leaders, Alfonso Armada, had with the King, was to force the monarchy's hand and enlist its support. It rapidly became obvious that Juan Carlos was not going to cooperate. Tejero seized the Congress at around 6.30 p.m. on 23

February 1981 and held all the members hostage. The leaders of the main parties were led to another room and both González and Carrillo were certainly concerned for their lives. Suárez gained a place in history (Abella 2006) with his valorous attempts to defend the indignant Gutiérrez Mellado, who remonstrated with his military companions and was roughly manhandled by Tejero himself.

The attempted coup failed due to the insistence of the King in his televised message at 1.10 in the morning of the 24th on maintaining Constitutional propriety. He contacted all the leaders of the military divisions and made clear his lack of support. It emerged that Armada wanted to lure the King into a meeting with him that night, which would allow him to present to his co-conspirators an impression of royal implication. Cleverly, the King's aide, Sabino Fernández Campo, prevented Armada from accessing the Zarzuela that night and, in this way, possibly, offset the greatest threat to Spanish democracy since the death of Franco (Abella 2006).

The failure of the coup attempt had many implications, but there are three principal ones: first, it reinforced, if anything, the institution of the monarchy but also of democracy itself. Numerous Spaniards took to the streets the following day to proclaim their support for the two. As the philosopher Elías Díaz notes, it 'served to stir the weary, impotent victims of disenchantment from their slumber' (Díaz 1999: 31). Secondly, it affected subsequent political action and government policy. For example, in relation to decentralization it had a profound effect on the government's decision to try to slow the process down through the LOAPA legislation which, although subsequently overturned by the Constitutional Court, still sent out a message to the military and the right about the government's intentions. Thirdly, it speeded up the plans, subsequently implemented by Felipe González, to demilitarize the control of the armed forces. In the immediate term, it undoubtedly influenced Calvo Sotelo's decision to speed up negotiation on Spain's entry into NATO.

3.13 Normality is Restored

The Calvo Sotelo government, though in many regards a care-taker government between the resignation of Suárez and the celebration of general elections in October 1982, made some highly significant and controversial decisions. The LOAPA was an important attempt to assert legislative control over a devolution process that the Constitution had, deliberately, left very open-ended and vague. It tried to privilege central government's control over regional authorities in cases of discrepancy of legislation, but in 1983 the Constitutional Court overruled the key aspects of the law (Colomer 1999: 47; Gibbons 1999: 20–1). The decision to enter NATO, while done without consultation, was, as Angel Viñas observes, a momentous step, 'one of the major doors that had been kept stubbornly closed to the Franco regime had opened. A whole set of shackles was thus simply cast off' (Viñas 1999: 248). It marked an attempt to reorient Spanish foreign policy in a direction that, despite the Socialists' opposition, they would eventually maintain and deepen.

Suárez had been successful in re-establishing Spain's links with the international community, however, for understandable reasons, Spanish foreign policy during the Transition had 'remained largely undefined due to the fact that the domestic agenda was more important than the international stage' (Magone 2004: 210). Still, from early on Suárez's team realized that foreign relations were an essential part of both shaking free from the past and consolidating the new democracy (Viñas 1999: 250). The monarchy had made a start with a successful visit to the USA in June 1976 and Suárez laid out a set of principles in July 1977 which included the aim of integration in the EC and initiating a parliamentary debate on membership of NATO. It also included the intention of retrieving Gibraltar and strengthening relations with the Arab nation and its 'just causes' (Pereira Castañares and Martínez de Lillo 2004: 1004). However, in practice Suárez's foreign policy tended more towards relations with third-world or non-aligned nations, in

Latin America especially, where he visited Cuba in 1978, and Spain sat as an observer in the 6th Conference of Non-Aligned Countries held in Havana in 1979. He was the first European leader to receive Yasser Arafat (Viñas 1999: 254).

Calvo Sotelo's short term in government undertook to undo this trend and move Spanish foreign policy in a more 'Western' direction. The disappearance of the principle of consensus which had characterized most of Suárez's premiership and prevented the discussion of contentious issues such as membership of NATO allowed Calvo Sotelo more leeway, and it was already part of his programme for government when the coup attempt occurred. The haste and the lack of parliamentary consultation in taking the final decision to join the organization were seen as a clear attempt to appease the military and guarantee their commitment to democracy. However, for many in the military, Spain missed an opportunity to hold out for more concessions in return for entry, and even saw the rush to join as humiliating (Preston 1986: 206).

On the issue of EC membership there was more agreement among the different political forces, and an application was formally made in July 1977 and accepted by the Community that September with negotiations officially beginning in September 1979. Subsequent delays until Spain's eventual accession in 1985 were due to internal EC politics, concern over the impact of Spain on agricultural policy and, in large measure, French obstructionism (Judt 2007: 527). The issue of NATO had effectively been shelved in the light of an absence of consensus but in 1981, partly under pressure from the USA, it was reactivated by Calvo Sotelo's pro-Atlanticist foreign minister, José Pedro Pérez Llorca, as a means of unblocking the EC negotiations and possibly advancing negotiations on Gibraltar. The measure was pushed through parliament and, in the absence of the debate promised by Suárez and without any formal discussions on the terms and conditions of membership, Spain became a member in May 1982.

Although seemingly marginal to the dramatic internal politics of the period, foreign policy developments were, in fact, crucial to the positive outcome of the Transition, much as they had been during the Franco regime itself for, as Tony Judt observes, Spain, along with Portugal and Greece – the other successful Mediterranean transitions – 'were able to enter or re-enter the "West" with such little difficulty, despite their self-imposed political isolation, because their foreign policies had always been compatible – indeed, aligned – with those of NATO or the EEC states' (2007: 525).

3.14 Conclusion

The Transition is, as we noted at the beginning of this chapter, a success story but one which is now coming under more critical scrutiny. Edles considers the Spanish experience as 'phenomenal simply because it is the first time in Spanish history that parliamentary democracy has worked ... has been self-sustaining'. By this she means 'one in which there is (1) a real possibility of partisan alternation in office, and (2) a real possibility of reversible policy changes resulting from alternation in office and (3) effective civilian control over the military'. She highlights what she calls 'the Basque and corresponding centralist violence and terrorism which plagued the new democratic regime' as the only exception to this success and as the 'most threatening and divisive issue in Spain' (Edles 1998: 4–5, 151). The successful management of the process led to it being credited, often over-simplistically, with influence as a model on other similar situations, both in terms of a process to be imitated or a framework for historical analysis (Pérez Serrano 2007: 65). Latin America in the 1980s experienced a succession of transitions which were said to have learned from the Spanish example (Ward 1997: 61; Tusell 1999: 12). The ingredients for Spanish success were various and they contained several fortuitous factors that could not easily be reproduced artificially in other circumstances. The pre-Transition process of the 1960s modernization and the effects of emigration and tourism meant that Spanish society was ready for the changes that the Transition made formal.

What characterized the Transition was the speed of change. Spaniards had gone from democratic euphoria to political disenchantment in the space of half a decade. The disenchantment was a sign that in the interests of consensus and moderation, much had remained unchanged. Ironically, however, one of the effects of the Tejero coup attempt was to slow down a process that perhaps was moving too fast for its own good and to remind both politicians and the ordinary Spaniard of the value of what was threatened by the events of the 23-F. In Calvo Sotelo's government there was an element of return to the spirit of consensus with the reintroduction of a policy of *concertación*, or cooperation between the principal political and social partners (Powell 2001a: 304; Edles 1998: 145).

It remained the case, however, that in the new political scenario, the people in charge were still the representatives, albeit reformist ones, of the previous regime, a fact that would impinge especially on Basque non-acceptance of the process (Aguilar 2001). At the end of the Transition the Prime Minister was a former Francoist minister and nephew of the same José Calvo Sotelo, conservative minister in the dictatorship of Primo de Rivera, whose assassination had been one of the sparks of the Civil War. Paloma Aguilar has pointed out how important the awareness of the past was in the process of construction of the Transition, in particular the failure of the Second Republic, and how it explains the compromises that were made. Any 'repetition of the institutional design of the Second Republic was almost superstitiously avoided' (Aguilar 2002: 269). Most of the institutional decisions from the monarchical system, the electoral procedure and the drafting of the constitution were made as corrective versions of the measures taken by the Republic. The pact of silence was a necessity for the larger goal of democracy.

However, the necessary concomitant was a mood of disenchantment at the time that change was not as spectacular as might have been expected. It was this disenchantment and desire for real change, for example, that lay behind the cultural movement in the late 1970s and early 1980s known as the

Madrid *movida* (which some saw as a pun on the Francoist *Movimiento*), involving figures such as the director Pedro Almodóvar attempting to institute real change by casting off the last shackles attaching it to the past of the regime and looking towards the future (Triana Toribio 2000: 275). It was the promise of change which, in the elections of 28 October 1982, swept the Spanish Socialists into power.

4

FELIPISMO, 1982–96

4.1 Introduction

The slogan for the electoral campaign of the Spanish Socialists in 1982 was *Por el cambio*, 'Time for a Change', and their very victory showed that Spain had in fact undergone a major change in allowing a party of the left to assume power a mere seven years after Franco's death. The Spanish people were not expecting with the idea of change anything more radical than the possibility of a government of a different hue and one of greater honesty and openness. In other words, the ambitions that had once been cherished for the Transition itself but which, colliding as they did against the hard rocks of political pragmatism, had resulted in the *desencanto* of the latter half of that period. With democracy restored, Spaniards now looked to the possibility of harmonization with its Western neighbours. This was an aim that the Socialists would be able to deliver, albeit imperfectly. The period was dominated by the charismatic party leader, Felipe González, and his almost fourteen years in power is still the longest term of any Prime Minister in the democratic period. Unsurprisingly, it was punctuated by highs and lows, and the four governments over which he presided traced an almost perfect arc from youthful optimism in hard times, through international success and economic boom, to the final weary decline into the mire of scandal and controversy. Nevertheless, if we take, as many do, its overall aim as that of making Spain 'a player on the world scene', then it is hard to deny that it succeeded. Sadly, they were also victims of their own success.

4.2 A Historic Victory

One of the unexpected outcomes of the Transition was the way Spain had moved towards a traditional, if still rather unequal, two-party system. The consensus of the early period of the Transition was no longer necessary, although a measure of political moderation was ushered in by the shock of the failed coup in February 1981. Felipe González's sensible manoeuvring of the party, with the help of party ideologues like the sociologist and first Education Minister, José María Maravall, towards a social democrat platform had worked to ensure that his party responded to the natural left-leaning 'sociological majority' of the Spanish population (Gillespie 1996: 429; McDonough, Barnes and López Pina 1998: 84). The break-up of UCD left Spain without a significant centrist party. Suárez had founded the Social and Democratic Centre (*Centro Democrático y Social*, CDS), but at the elections the party won only two seats, one for Suárez and one for his brother-in-law, though this would rise briefly to 19 at the following elections.

The conservatives were saddled with Manuel Fraga as their standard-bearer and, while he succeeded in making the AP the principal party of opposition, his past association with the Franco regime gave the AP an unbreachable electoral ceiling. Although the party had undergone considerable reorganization since the 1979 elections and realigned itself as a conservative party under Fraga, he would eventually give way to a younger successor in 1987.

The Socialists swept to victory by deliberately presenting themselves to the electorate with a modest, non-radical agenda for the change that they so boldly heralded, with nothing more controversial than proposals for nationalization of the power grid and a 40-hour week. Ironically, of the two simple promises with which they did try to fire the electorate, one was a last-minute decision that they would fail to live up to and the other a commitment upon which they almost reneged. The former was the promise, insisted on late in the day by the sister trade union *Unión General de Trabajadores* (General Workers' Union, UGT), to create 800,000 jobs within the first four years of being in power. The latter was their promise to hold a referendum on Spain's membership of NATO. Although not a plank of the electoral campaign, it was also their determination to push for entry into the EC, a process already initiated by Suárez in 1978. Joining the EC was to become one of the principal driving forces of government policy throughout its period in power and probably Felipe González's greatest achievement. Preparing the country for survival in the EC would also contribute to the split between the party and UGT as well as between UGT leader, Nicolás Redondo and González, once close personal friends.

The sweeping victory at the elections in 1982, with over 10 million votes, granted the Socialists an absolute majority not intended by the drafters of the Constitution. It permitted the implementation of a programme of reforms on education, health, defence and women's rights, but it also allowed them to carry out a series of unpopular measures to modernize the industrial infrastructure and to strengthen the economy in preparation for EC membership. They did this in the face of mounting unpopularity among the public and their trade-union base, which became increasingly disillusioned at not just the lack of fulfilment of the electoral promises but also González's strategy of austerity measures, industrial modernization and privatization policies. However, González benefited from the lesson of the French Socialists' failed attempt at Keynesianism in the early 1980s (Powell 2001a: 344; Ardagh 1988: 39–43), as well as the example of Margaret Thatcher's neoliberal reforms and battles with the trade unions in the UK. As Judt points out, Spain in the 1980s was part of a south Mediterranean trend, along with Greece and Portugal, whereby peaceful transitions to democracy were carried out by 'conservative statesmen from the old regime itself' such as Karamanlis, Spinola and Suárez, and 'they, in turn, were succeeded by Socialists – Soares, González, Papandreou – who convincingly reassured their own supporters of their unbroken radical credentials while implementing moderate and often unpopular economic polices forced upon them by circumstances' (2007: 524–5).

4.3 The 'Window of Change', 1982–6

A landslide victory in the general elections of 28 October 1982 (see Appendix 3) gave the Socialists 202 seats in parliament compared with 107 for the Popular Coalition. The nationalist parties had improved their position with the Basque Nationalist Party, winning eight seats, and the centre-right coalition in Cataluña, *Convergència i Unió*, did even better with twelve. The great loser in the contest was the Spanish Communist Party, which only managed to obtain four seats, confirming its relegation to the sidelines of national politics after a heroic record under Franco and a noble role in the Transition process.

The Socialists' first phase was dominated by the drive to join the EC, essential to its more fundamental aim of socioeconomic modernization. Despite the concessions to modernity made by the regime in the economic ambit, there was still a heavy dependency on traditional industries such as iron and steel which, in the 1980s, were entering a deep crisis on a global scale. In addition Spain's lingering overprotective Francoist labour laws made it difficult for companies to cope with fluctuations in the economy. Finally, Spain's history of protectionism and nationalization of state utilities meant it was unused to competing on the level economic playing field that membership of the EC would inevitably introduce.

Unpopular decisions were necessary to prepare for accession. The buzzwords of this period were *reconversión industrial*, modernization and restructuring of industry, and *ajuste*, an 'adjusting' of the economy to new circumstances. In practical terms this meant closures of many unnecessary or unproductive industries and streamlining the workforce in the rest. As a result, the electoral promise of creating 800,000 jobs in four years, which Employment Minister, Joaquín Almunia admitted had been a 'rash promise' and Carlos Solchaga in 1983 declared unrealistic (Soto 2005: 355), became a job loss of almost equal proportions within the same period. Unemployment rose from just over 16 per cent to nearly 22 per cent (Powell 2001a: 353).

The PSOE earned the enmity of its own rank and file through its allegiance to neoliberal, monetarist economic thinking. González's priority was to reduce inflation, give incentives to the business sector and control wages. Initial trade-union support with this strategy was based on the social redistribution of economic gains. González achieved pacts with both the UGT and the CC OO trade unions and the employers' body, the Spanish Confederation of Business Organizations (CEOE), in 1983 and again (this time without the participation of CC OO) in 1984. The results were undoubtedly successful, if painful for many. Inflation was reduced from 14 per cent to 10 per cent, its 1972 level. Economic problems which, due to the political instability of the Transition period and the weakness of the Suárez governments, could not be tackled at the time, could now be addressed. Between 1975 and 1985, the economy had grown by a mere 1 per cent. Soaring interest rates put a stop to investment. The cost of social security payments during this period led to a sharpening of the public deficit, reaching 5 per cent of GDP in 1982 (Salmon 1995: 7–12).

The crowning achievement of this first term was entry into the EC on 12 June 1985. From then, the economy grew strongly, at 4.5 per cent compared with the EC average of 3.2 per cent (Soto 2005: 364) due to the Socialists 'adopting more market-centred economic policies and seeking to be in the vanguard of European integration' (Salmon 1995: 12). It was the service sector that experienced the greatest expansion, and Spain became a magnet for foreign investors (Cabrera and Del Rey 2007: 142).

On a political level, with the Tejero incident still fresh in the collective psyche, the government set military reform as a priority, with a view to eradicating the risk of future coups. If the mildness of the Socialists' 1982 electoral campaign can be interpreted as a desire not to alarm this particular *de facto* power, the party was determined to introduce change. It was no coincidence that one of the first visits made by González in December 1982 was to the División Acorazada Brunete, a unit that had played a prominent role in the February coup attempt but which had also lost one of its generals in an ETA attack in October (Soto 2005: 216). Alfonso Guerra summed up their approach as the 'perfect application of the strategy of establishing relations with the military founded on loyalty but always on the firm basis of respect for Government authority' (2006: 47).

By the end of the first term, the threat of coups (*golpismo*) was effectively eliminated. Two attempts since the 23-F, one just before the 1982 elections and another in June 1985, were successfully thwarted. The strategy was to reward the democratic elements in the armed forces and ease the more reactionary elements into retirement. In 1984 a reform of the 1980 Defence Bill (*Ley Orgánica de Criterios Básicos de la Defensa Nacional*) placed the armed services firmly under the control of government, strengthening the role of the Minister for Defence (Powell 2001a: 374).

4.4   Riding the Wave, 1986–9

In spite of U-turns and failure to deliver on the electoral promises of 1982, surveys showed that at the end of their first period in office 53 per cent of Spaniards approved the government's performance, a fact that was confirmed at the polls on 22 June 1986. In spite of an additional 2 million potential voters, the Socialists managed to lose over one million votes and still win an overall majority with 44 per cent of the votes (see Appendix 4). The Popular Alliance formed a coalition with smaller Christian Democrat and Liberal Parties (*Partido Democrático Popular* and *Partido Liberal*, respectively) to form the Popular Coalition, but their vote remained virtually unchanged. Manuel Fraga had tried to outmanoeuvre the Socialists during the referendum on NATO with a call for abstention which went unheeded (see **4.8**), thus sealing his own and his party's fate in the general elections. Despite his party's success in the Galician elections in 1985, the limit of Fraga's potential as party leader was clear and he would eventually be succeeded, first in 1987 by a young Andalusian lawyer, Antonio Hernández Mancha, who failed to make his mark, and then permanently by José María Aznar in 1990.

The Communist Party, which in its new formation, United Left, won only 7 seats with less than 5 per cent of the vote, was unable to exploit the anti-NATO vote nor the impact of a strike called by the Communist trade union in 1985. The PSOE, still strong in its enclaves of Andalusia, Castilla-La Mancha, Valencia, Murcia and Aragón, survived a loss of 18 seats and subsequently in the municipal elections of 1987, a loss of nearly three million votes. In addition, in the Basque Country splits within the PNV due to former leader Garaikoetxea's departure to form Eusko Alkartasuna (EA) led to a need for a pact with the Basque wing of the Socialist party (PSE–PSOE) in the regional government.

Spain after 1986 entered into a period of economic boom lasting until 1989, which saw it grow at a rate of 4.5 per cent, higher not only than its European partners, but also faster than any other country except Japan (Salmon 1995: 12). The period of prosperity ushered in led to the coining of the term *cultura del pelotazo*, the get-rich-quick culture, to describe the mood (Cabrera and Del Rey 2007: 143). There was a boom in property prices, fortunes were made in speculation and the Socialists soon acquired a reputation for presiding rather too contentedly over a period of wealth and prosperity that saw them characterized as 'champagne Socialists'. But González was governing Spain at a crucial juncture in its history, summed up at the time as one in which the 'great, heroic, unifying work of transition to democracy and economic adjustment is behind it; ahead lies the more prosaic task of broadening political participation while keeping control of the economy' (*The Economist* 1989: 3).

Nonetheless, ostentatious enjoyment of the proceeds of prosperity was bound to jar with traditional Socialist values and with the ordinary worker for whom Spain's providential situation was a result of their effort and wage sacrifices. The clash with the trade unions was not long coming, and at the end of 1987 Redondo, for many the conscience of the party, resigned his seat in parliament. Worse still, talks began between the Socialist trade union and its arch-rival, the Communist Workers' Commissions (CC OO), over plans for a general strike. A general strike in any circumstances is bad for a government, but the 14 December 1988 strike to challenge a Socialist government was a sign of the depth of the discontent. Under the slogan 'For a Change in Social Policy' (*Por el giro social*), the unions wanted the government to direct its attention less at businesses and banks whose profits were 'skyrocketing' and more at the plight of the jobless. The government's anti-inflationist policy had had the effect of cooling down the economy, with a knock-on effect on employment. By 1985 the unemployment figure had risen from 16.2 per cent in 1982 to 21.3 per cent, the highest in Spain's history (Powell 2001a: 353). It was in that year that the CC OO had organized its first strike on 20 July 1985 in response to the government's pension reform.

The impact of the strike was negligible but it led the Socialist UGT trade union to contemplate a rapprochement between it and CC OO, each eager to retain support among an increasingly disgruntled working class. The more damaging 1988 strike was motivated by the unions' impatience at government failure to respond to a series of moderate social demands. These involved preserving pensioners' and civil servants' purchasing power, creation of non-contributory pensions and the extension of unemployment benefit. One of the most publicized issues was the unions' outright rejection of the government initiative to get young people into work, the Youth Employment Plan (*Plan de Empleo Juvenil*), with what were soon branded 'junk contracts' (*contratos basura*) by the unions (Ruiz 2002: 90–1). In 1987 the Economy minister, Carlos Solchaga, recommended a 5 per cent limit on wage rises to employers, a proposal flatly rejected by the unions.

The strike was supported by an estimated 90 per cent of the active population including students, actors and even the Football Association (Ruiz 2002: 91). González was badly shaken by the strike and considered resigning. Its success did prompt the government to try to meet the unions' demands, which, given the healthy economic growth in 1988, it was able to do. By the tenth anniversary of the Socialists' victory, social spending had risen from 17 per cent of GDP at the time of the strike to 20 per cent, and unemployment benefit was extended to cover 67 per cent of those out of work, compared with the previous figure of 34 per cent. Non-contributory pensions were also introduced (Méndez Lago 2005: 179). The prosperity during this second term allowed the Socialists to increase spending on health and, in fact, investment in the sector, following the passing of the 1986 Health Act, in the last five years of the decade doubled that of the first half (Ruiz 2002: 87).

Studies of electoral participation reveal, rather unsurprisingly, that turnout at the polls increases when voters want to see political change (Magone 2004: 106). If that is the case the results suggest that in the 1989 elections Spaniards' lack of interest in change was only matched by the 1979 elections, when Suárez was riding the crest of his wave. Both were what Powell calls 'elections of continuity', not change (Powell 2001a: 618). In the 15 June 1989 elections the People's Party (*Partido Popular*) as the Popular Alliance was now called, was unable to break through their old electoral ceiling but now, under the leadership of José María Aznar, was in a position to project a fresh image, though limited somewhat by Aznar's notoriously dour demeanour. The Communist Party, which had also elected a new leader, Julio Anguita, in February 1988, showed itself unable to capitalize on the December strike. The Socialists had been encouraged by their trouncing of the opposition in the European Elections in June 1989 to call a snap election for October. The result, however, was a loss of their absolute majority (see Appendix 5). Moreover, a victory for the PP in the Galician regional elections in December, where Fraga won the presidency, combined with the continued superiority of the moderate PNV and the moderate Catalan nationalists (CiU) in their respective regions, showed the emergence of a strong political opposition in the periphery of the country to challenge the central Socialist government. The 1989 elections also revealed a changed trend in the profile of the PSOE voter from a predominantly young male, highly educated urban voter to an older, female rural voter, a trend confirmed in 1993 (Cabrera and Del Rey 2007: 159). The PP was starting to capture the vote of the upwardly mobile younger generation eager for change.

4.5 Celebrations amid the Crisis, 1989–93

Still, in practice the Socialists managed to hold onto their absolute majority owing to the technicality of the boycott of the Madrid parliament by the radical Basque party, HB, which had 4 seats. However, it was beginning to lose its support among the young and in urban areas, traditional constituencies of the left, as would be evident in the municipal and regional elections of 1991, in which it lost the important mayorships of Madrid, Valencia and Seville. These municipal elections saw the end of Suárez's career as his CDS party slipped to 4 per cent of the vote. Socialists held on to ten regional governments and the PP won five. The 1989 elections saw the confirmation of the bitter split between the PSOE and the UGT with Nicolás Redondo taking the extraordinary step of urging his supporters not to vote for the Socialists. The government in its third term would face another general strike, not as damaging as in 1988, on 28 May 1992 in protest at unemployment benefit cuts.

The third government of the Socialists was dominated by two phenomena which were to spell the eventual demise of the party. One was the growing incidence of political corruption which, though affecting all parties in some form or other, was most notable in the ranks of the Socialist party and clearly most damaging. The second was the improved fortunes of the People's Party (*Partido Popular*), with José María Aznar leader of the party from 1990. A further factor, linked to the second, would be a concerted policy of hounding by the press, especially *El Mundo*, led by its rabidly anti-González editor Pedro J. Ramírez (Tusell 2004: 28). *El Mundo* and the Church-linked radio station COPE are considered by some to constitute a 'neocon media base in Spain' which have shown a talent for smear campaigns often 'without offering any empirical base' (Sampedro and Seoane Pérez 2008: 341).

Within the Socialist party, the division between the left and right factions, the *guerristas* (supporters of Alfonso Guerra) and the *renovadores* (modernizers), became more pronounced and it was no longer possible for Felipe González to sit on the fence. The modernizers advocated a move towards social democracy and opening the party up to Spanish society as a whole. Their aim was to make the PSOE the natural party of government in Spain, and in the end González came down on their side. When in 1991 Guerra resigned the Deputyship in the wake of the scandal involving his brother, Juan, González was able to replace him with a modernizer, Narcís Serra.

Towards the end of the Socialists' third term, Spain staged a series of international events that earned 1992 the accolade of being 'the Year of Spain', its *annus mirabilis*. The Barcelona Olympics, Expo 92 in Seville and Madrid as the European Capital of Culture guaranteed the attention of the world's media. It was to be Spain's coming of age as a fully modern western democracy and in general it passed with flying colours. However, to keep up the spending needed for such projects as well as the infrastructure to support it, Spain had to postpone the belt-tightening which the recession was causing elsewhere. A year later, the Socialists headed into an election in the context of a crippling recession with the peseta devalued three times in eight months and the unemployment figures rising at a rate of 3000 a day. González, realising the economy was not going to improve and counting on his greater electoral appeal to the voters, decided to call early elections, although his confidence was badly shaken when, in the first of two televised debates with Aznar, he was over-confident and under-prepared, and was judged to be bettered by his young rival. The difficulty for the conservatives was not simply Aznar's inexperience, but the fact that in economic terms little separated the neoliberal economic policies of González from those of his more right-wing opponents.

4.6 A Surprise Fourth Term, 1993–6

Despite being rocked by a succession of scandals (see **4.15**) the Socialists went into the 1993 elections buoyed by the presence in its electoral lists of significant, high-profile independents such as the feminist lawyer Victoria Camps and the much-admired judge Baltasar Garzón, who at the time was still investigating the GAL case (see **4.17**). While to outsiders this seemed a desperate attempt to offset the taint of corruption that was beginning to be associated with the party as a whole and, even more cynically, to neutralize Garzón, it was clear that a chastened González wanted to convince his supporters that the battle against corruption was high on his list. The electoral slogan 'Change within Change' (*El cambio del cambio*) implied both a renovation of the promise of change that had won them their first historic victory in 1982 and a correction of errors made. It was a campaign that based itself on the leader, known popularly as Felipe, and as such was a personal victory (Sánchez Cervelló and Tubau 2004: 109). In the event, the party won 159 seats, 17 short of an absolute majority, so it required them to negotiate support among the small but powerful nationalist parties representing the Basques and the Catalans in the Madrid parliament (see Appendix 6).

While at the time the loss of the overall majority was seen by many, even among PSOE supporters, as a positive thing, as it would redirect a party that had become accustomed to wielding absolute power, in other ways it created a headache for the party. The result was a new era of pacts and consensus, eventually with the Catalan nationalist party, the CiU. It was a measure of the bitterness between the two parties of the left that no cooperation could be sought with the Communist United Left whose 18 seats would have carried the Socialists over the 176 threshold for an absolute majority. Indeed González had moved so far towards the centre that such an option was not seriously entertained by either side. Moreover, the anti-EU stance of the Communist IU would have seriously hindered the government's plans for economic convergence with Europe (Powell 2001a: 519).

González created a predominantly modernizing government in which women increased their presence with the appointment of Cristina Alberdi, Carmen Alborch and Angeles Amador, though still to the 'caring' portfolios of Social Affairs, Culture and Health, respectively. It was still afflicted with internal divisions. Guerra's more traditional, left-wing supporters figured prominently in the new Party Executive elected in 1994. In addition, his supporters were quick to note that in the regional elections, the party had hung on to power in those regions where the *guerristas* dominated, such as Andalusia and Extremadura, and lost to the PP in those regions where the modernizers held sway (Valencia, Madrid, Castilla y León, the Canary Islands). Hence the internal problems were not resolved and in a survey in 1994 only 24 per cent saw the PSOE as a united party, against 58 per cent that saw it as divided (Powell 2001a: 520).

4.7   Europe and Foreign Policy

One of the primary aims of the Socialists was to strengthen Spain's reputation and standing abroad. In place of the traditional pro-American and pro-Arab strategy followed by the regime and UCD, it pursued one which was more Atlanticist and pro-European (Romero Salvadó 1999: 178). In this it represented continuity with Calvo Sotelo, who had taken Spain into NATO but, under González, allegiance to that body was combined with maintaining a distance from American policy. González's first foreign minister, Fernando Morán, favoured a certain independence from the USA and Europe and the fostering of relations with Latin America, but was substituted in 1985 by Francisco Fernández Ordóñez, who saw his country's role much more as a bridge between Europe and Latin America. Though initially Spain's lack of clout in the EC meant that it was unable to negotiate privileged status for Latin American countries, it did manage to raise the profile of the region on the European agenda, specifically with regard to economic and political issues. Spain was active in helping the process of debt repayment and promoting economic growth in the area. Between 1985 and 1995 EU economic aid to the region increased from €37 million to €367 million (Heywood 1995: 274; Closa and Heywood 2004: 225–9).

Spain played a significant role in furthering democracy and collaborating in resolution of conflicts in Central America and Colombia (Soto 2005: 255). González enjoyed an initially friendly, though not uncritical relation with Cuba's Fidel Castro (Heywood 1995: 276–7), though this was soured owing to the NATO volte-face and Castro's implication that Felipe was aware of the GAL operation (Ramonet 2007: 483–5). González aided the democratization processes in Argentina, Chile and Uruguay, and he opposed the American-backed *Contra* war against the left-wing Sandinista government of Nicaragua, showing support for the Contadora plan for the region. In addition Spain cancelled its debt with that country and with Bolivia, and granted Mexico a 50 per cent reduction. In 1992, as part of the celebration of the fifth Centenary of the Discovery of the New World, the government instituted a series of programmes of cooperation, such as the *Fondo Quinto Centenario* (Fifth Centenary Fund) (Heywood 1995: 274–6). For the Franco regime the link with Latin America had been part of a strategy of escaping isolation (Preston 1995a: 582) and thus it fostered the concept of *Hispanism*, a concept popularized among the right wing in the 1920s and evolving under Franco into the idea of *Hispanidad*: 'a spiritual community of Hispanic nations united by Catholic, universalist principles that were the legacy of Mother Spain to her daughters' (Boyd 1997: 185–6). Under the Socialists Spain moved away from this towards a more modern concern for conflict resolution and aiding economic development. Thus Spain was instrumental in setting up the first of a series of annual Ibero-American summits in Guadalajara in 1991 with the aim of promoting 'greater and more efficient integration in a changing global context'.

In 1982 Spain belonged to NATO and the Council of Europe. Its position in NATO was somewhat compromised by its position at the same time as an observer in the Non-Aligned

Movement (Powell 2001a: 278). González's government decided to launch a charm offensive with the USA and with those members of the EC with which it either had outstanding disagreements, such as Britain, or whom it saw as crucial to its negotiation of entry into the organization, such as France. One result was the meeting in 1983 with Mitterrand in which greater cooperation was achieved in dealing with ETA terrorism. Another was Spain's decision to open the border with Gibraltar in 1982 which, in turn, led to the Brussels Agreement of 1984 by which both Britain and Spain committed to maintaining a dialogue over the issue. Discussions with Germany led to that country's support for Spain and Portugal's entry at the European Council meeting in Stuttgart in 1983 (Powell 2001a: 359).

4.8   Saying Yes to NATO

In relation to NATO, the Socialists soon became convinced of the need to remain in the organization if membership of the EC was to be secured. The lesson of the past in general and the Tejero coup attempt in particular had shown the advantages of membership as a way of appeasing the armed forces and a route to its modernization. González, therefore, set out in 1984 a set of ten points, his famous *decálogo*, which mapped out the parameters for the Socialists' change of heart, playing on the enduring anti-military, anti-nuclear and rather anti-American sympathies of many of his supporters. This turnaround, described by Alfonso Guerra as 'Copernican' (2006: 180), on the part of the government allowed the Treaty of Accession to be signed on 12 June 1985. The time was now propitious to fulfil the long-postponed promise of the 1982 electoral campaign to hold a referendum on NATO on 12 March 1986. Riding high on the tide of optimism accorded by Spain's entry into Europe, González used his party's control of the media to the full to campaign for a yes vote for remaining within the organization. González explained his U-turn, saying that the party's real objection to NATO was not the issue of membership but the fact that the previous government of Calvo Sotelo had taken Spain into the organization without consultation. The referendum therefore rectified that situation. Much thought was given to the phrasing of the referendum question and, in the end, a favourable response was encouraged by linking the question with continued membership with Spain's commitment to stay out of the military structure, keeping Spain a nuclear-free zone and progressively reducing American military presence on Spanish soil.

The biggest threat for the Socialists was the decision by the Alianza Popular leader, Manuel Fraga, to recommend abstention, to the consternation of his European conservative colleagues. Given that Fraga would in normal circumstances have voted in favour (Powell 2001a: 420), this decision seemed perversely intended to precipitate a defeat for the Socialists that would weaken their chances in the imminent general elections by robbing the government of the substantial support of the traditionally pro-NATO right. In the end the government won with 53 per cent of the vote, compared to 40 per cent voting against, all the more impressive for having been gained by the Socialists alone (Guerra 2006: 238). The extent of the party's changed view on NATO would be confirmed when, in 1995, Javier Solana, at the time González's Foreign Minister, was appointed the organization's Secretary-General.

It was shortly after the NATO referendum when Fernández Ordóñez replaced Fernando Morán as Foreign Minister and, as a result, Spain's foreign policy took a more moderate, pro-American direction. In 1987 Spain signed the Nuclear Non-Proliferation Treaty and the following year joined the Western European Union and renewed the Defence Agreement with the USA (Heywood 1995: 263). On 17 January 1986, Madrid restored full diplomatic relations with the Israeli government, boycotted by the Franco regime, and shortly after it granted the office of the PLO in Madrid the status of embassy. This new role was aptly illustrated when in 1991 Madrid hosted the Arab–Israeli Peace Conference. Thus, one can say that under

the Socialists, Spain's international relations, probably for the
first time in history, were put on a relatively even keel.

4.9   Spain and the EC

With regard to the EC, the Socialists benefited from the overwhelming Europeanism that characterized the Spanish. For
many, membership was a guarantee that the country could
never slip back to its former dictatorial ways nor suffer isolation-
ism again and a consolidation of the new democratic system.
Those on the right saw the opportunities for business and those
on the left were won over by the promise of a higher standard of
living for workers. Fishing and agriculture were the two main
risk areas, but the Socialists made the wise move, subsequently a
characteristic of Spain's approach to the EC in general, of
taking its role seriously and sending in heavyweight politicians.
As a result it could be said that Spain has consistently managed
to punch above its weight in the Community, with many of its
representatives occupying key positions from the start, such as
Enrique Barón, President of the European Parliament from
1989 to 1992, and Manuel Marín, appointed Commission
Vice-President for social affairs, education and employment in
1986.

The final deal involved Spain accepting a seven-year transition period before EC tariffs would be removed from Spanish
exports. In 1989 Spain signed the Single European Act and,
while it chose to become a member of the European Monetary
System in spite of the difficulties of convergence owing to the
recession of 1991–3, the lack of social dialogue and corruption
cases, a change was detected in the government's EU rhetoric
away from the emphasis on collective principles and 'economic
redistribution' towards a 'more nationalistic stance', particularly
in the light of the renewed PP opposition and imminent elections (Closa and Heywood 2004: 45). In fact the difficulties of
the ERM in the early 1990s made it an opportune moment for
González to win a good deal for Spain in return for supporting

Spain since 1939

the process (Farrell 2005: 217–18). It also was a sign of the new focus on national interest which was now characterizing Spain's relationship with the Community. Spain continued to show its pro-European credentials with wholehearted support for the Maastricht treaty in 1992, for which it instituted and adhered to a Convergence Plan to meet the EU criteria, as well as becoming a founder member of Eurocorps and a signatory to the Schengen Agreement in 1991.

Such enthusiasm was undoubtedly coloured by the financial benefits that Spaniards saw from membership. From 1989 to 1993 Spain received 12 billion ecus in Structural Funds, a quarter of the EC's expenditure on such aid. At the Edinburgh Summit in 1992, González had threatened to scupper negotiations entirely on the Maastricht Treaty if he did not get his way in a deal on Cohesion Funds for the poorer member states (Ross 2002: 116). In the end he succeeded not only in securing these funds for countries such as Spain, Ireland, Greece and Portugal but also managed to win increased amounts of Structural Funds. Between 1995 and 2000 Spain received approximately half (1576 million ecus) of all structural funds.

4.10   Spain's Second Economic Miracle

On the economic front the Socialists inherited a difficult situation, as the country 'had not yet recovered from the worst of the economic crisis that had begun in 1974: GDP was stagnant, inflation remained stuck at 14 per cent per year and unemployment had risen steadily to 16.5 per cent' (Juliá 2000: 331). It was decided early on to devalue the peseta and apply a strict monetarist policy which had an immediate effect on the current account deficit. Improvement in the petrol prices, tourist revenue and the increase in foreign investment meant that by 1987 Spain's economic health was restored, though not without taking its toll on the unemployment figures, which had risen to 17.8 per cent in 1983 and reached a record high of 21.5 per cent in 1986 (Rodríguez Braun 1992: 56). Industrial restructuring

126

cost the Spanish Treasury a substantial amount. Not only the money needed to cushion the effects of redundancies, but also the cost of investment in new industrialization projects in those areas hardest hit by the closure of traditional industries.

Added to this was the cost of expanding the welfare state system. By 1995, Spain was spending around half of its GDP on public-sector spending, half of that going towards the welfare state, thus bringing it into line with the EU average. The Socialists had universalized free health care and pension rights. Spain was first in the OECD for the number of doctors per capita while expenditure on education rose fivefold and spending on unemployment benefit doubled (Kennedy 2007: 188). Such social measures, needed to keep the trade unions on board, meant an increase in taxes, which rose by a third, and the public debt, as well as a reduction in investment in infrastructure.

The result, however, was that Spain was well placed to benefit from the economic boom enjoyed by Europe in the second half of the decade. Under the Economy Minister, Carlos Solchaga, Spain's spectacular growth outstripped that of its partners. Spain was a popular target for foreign investment, rising by over 13 per cent between 1986 and 1989 (Rodríguez Braun 1992: 58). Inflation dropped to 5 per cent, industrial investment rose by 10 per cent, foreign investment constituted 4 per cent of GDP and in the period between 1986 and 1990, almost 2 million jobs were created, with unemployment decreasing by half a million. One of the problems for the Socialists was that after the initial period of forced job losses owing to the *reconversión* programme, its record on job creation was actually quite good. However, it was accompanied by a huge growth in the labour market, especially with women and young people entering it for the first time. As a result, although job creation was a success, the unemployment figures remained high.

While Spain's economic performance under the Socialists was undoubtedly a success and involved much needed restructuring, the boom of the late 1980s was based on rather ephemeral factors. Foreign investment was attracted by the high interest rates and the low labour costs. Spaniards, starting from a low base, were eager to spend their new wealth on consumer goods. But the low labour costs soon disappeared as the Spanish workforce acquired parity with their European neighbours and, by the early 1990s, after several devaluations of the peseta in rapid succession, Spain was, like many other European countries, entering recession. Unemployment shot up to 20 per cent and Spain's economic figures were the worst they had been in over fifty years. In the early 1990s Spain was one of the fastest growing nations, but also one where unemployment was highest. In part this was due to an expanding active population, as women and the generation of the 1960s baby boom entered the job market.

Despite this the government, under Finance Minister Pedro Solbes, continued to work towards convergence. Meeting the criteria for monetary union was difficult enough, but exacerbated by the impact of the European recession. In 1993, to retain the competitivity of its exports, Spain had to devalue the peseta beyond the limit permitted by the EMS. The sacrifices made to achieve entry to Europe were compounded by the need to be in the first wave of countries signed up to monetary union. The result was new general strikes on 24 May 1992 and 27 January 1994.

4.11   Education

In education the Socialists introduced important democratic reforms. At secondary level, a key concern was to regain government control over the prestigious subsidized private schools. The Right to Education Act (*Ley Orgánica del Derecho a la Educación*, LODE) in 1984 obliged private schools that wished to benefit from government funding to observe the same criteria for admission as those in the public sector, teach the national curriculum and submit themselves to government inspections. In addition, a new body, the School Council, with 80 per cent representation from teachers, parents and pupils, effectively managed the school. The law met with strong protest from conservative and ecclesiastical sectors, who tried unsuccessfully to overturn it through the Constitutional Court in 1985.

The most wide-ranging and visionary reform was the General Educational System Act (*Ley de Ordenación General del Sistema*, LOGSE). It attempted to tackle deficiencies in state provision at pre-school level by creating and funding infant schools for the 3–5-year-olds, which ceased to be a privilege of children the well-to-do. It also brought the Spanish system into line with most of Europe by having compulsory secondary education (*Educación Secundaria Obligatoria*, ESO) extend from 12 to 16, bringing it into line with the labour laws and ending the exploitation of young people between those ages. Choice of academic or vocational routes is made after 16, with particular emphasis given to restoring much-needed prestige to vocational courses to address a deficit in training for the modern job market. The LOGSE, while idealistic in its motivation, was generally credited with leading to a drop in academic standards, the progressive values underpinning it militating against the more conservative concern with standards. Furthermore, the LOGSE's deference to the Autonomous Communities in regard to much of the curriculum content would be controversially reversed by the Conservatives when in power, particularly in relation to the teaching of history (Resina 2000: 114–15).

At university level, the 1983 *Ley de Reforma Universitaria* (LRU) granted greater autonomy to universities over their own affairs and, as with the LODE, made their governing bodies more representative. It sought a reduction of the reliance on temporary teachers, who had come to represent 60 per cent of staff, and in an attempt to extend provision and promote competition it encouraged the establishment of further private universities, up to then restricted to four prestigious centres, three founded by the Jesuits and one belonging to Opus Dei. Granting universities the power to design their own degrees allowed greater adjustment to the needs of the labour market and allowed students greater mobility to attend universities outside their local area, thus increasing competition between institutions. While not a panacea, the reforms were seen as a much-needed loosening of an out-of-date, hidebound system. Student numbers rose from 692,000 in 1982 to 1.2 million in 1992 (rising to 1.5 million in 1997) and the number of lecturers rose from 35,000 to 53,000 in the same period. Spending on education rose from half a billion to two and a half billion pesetas. Spain rose to fourth place in world rankings in terms of the proportion of the population in education between the ages of 4 and 23 (Martín de la Guardia 2004: 1042).

Still, the perennial complaint was that government measures to expand and improve the sector were not always matched with adequate resources, Spain's budgetary allocation to education being approximately half the EU average. The private sector continues to occupy an important position in the Spanish system, although the Socialists' measures have managed to redress many of the social imbalances, perhaps to the detriment of attention to quality. Nonetheless, in addition to aggravating the right, the Education Minister, José María Maravall, had incurred the wrath of trade unions and the student body over the LRU. Protests culminated in a student strike in 1987 and led to government capitulation to demands for more investment in grants (Martín de la Guardia 2004: 1040).

4.12 Social Change

In addition to education, the Socialists carried out substantial reforms in the areas of health, welfare and pensions. A 1986 Health Act (*Ley General de Sanidad*), accompanied by huge investments in equipment, established the universalization of health cover (Brooksbank Jones 1997: 51), and a network of primary health care had reached 80 per cent of the population by 1994. The financing of the system through taxation was also placed on a firmer footing.

As a result of educational reforms and social investment by the Socialist government in the 1980s, average living standards of most Spaniards rose by 40 per cent, which for some made the trade union demands at the time hard to understand. However, the Socialists incurred the trade unions' wrath in 1985 by tackling the outdated and costly pensions system inherited from the Franco regime. Early retirements as a result of *reconversión* and a rapidly ageing population meant that the government could no longer afford the relatively generous system instituted by the dictator. In the 1985 Pensions Act, the government increased the number of years' contributions required to qualify for a state pension from 10 to 15, with the amount of the pension depending on the amount contributed over the previous eight years (Ruiz 2002: 90). The Socialists' overall majority and the need to drive through these unpopular measures also meant the end of the system of *concertación social*, i.e. cooperation between the main social agents such as trade unions and employers, to ensure consensus on economic policy.

Throughout the 1980s Spain became a society dominated on the one hand by young people, product of the baby boom between 1964 and 1974, but also with an increasingly ageing population which would put pressure on its social security and pensions system to cope (Harrison and Corkill 2004: 33). The pattern of the typical Spanish family would also change. Growing numbers of people lived on their own and there was an increased tendency for young people to prolong their dependency on their parents owing to difficulties of integrating into the labour market or buying their own home. It was also a country of great inequalities between wealth and poverty as a result of the precipitate nature of the growth (Toharia 1992)

In other respects, the Socialist period brought about a social, as well as an economic, convergence with its European neighbours. The number of people working in agriculture dropped over the decade of the 1980s and the service sector grew by over 2 million. Women and young people became more prominent in the workplace, though with the negative consequence noted earlier. Salaries doubled and this, added to a reduction in inflation of 8 per cent, led to a major improvement in Spaniards' lifestyle. For women the 1980s saw a massive increase in their presence in higher education (Harrison and Corkill 2004: 28).

The Socialists promoted the role of women and a major development was the founding of the Institute for Women (*Instituto de la Mujer*) in 1983 to carry forward the Constitution's provision for sexual equality. This autonomous body, linked from 1988 to the Ministry for Social Affairs, benefited from input from those involved in the wider women's movement and its brief was 'the promotion and encouragement of the conditions necessary for the social equality of the sexes and women's participation in public, cultural, economic and social life' (Brooksbank Jones 1997: 40–1). While tensions set in between it and the wider feminist body in Spain, there is little doubt that it was a positive initial step in giving a higher profile to women in Spanish society.

The Socialist period also saw a progressive decline in the birth rate, with the average number of children per family dropping to 1.2 in 1994, well below the replacement level of 2.1. This trend would continue to the present, with Spain's population decline only rescued by the not unproblematic factor of immigration from the late 1980s onwards. Although not a factor in this trend, the Socialists had exploited the Constitution's ambiguity to introduce a law in 1985 permitting abortion in three cases: rape, malformation of the foetus and when the mother's life is in danger. This was still a very restrictive arrangement and when, in 1994, the government tried to introduce a fourth category for termination during the first 12 weeks 'in cases where serious personal, family or social conflict was likely to result from the birth', it was rejected (Brooksbank Jones 1997: 87). Spaniards have a notorious attachment to family and in particular the raising of children, possibly a legacy of Francoist pro-natalist propaganda. When in 1981 a divorce law was introduced, after an initial flurry due to 'pent-up demand' the figure stabilized at a moderate level. Spaniards are more likely to separate than divorce and women's greater willingness to initiate the process in part 'reflects the erosion of women's affective and economic dependency on men' in the democratic era (Brooksbank Jones 1997: 91) (see **6.6**).

4.13 Immigration

A further aspect of Spain's social transformation as a result of the Socialists' drive for European integration was the growth of immigration, with its consequent impact on the social dynamic. Spain, traditionally a country of emigration, was to become an increasingly multicultural society with the attendant advantages and problems such a development brings. Faced with one of the lowest birth rates in Western Europe, immigration would act as a demographic supplement and source of cheap labour which would drive the economy, especially the housing and agriculture boom of the 1990s. The predominance of illegal immigration would impose a strain on the system and lead to social tensions such as the riots that occurred between Moroccan agricultural workers and local inhabitants in El Ejido in Almería in February 2000.

The Franco regime had been constructed on a xenophobic intolerance that fostered, not entirely successfully, an exaggerated pride in Spanishness and Catholic values. Monoculturalism was both a reality, born of Spain's socioeconomic history, and an ideal that was only moderately challenged by the cultural variety that Spain contained at a sub-national level (Corkill 2000: 50) (see **6.15**). Such a scenario changed in the 1980s. Before this, Spaniards only really knew of their own emigration, either the nineteenth-century wave to Latin America or the more recent 1960s exodus to the factories of Europe. Immigration tended to mean internal immigration and racism was not a major social problem, though it had existed for centuries, directed at the long-standing gypsy community (Hooper 2006: 290).

Membership of the EC had the effect of igniting immigration. The word *patera* entered the Spanish lexicon – the small flimsy boat in which African immigrants risked their lives, often unsuccessfully, to cross the Straits of Gibraltar. The African invasion was soon added to by the Latin American wave. As well as its prime motivator, the EC factor determined its treatment. The matter was dealt with by the Interior Ministry, which promoted an Aliens Act (*Ley de Extranjería*) in 1985, mainly targeted at those immigrants already present in Spain, giving strict powers of deportation within 72 hours with no right to appeal. Its draconian nature surprised many on the progressive left, and its harsh treatment of immigrants' rights had to be softened by the Constitutional Court (Jiménez 2000). Still, in the long run this may have had the positive effect of defusing a hard-right backlash. While Spain does have some ultra-right activity, it has never had an equivalent in the post-Franco era of a movement such as that of Jean-Marie le Pen in France. Successive Spanish governments, especially the conservative PP, would take advantage of the 'blame allowance' granted by the need to conform to EC/EU norms as justification for harsh immigration policies (Closa and Heywood 2004: 233). Difficulties in implementing the 1985 Act forced the government to agree on an amnesty in 1986, the first of many, to allow illegal immigrants to 'regularize' their situation. Such legalization at least ensured social security contributions to fund an increasingly stretched welfare state. A total of 23,000 were regularized in the first wave in 1986 and over 110,000 in a further amnesty in 1991 (40 per cent of whom were from Morocco) (Cornelius 2004: 413).

It is important to set immigration in Spain in context. First, given Spain's decreasing birth rate, it is a demographic and economic necessity. Secondly, in terms of numbers, Spain's immigrant community does not present a serious problem. In 1992 immigrants accounted for a mere 2 per cent of the population, compared with 6 per cent in France and 9 per cent in Germany (Harrison and Corkill 2004: 39) though this has now risen to around 8.7 per cent (see **5.11, 6.15**). Still, Spain was under pressure to comply with EC regulations, though, as suggested above, this could conceal xenophobic motives. As a party to the Schengen Convention in 1991 which permitted free movement of labour within the EU, Spain acquired a large responsibility in policing Europe's vulnerable southern border, especially at a time when not only affluence was on the rise but also its 'unwanted features, including unemployment (the

highest percentage in the EU), the erosion of social solidarity'
and social prejudice (Corkill 2000: 51).

4.14   The Regions

While the elections of 1982 heralded a period of hegemony for
the Socialists it was the beginning, too, of the emergence on to
the national parliamentary scene of the Nationalist parties,
particularly the moderate Catalan CiU and the Basque PNV,
both Christian Democrat in their leanings. While numerically
small, they would occasionally assume important roles as
power-brokers, in particular towards the end of the Socialist
period (1993–6) and the first government of José María Aznar
(1996–2000). In their own regions, the CiU, a conservative
coalition under Jordi Pujol, enjoyed its own period of uncontested hegemony between 1981 and 2003, while in the Basque
Country the PNV dominated until an internal split in 1987
required it to enter a coalition with the Socialists that lasted until
October 1998.

On the other hand, from 1983 the Socialist party controlled
the majority of the other 15 regional governments (exceptions
being Galicia, the Baleares and Cantabria, all in the hands of
the conservative AP) and at council level, they were in charge in
most of the cities and large towns. The Socialists had set as one
of their aims to advance the devolution process outlined in the
1978 Constitution. Throughout the 1980s the 'system of
autonomies', as the devolved arrangement was called, gradually
settled down. In the end, seven regions – Catalonia, the Basque
Country, Galicia, Andalusia, the Canaries, Navarra and
Valencia – had been fast-tracked to a high level of autonomy,
and the rest were taking the slow route laid down in Article 143.
As the regional role intended for the Senate by the Constitution
was (and is) still not worked out, early tensions were dealt with
by the Constitutional Court, but the process became progressively less contentious, with the number of appeals to the
Constitutional Court decreasing from 135 in 1985 to 9 in 1991.

A regional distribution fund, the *Fondo de Compensación Interterritorial*, was established in 1984 to ensure an equitable financing of the varied regions. Progress was such that by 1992 many of the slow-route regions were given control over areas such as Education and Social Services, hitherto the prerogative of the fast-route regions.

The period witnessed the increasing prominence of regional politics, naturally within the regions themselves but also occasionally impacting on the national level. This was mainly the case in Catalonia and the Basque Country.

Basque regional politics divides into the nationalist and the non-nationalist camps. The latter is made up of the Basque branches of the Socialists (PSOE-PSE, then PSE) and the PP (PPE). There is also the Basque branch of the communist United Left, which often sides with the nationalist parties, as, for example, in signing the Estella Pact (see **5.9**). The nationalists divide into the anti-ETA and the pro-ETA camps. Of the former, the dominant party is the Basque Nationalist Party, the PNV, formed by the founder of contemporary Basque nationalism, Sabino Arana, in 1895. Arana's peculiar brand of ultra-orthodox Catholicism and radical ethnic nationalism has evolved into a more moderate brand of nationalism which, until towards the end of the 1990s, maintained an ambiguous stance between advocacy of independence and contentment with the constitutional arrangement within a Spanish state. During the 1980s it had to contend with a more radical rival, HB, which was founded in 1978 as part of a wider nationalist movement called the Nationalist Socialist Coordinating Council (the KAS Alternative) which includes the terrorist group Basque Homeland and Freedom (*Euskadi ta Askatasuna*, ETA). The aim of this movement is an independent Basque Homeland, which would incorporate the three provinces of the current Basque Country (Vizcaya, Guipúzcoa and Alava), as well as the region of Navarra and the three French Basque provinces (Soule, Labourd and Basse-Navarre). In the regional elections HB polls between 10 and 18 per cent of the vote and in 2005 and 2009 was banned for its support of ETA, though in 2005 its 'front' party, the Communist Party of the Basque Land (PCTV-EHAK), managed to gather 12.5 per cent of the vote and gain nine seats in the Basque Parliament (see Appendix 11).

The PNV had a split in 1986 when a former regional Prime Minister Carlos Garaicoechea abandoned the PNV to form *Eusko Alkartasuna* (Basque Solidarity, EA), with a slightly more radical, social democratic agenda. The PNV ruled since 1980 either on its own, or between 1986 and 1994 in coalition with the Basque Socialists (PSE-PSOE) and thereafter with Socialists and EA from 1994 to 1998. However, following the signing of the pan-nationalist Estella Pact, which included HB, the Socialists abandoned government and the PNV ruled in coalition with EA, and the Basque branch of United Left (IU-EB), the tripartite government or *tripartito*, until 2009.

The Basque region during the Socialist period was one of reasonable success. It was badly affected by the industrial *reconversión* exacerbated by having its businessmen targeted by ETA for their 'revolutionary tax', with 64 per cent in a 1984 survey saying they were persecuted (Cabrera and Del Rey 2007: 141). The region fought back to remain a thriving economy on the back of the SMEs, a vibrant service sector and a thriving tourist industry based around a regenerated Bilbao and its centrepiece, the Guggenheim Museum. ETA remained a problem, but there was cross-party unity against its violence, formalized in the Ajuria Enea Pact of 1988.

Catalan politics during the Socialist period was dominated by Jordi Pujol and his CiU. It governed from 1980 to 2003, three times (1984, 1988 and 1992) with absolute majorities. CiU is, like the PNV, a combination of centre-right in traditional politico-economic terms and staunch nationalist but not secessionist in its regional politics. Under Pujol Catalonia was vigorous in defence of its autonomy within Spain and towards the end of the Socialist period, in González's fourth term (1993–6), it lent its support to the government and in return negotiated a 15 per cent control of the levying of income tax in the region. This would be raised to 30 per cent when the party played the same supportive role in Aznar's first term, thus illustrating what is seen as the greater pragmatism of Catalan nationalism compared to that of the Basques. However, there were attempts, fruitless in the end, to have the leverage it had acquired in the last González government used for more ambitious aims, such as forcing the government to recognize Spain as a plurinational state and to allow the Catalan government to have direct dealings with the monarch (McRoberts 2001: 75).

The Socialist government advanced the decentralization process throughout the 1990s to the extent that the only areas which the seven 'fast-route' regions controlled and the other ten did not were health services, social security and the police force. As such Spain was, much to the Basques' and Catalans' discontent, creeping steadily towards a *de facto* federalism.

4.15   Scandal and Corruption

The end of the Socialist period, sadly, was characterized by a wave of corruption scandals and, ironically, this was perhaps one of the principal signs that the party's modernizing transformation had worked. Corruption of one sort or other seemed to be the democratic disease in the 1980s and it was not limited to the southern European nations. One of the major taints on the Socialist period of office was the accusation of clientelism, *enchufismo*. This has commonly been seen as a Spanish vice, with its roots in 'a specific form of southern European *caciquismo*' (Pujas and Rhodes 1999: 51), but under the Socialists it reached new heights. It became the source of one of the most prominent kinds of corruption under the Socialists, *tráfico de influencias*, or influence-peddling. This brought down the civilian head of the Civil Guard, Luis Roldán, and the Governor of the Bank of Spain, Mariano Rubio. Roldán, tipped initially to succeed González as leader, turned out to have falsified his qualifications and exploited his position to charge illegal commissions, and Rubio stood accused of favours to the Ibercorps bank, considered the favourite bank of the Socialist jet set. Both incidents shamed the party and were a cause of deep embarrassment for

González. While the opposition PP, the Basque PNV and the Catalan CiU had similar cases, and even the UGT had its own scandal, that of the Promotora Social de Vivienda (PSV), when a trade-union housing scheme fell through in 1993, and led to the union having to borrow over 76 million euros from the Instituto de Crédito Oficial, the major casualty was naturally the government, especially that of a party which had historically proclaimed its own probity, encapsulated in its 1979 centenary slogan, 'A hundred years of honesty'.

In many ways, the Socialists can be seen as victims of their own absolute majorities and the nature of the Spanish system. Parties in Spain have a low membership and so a high proportion of members actually held office and treated the 'Administration as their own personal property' (Cabrera and Del Rey 2007: 159). Some scandals were the result of genuine social policies, designed to help the most vulnerable in society, being mishandled at a local level for electoral purposes. One example was the PER scandal in the south of Spain. The Plan de Empleo Rural (Rural Employment Scheme), intended to combat seasonality in the poor Andalusian south and Extremadura, led to an illegal trade in certificates of employment so that subsidies could be claimed.

Very damaging for the PSOE was the FILESA scandal where, following a model used in France and Italy, money for fictitious business reports supposedly supplied to businessmen by a paper consultancy firm (FILESA) made its way into Socialist Party coffers. The BBV bank paid 168 million pesetas for such reports. In another case a supermarket chain store paid over 33 million pesetas for a 17-page report, 14 pages of which were photocopies of local council planning documents and another 2 a photocopied press article (Soto 2005: 310). The person running FILESA was a Socialist MP in charge of the party's finances. While not strictly illegal, this scam was one solution sought by PSOE activists to finance the high level of electoral campaigning which the Spanish system imposed on parties (Guerra 2006: 234). The irony was that this desperate measure was a response to the Socialists' own attempt to limit the donations given to parties through the 1985 electoral law (Ley Orgánica de Régimen Electoral General). However, the increasing costs of electioneering and the greater competition from the PP in the early 1990s are seen as pressures on the Socialists to find ways around their own legislation (Pujas and Rhodes 1999; García Viñuela 2008: 178–9). The problem was that although 'the final destination was the party account, the money did not always make it there' (Cabrera and Del Rey 2007: 160).

4.16   Terrorism and the GAL

The most damaging scandal to hit the Socialists in power related to a dirty war waged by the Spanish government against ETA by the *Grupos Antiterroristas de Liberación*, or GAL. The affair is so murky that even now, over twenty years later, the full facts are still debated. The incidents themselves occurred in the mid-1980s, but they only made an impact on Spanish politics in the early 1990s, just in time to scupper the Socialists' chances of a fifth victory at the polls.

In 1983, two young ETA sympathizers, José Antonio Lasa and José Ignacio Zabala, each 20 years old, were captured in San Sebastián, tortured, shot, and their bodies buried in quicklime in Alicante and only identified ten years later. The most widely publicized event in the whole GAL saga took place earlier in 1983 and involved a botched kidnap. Segundo Marey, a French furniture dealer and resident of the French town of Hendaye, just on the border between France and Spain, was taken from his home, and although released ten days later, he never fully recovered from his ordeal. Another victim of the GAL, Juan Carlos García Goena, was blown up by a car bomb in 1987. He too was innocent. In the end, the GAL were responsible for the deaths of 28 people, most of whom had no connection whatsoever with ETA.

The crucial question in the GAL affair was not whether the Socialist administration was guilty or not, but rather how far up the chain of command the responsibility went. José Amedo, a police superintendent in the Basque country, and his deputy, Michel Domínguez, arrested in 1988 and convicted in 1991 of involvement, were clearly seen as mere pawns. In 2000 leading Socialist politician, Julen Elgorriaga, the civil governor of San Sebastián and one of the most respected Civil Guard generals, Enrique Rodríguez Galindo, would be sentenced to 75 years in prison, although the general, for whom there was much support among the Socialist elite, would be released in 2004 on health grounds.

When the story broke the most talked-about factor was who was Mr X, the highest point in the hierarchy to sanction the fight against the terrorists using their own methods. The right-wing press insinuated, and many in the country believed it was Felipe González himself, and Julio Anguita, the leader of the communist coalition, the IU, made the explicit accusation. More seriously at the time, a leading Basque Socialist, Ricardo Damborenea, told the judge that he had spoken to González on three separate occasions in 1984 about setting up the GAL (Soto 2005: 239). Damborenea subsequently shared a platform with the opposition leader José María Aznar, as a sign of his disillusion with his own party leader. From 1988 the principal investigator of the GAL was the judge Baltasar Garzón, and his investigations pointed to the involvement of the Interior Minister, José Barrionuevo, and the use of government slush funds, the *fondos reservados*, not only to finance the operations but to pay for Amedo's and Domínguez's continued silence while in prison.

González successfully neutralized Garzón for a while by inviting him to stand as an independent for the Socialists in the 1993 elections. It gave an impression not only that González was innocent but that he was siding with Garzón in the search for the truth behind the GAL. Disillusioned perhaps by only being given a post as anti-drugs czar, Garzón resigned in May 1994 and resumed his GAL investigation in the face of much pressure and opposition. Amedo and Domínguez, convicted in 1991 of organizing mercenaries to carry out the GAL activities, felt abandoned by an absolved Socialist government, and soon talked and eventually implicated senior government officials such as José Barrionuevo, a former Interior Minister and his second-in-command, Rafael Vera. These and other officials would be sentenced to jail terms in 1998, by which time the damage had been done and the Conservatives were by then the party in government.

Most commentators now agree that, aside from the actual responsibility for particular actions, the Socialists colluded in a counter-terrorist practice that was a hangover from previous regimes and, when it was discovered, neither the government nor Felipe González distinguished themselves by their reaction to the investigations and the outcome. The general stance was to either deny responsibility or tacitly imply that the actions were justified and indeed supported by the majority of Spaniards. González's defenders and even some of his opponents, on the other hand, recognize that one of his characteristics was a complete trust in those under him to look after their own area. Such unwillingness to interfere in the work of his subordinates may justify his claims to ignorance (Sánchez Cervelló and Tubau 2004: 111). Be that as it may, surveys showed that only just over a quarter of Spaniards believed González's denials of involvement (Powell 2001a: 536). One aspect of the events which did cast Spain in a reasonably positive light was the success of the judicial system in bringing former ministers to account (Woodworth 2005: 76).

Paddy Wordworth explains the GAL as a result of the new Socialist government's panic at renewed terror attacks by ETA and its fear of losing the tenuous support it had from the Spanish armed forces, which led it to return to dirty-war tactics against ETA that had already been used throughout the Transition. Such tactics had been initiated by Carrero Blanco in the early 1970s and carried on after his death by an intelligence agency he set up (Woodworth 2005: 67). The Basque Socialist Ramón Jáuregui dismissed the idea of González's involvement but recognized that the GAL scandal showed that the Spanish police had not undergone the same transition to

new democratic methods as the political class (Sánchez Cervelló
and Tubau 2004: 111). Faced with a recrudescence of Basque
violence after the 1982 elections, senior military figures and
certain Socialist politicians in the Basque country decided to
target ETA members with kidnapping and, later, bombs and
gun attacks.

ETA, too, had stepped up its terrorist campaign with the aim
of dragging the government to the negotiating table. The
Hipercor bomb in Barcelona in June 1987, with a death toll of
21, contributed to a year which, with 52 deaths, was the fourth
worst in the history of the conflict. It led to the signing of the
Ajuria Anea Pact in January 1988 by all democratic parties,
national and nationalist, except HB, and as an attempt to isolate
the latter party. This coincided too with greater cooperation
between the French government and Spain allowing the arrest
of Santiago Arrospide in 1987 and the arrest in 1992 in the
French Basque town of Bidart of three top figures of the terrorist organization. The policy of police repression and dispersal of
ETA prisoners was combined with the start of talks between the
government and ETA leaders in Algeria from 1986 until their
break-down in April 1989. The elections of 1991 in the Basque
region saw progress for the PNV and, as a result of disagreements with the Basque Socialist party (PSE), the nationalist-
national coalition briefly came to an end, replaced by a
tripartite nationalist government formed with EA and EE, only
to reassemble in September 1991.

4.17 The End of Felipismo and the Return of the Right

In spite of his achievements and his undoubted status abroad,
many see González's legacy as permanently tarnished, not just
by the scandals that beset his governments towards the end, but
by the way the PSOE was transformed from a party of the
people into a highly efficient organization aimed at gaining and
retaining power. Nonetheless, the astonishing support for a

González-led party in the 1996 elections when it narrowly lost, despite the barrage of negative publicity furnished by the GAL scandal and others, is a testament to its leader's standing and explains Alfonso Guerra's description of it at the time as a 'sweet defeat'.

Within the Conservative opposition, concerns over the ability of Manuel Fraga ever achieving outright success at the polls began in 1986. The collapse of the Alianza's vote in the 30 November Basque elections, where they were reduced to just two seats in the regional government, signalled the need for action. A young Andalusian lawyer, Antonio Hernández Mancha, hoped to add new vigour to the party's image but such was his failure, the low point being a botched censure motion against Felipe González, that in January 1989 Fraga was voted back as party leader. One hopeful was a moderate Christian Democrat, Marcelino Oreja, chosen to fight alongside Fraga in the June 1989 European elections. The disastrous loss of over 1.3 million votes compared to 1987 scotched his chances (Heywood 1995: 205). When the Socialists took advantage of this weakened position and called early elections in October 1989, the party had to choose a candidate quickly and Fraga was persuaded to pick José María Aznar, a successful President of the staunchly conservative region of Castilla y León since July 1987. Aznar's aim was to transform the AP into a more inclusive centre-right party, and although the party's vote in the 1989 elections was virtually unchanged the gain of two extra seats was a sign, albeit a symbolic and tenuous one, that Fraga's ceiling was broken.

Aznar benefited, also, from the waning fortunes of the other centre-right parties that temporarily established themselves in the 1980s. The most significant of these was Adolfo Suárez's CDS which, in the 1986 elections, had managed to win 1.8 million votes and raise its fortunes in parliament from two seats to nineteen. Nonetheless, in a virtual repetition of what happened with UCD under Suárez in the aftermath of establishing democracy, he was unable to stamp a clear political identity on the CDS and the support seemed largely to reflect the admiration for Suárez the man rather than his party's policies. Thus, when he failed to consolidate his party's success in the 1989 elections, where the CDS slipped to 14 seats, Suárez resigned in 1991 and it would not be long until the party folded with him after failing to win a single seat in the 1993 elections.

4.18   Conclusion

Hence in spite of signs of a moderate economic recovery in 1994, the benefits of which were tempered by the government's measures to achieve economic convergence with Europe, and in spite of Spain's successful presidency of the EU in 1995, the Socialists' decline in popularity could not be halted. In the new People's Party it faced an opposition which from 1995 had triumphed at municipal and regional level. Some even suggested that Aznar's near miraculous survival of an ETA car-bomb in April 1995 had added a certain allure to his hitherto lacklustre image and it had certainly suggested the terrorists saw him in some way as the future Prime Minister. When Pujol's Catalan coalition, *Convergència i Unió* (CiU), refused to support González's 1995 budget proposals, elections were inevitable. On 3 March 1996 the People's Party won a historic victory, with a surprisingly narrow margin of 300,000 votes, giving it 156 seats compared to 141 for the Socialists (see Appendix 7). The margin, which both reflected well on González's ability to almost carry off victory in the worst possible circumstances and also robbed the PP of the ability to govern without support from other parties, led to Alfonso Guerra's infamous comment: 'Never was a defeat so sweet nor a victory so bitter' (Gillespie 1996: 428). Given the polls' indication of a close result, the PP had refrained from presenting the more radically neoliberal policies it would have liked, but the scale of its victory was even less than hoped. Twenty seats short of an absolute majority forced Aznar into humiliating collaboration with the Catalan nationalist Pujol, who his supporters had been mocking in the most pejorative of terms the night before the election. What proved more important, however, was that the PP were now in a clear majority in terms of the urban and youth vote, precisely where the PSOE had been in 1982. The power-change from left to right, the first in the post-Franco democratic period, was as historic if not more so than the 1982 victory of the left and for many, in spite of the Socialists' scare campaign likening Aznar to Franco and Hitler, it signified that in one sense at least the dictator's ghost had finally been laid to rest.

5

THE RETURN OF THE RIGHT, 1996–2004

5.1 Introduction

José María Aznar's victory in 1996 was both the successful result of a process that commenced within the opposition a decade before and an inevitable effect of evolving difficulties for the Socialist Party in government. Given that the latter would not always be the case, Aznar supported Fraga's view that the party needed a more populist orientation to capture the 'natural majority' (Balfour 2005a). The party had to escape its Francoist past and project a more moderate image, something Aznar planned from the party's 1990 Seville Congress (Aznar 2004: 68). That this was clearly an electoral strategy rather than a genuine ideological shift can be judged from the contrasting patterns of the two legislatures between 1996 and 2004. Aznar's first period in office was characterized by the need to establish pacts with Basque and Catalan regionalist parties that, while not dissimilar in terms of economic principles and conservative values, were diametrically opposed to the PP when it came to constitutional matters and their vision of a future Spanish state. However, after the 2000 general elections when the PP won an overall majority, such a need for conciliatory politics became unnecessary.

5.2 José María Aznar and the PP

Aznar himself was ideologically right-wing. His early political career had evolved as a member of a branch of the Falange that

147

had distanced itself from the Francoist establishment, though as Manuel Vázquez Montalbán makes clear, was 'never anti-Francoist' (2003: 14). He joined the Popular Alliance in 1979 when he was working as a tax-inspector in La Rioja, near the Basque Country, and in those early days displayed reservations about many aspects of the Constitution passed the previous year. When he took over the leadership of the People's Party, Aznar showed himself capable of imposing discipline on the party without alienating its members, and his success was to put together a fresh young team that unified the party (Aznar 2004: 70). He also sought to ensure that the party's structures fitted into the new regional framework to improve success at that level and forge alliances with like-minded regionalist parties. Links were forged also at European and international levels with incorporation into the Christian Democrat International and their grouping in the European Parliament, the European People's Party (EPP), though in relation to these groupings Aznar's party was much more neoliberal (Ross 2004: 182).

The early opposition years were difficult because in spite of the scandals which were starting to afflict the Socialist party, the charismatic shadow of González still hovered over the political stage. Also, public opinion tended to dislike the oppositional strategy of Aznar's party, the majority seeing it as unable to offer a positive and constructive vision (Tusell 2004: 30). Still, his eventual success in 1996 would not have occurred had he not set as his mission to capture the political centre. This aim was dubbed by Aznar in one of his own books as a 'second Transition', a phrase which, in one sense, for Tusell, seemed to express a wish to correct the process that had occurred between 1975 and 1978 (2004: 47). In the book Aznar implies that the Socialist government had failed to capitalize on the achievements of the Transition whereas, as Balfour notes, 'the PP government owed an enormous debt to the Socialists who had persuaded and fought with the left to accept privatisation and deregulation in a way no conservative government could have done' (Balfour 2005a: 154). If the economy Aznar inherited owed much to his socialist predecessors, and the rebuilding of the PP had begun in the 1980s with the incorporation of many Christian Democrats fleeing the sinking ship of UCD, its success as an electoral machine was in no small measure attributable to the personal qualities of Aznar. Commentators have alluded to his coldness, his discipline and his rigid, self-oriented style of government. His principles were largely pragmatic and he was unhampered by a strong ideological doctrine, a sign of which was his close ties throughout his presidency with Tony Blair and the Portuguese António Guterres, both leaders of leftist social democrat parties (Barrera 2002). In fact, the PP's success in the 1990s can be ascribed to Aznar's canny decision to eschew both the traditional conservatism of the Alianza Popular in the 1970s and the neoliberalist trend of the 1980s in order to embrace a more marketable mixture of a neoliberal economic strategy with popular social policies on issues such as pensions and welfare that had made the Socialists so electable in the 1980s (Astudillo and García-Guereta 2006: 411).

5.3   A Government of Moderation

The only thing that for the victors tainted the success of the 3 March 1996 elections was the fact that Aznar had to negotiate the support of those parties, the Catalan CiU and the Basque PNV, whose policies and in some cases whose personalities his party had spent the previous four years attacking, in particular their propping up of a mortally wounded Socialist party after 1993. To his credit, Aznar was determined to win support for his candidacy as president from both the main regionalist parties, even though numerically he was safe after securing the support of Jordi Pujol's CiU. It was as if he wanted to balance his simple majority electoral win with a more cross-party support in government. The two parties did not yield their support cheaply, and in the case of the Basques, their support was solely for investiture and not for government. The Catalans agreed to the latter and exploited their renewed status as a 'hinge party' to raise the degree of fiscal co-responsibility from the 15 per cent won under the Socialists to 30 per cent. The reward for the PNV was a renegotiation of the terms of its *cupo*, the financial arrangement whereby the Basque government transferred money to central government from the taxes it raised, and also a promise to revisit the regional constitution, the Guernica Statute.

5.4 Achieving a Stable Economy

Aznar's cabinet reflected a moderate hue less in the consistent nature of its components and more in the balance between hardliners, moderates and independents. It set as its target achievements that were principally economic and in this it was undoubtedly successful. According to Balfour, the 'PP government's most important achievement during its two terms of office was macro-economic. It oversaw Spain's incorporation into the EMU and fulfilled the conditions of the EU Growth and Stability Pact' (2005: 146). Under the stewardship of Rodrigo Rato, Deputy Prime Minister in charge of the economy, the *populares* introduced a series of austerity measures aimed at lowering public spending. The determining aim was to locate Spain among the first group of countries entering into the single currency by January 1998, a target that became for Aznar a similar incentive, as did entry into Europe for González and the Socialists. It has been said that the 'PP expected to make its profile on economic issues distinctive by superior performance rather than by offering markedly different or specific policies' and that 'by participating in the euro from the outset ... would gain among the Spanish electorate a reputation for economic and political competence' (Astudillo and García-Guereta 2006: 413). It was an aim that was largely successful, and certainly *The Economist* could report that 'the PP's stewardship of the public finances was exemplary' (2004: 10).

Luckily for Aznar and his team, Spain's economy was on an upward turn from the recession suffered in the years 1992–4 both as a result of the general international economic climate and the mood of confidence that the process of European Union inspired (Jiménez 2000: 57); nevertheless, the degree of Spaniards' satisfaction with the progress of the economy – which rose steadily from just over 10 per cent in 1996 to close to 40 per cent by the end of 1999 – was unprecedented in the democratic period (Wert 2000: 214).

However, when he took over, Spain had still only met one of the Maastricht criteria, that of interest rates. Nonetheless, his measures undoubtedly helped, as did his success in reaching agreement, signed in April 1997, with the main trade unions, a task that had been beyond González in the later years. What distinguished Aznar from the Socialists was that Aznar was keener to give the employers and trade unions free rein to reach their own agreements in the interests of fostering economic confidence. In his weak parliamentary situation he certainly could not afford to provoke trade union unrest. One of his first moves on arriving in office was to meet with the two trade union leaders and emphasize his commitments made at investiture to maintain the level of social protection, the purchasing power of pensions and promote job creation (Soto 2000: 71).

The result was a signing of the Pact for Stability in Employment and Collective Bargaining in 1997, the first of its kind since the Socialists signed the Interconfederal Pact of 1983 (Powell 2001a: 588). Aznar still pursued a neoliberal agenda and his advocacy of reduced state intervention in the economy placed him on the right of the political spectrum. However, he balanced this with a progressive social policy in many areas, especially pensions and unemployment benefits. The PP government continued to respect the Toledo Pact of 1995, according to which a range of parties had agreed to maintain the level of pensions. From 1998 the thrust of the PP's stance was represented by the move to the centre, the 'reformist centre', as it was known.

As was said, the governing principle for Aznar was to place Spain in the group of first entrants into the euro, and so a priority was tight control of the budget. A budget office was set up under the distinguished academic José Barea and devised a convergence programme for the years 1997 to 2000, during which Spain's economy grew at the healthy rate of 3.4 per cent, 1.2 per cent higher than the EU average (Jiménez 2000: 56). There were also positive signs that as opposed to other periods, such as the late 1980s, Spanish growth was fuelled by demand in consumption and private investment rather than the public sector (Powell 2001a: 577; Jiménez 2000: 58). The government succeeded in lowering inflation, interest rates and public debt. Thanks to the 1997 employment pact, which went some way to reducing the rigidity of the Spanish labour market, job creation grew by 1.8 million over the period and the unemployment rate fell from 23 per cent in 1996 to 15 per cent in 2000 (Jiménez 2000: 62). For the first time Spain's active investment abroad exceeded its passive role as a destination for foreigner investment and imports. By 1998 Aznar was in a position to honour the pledge he made at the elections to cut taxes.

In general, with both the economy as a whole and the EU in particular the policy of Aznar's government was to continue the trend set by preceding Socialist ministers, and this applied to the approach to liberalization or deregulation, where public-sector involvement in the economy had dropped from 12 per cent in 1985 to 7 per cent in 1993 (Cabrera and Del Rey 2007: 166). However, Aznar's government was prepared to go much further than González's government would have wished, or indeed than the EU would permit. In the area of liberalization government was accused of blatant cronyism according to which large public utilities were privatized in such a way as to not only maintain their dominance of the market but also reap huge profits for those placed in charge, often longstanding friends of Aznar (Cabrera and De Rey 2007: 168). The most controversial case was that of the state telecommunications company, Telefónica, where Aznar had appointed a childhood friend, Juan Villalonga, as director in 1996. What was controversial was that after being appointed to oversee the privatization, he was allowed to stay on as director of the privatized company, profiting personally to an enormous extent, but also he proceeded to expand Telefónica's interests into extensive media ownership, such as the private TV channel Antena 3 in 1997, often acting in support of government interests, as was seen in the case of the 'digital war' (see **5.5**). Eventually he was ousted from Telefónica after a series of controversial ventures that put Aznar's government at serious risk of scandal.

The government achieved its aim of wholesale privatization by 2000, but this has been criticized as having shifted monopolistic control of companies in key sectors like electric, oil and gas into private hands with no discernible benefits for the consumer (Cabrera and Del Rey 2007: 169–70). Nonetheless, it is also undoubtedly true that the move towards consolidation in areas such as banking, telecommunications and energy had allowed Spain to become a major international player in those areas.

5.5   Media Wars

The People's Party had campaigned in 1996 on the promise of a reformed broadcast media landscape 'favouring a plural framework appropriate to a free democracy' (Aguilar 2000: 194). However, one of its most public controversies surrounded plans to introduce digital broadcasting and was seen as an example of Aznar's government flexing its muscles and attempting to impose its authority. In December 1996 the media group PRISA, well known for its sympathies towards the Socialists, had negotiated a deal with Antonio Asensio, the head of the private channel Antena 3, to share the rights to pay-per-view football. The viewing platform was to be the digital channel Canal Satélite, in which PRISA was the controlling stakeholder. Up to that point it had seemed likely that Asensio would work with a rival digital platform owned by, among others, the Spanish state TV channel, RTVE, and the telecommunications company Telefónica, politically much closer to the government. The popularity of football in Spain meant that this would be a determining factor in the success or failure of each platform.

Early the following year Aznar's government moved quickly to replace key people and also introduced legislation that made

life difficult for PRISA's satellite channel. Pay-per-view television had its VAT raised from 7 per cent to 16 per cent; a controversial 'Football Act' stipulated that certain key games had to be
shown on open-access channels and, finally, the Digital
Television Act obliged the industry to use a decoder that was not
compatible with Canal Satélite. The matter was finally resolved,
to an extent, by the surprise sale by Asensio of his television
rights to the football and his shares in Antena 3 to Telefónica,
thus obliging the two rival platforms, Via Digital – belonging to
Telefónica and others – and Canal Satélite to reach agreement
on sharing the rights. Later the European Commission forced
the government to retract some aspects of its Digital Television
Act.

The outcome of the government's intervention in the media
controversy was mixed. On the one hand, it was seen to act
effectively and rapidly against monopoly and in defence of free
competition and viewers' rights, even though the target being
PRISA meant that government self-interest was not an unre-
lated issue. On the other, it was interpreted as a government
abusing its authority against the free market and in pursuit of a
political enemy in the form of the PRISA group. In a further
and undoubtedly related incident in February 1997 PRISA was
pursued through the courts for supposed financial irregularities.
The basis of the accusation was a claim made by an extreme
right-wing journalist, Jaime Campmany, a favourite intellectual
mentor of Aznar's (Tusell 2004: 44). The case was taken up by
the Judge Gómez de Liaño, whose handling of the case was so
extreme and biased that not only was it thrown out of court but
he himself was convicted for abuse of authority, only to be
granted a pardon in 2000.

What was clear was that the electoral promise made by the
PP to carry out a reform of the broadcast media, including the
state channel, RTVE, in favour of greater impartiality and independence by 2000 went unfulfilled. Worse still, in July 1997
Telefónica, run by Villalonga, bought a controlling share of the
private channel Antena 3 and immediately a pro-government
bias was apparent in their news broadcasts (Tusell 2004: 161–5).

5.6 Aznar and the Regions

Aznar's determination in the first term was to serve it in its entirety, and his main weapon was controlled and successful management of the economy. In a policy that was referred to as *lluvia fina*, or 'the drizzle effect', the aim was that the gradual positive perception of the economic performance would impact on political perception and consolidate his position. To a large extent this was successful. Whereas the trend throughout the first half of the first term was for the positive social perception of the political situation to be higher at the start than that of the economic situation, this situation became reversed in the latter half. The implication that the political success of the PP among the electorate was underpinned by its economic achievements, while helpful, was also evidence of a weaker emotional and ideological attachment to the party as well as dependence for support on a factor, the economy, that was not always entirely within the government's control (Wert 2000: 214–15).

Nonetheless electoral performance between 1997 and 1999, at regional, municipal and European levels, proved highly satis-factory for the party and the government. In October 1997 former leader Manuel Fraga maintained his level of support in Galicia and won his third term as regional President, with the added satisfaction for the PP of the Bloque Nacionalista Galego taking over from PSOE as the second party in the region with nearly 25 per cent of the vote. In the Basque regional elections of October 1998, the PP, no doubt helped by the ETA truce announced the previous month, almost doubled its votes and became the second most voted party in the region, winning 16 seats to the PNV's 21 and the PSE-PSOE's 14. In the context of the newly inaugurated Estella Pact (see **5.9**) (named after the Navarrese town where it was signed, called Lizarra in Basque), the PP thus became the leading constitutionalist party in the region. In the June 1999 European elections the PP won, though in this case its lead over the PSOE dropped to 4.5 per cent compared to the 9 per cent it had enjoyed after the historic 1994 elections. In the regional and local elections held on the same date the PP lost some town halls and the regional governments of Aragón and the Baleares owing to the Socialists forming anti-PP pacts and also to local issues such as the transfer of water through the Plan Hidrológico Nacional (see **5.14**).

Overall in the regional elections in the 13 slow-route autonomous communities, both the major parties increased their votes and seats, the Socialists more than the PP, probably due to the losses incurred by the communist coalition IU. In October 1999 in the Catalan elections the vagaries of the D'hondt version of the proportional representation system meant that although it received a smaller percentage of votes than its Socialist rivals, led by the popular ex-mayor of Barcelona Pasqual Maragall, the CiU won the highest number of seats and received the support of the PP and their 12 seats to assure a sixth term for a much weakened Jordi Pujol. There had been a drop in the PP's vote in this election which many interpreted as a sign that the policy of moderation towards the CiU had failed. Nonetheless the fact that the CiU's vote had also declined, making it reliant on the PP for support, also effectively cancelled out the leverage the Catalans had on central government with regard to the reform of its regional statute (*Estatut*) and the Constitution.

5.7   The Basque Situation

The relations with the moderate nationalist party in the Basque Country, the PNV, were more fraught. Aznar had successfully sought their support for his investiture but they were not prepared to enter into a pact for government. In return Aznar's government agreed to consider reform of the Guernica Statute and to renegotiate the financial framework known as the *concierto económico* which regulated the funding of the region. Other matters of more symbolic resonance were also placed on the table such as doing away with the figure of the civil governor, a long-standing source of resentment for nationalists, greater participation of the regional government in EU affairs and the possible return of the PNV's patrimony confiscated during the Civil War. Neither of the last two was met. The PNV was eager, also, to extend the transfer of powers from the centre to the region. By May 1997 progress had been made on updating the *concierto*, but shortly after there occurred something which was to radically alter the social mood and political reality of the Basque region and, in effect, Spain as a whole in terms of its relation to and handling of the problem.

5.8   The Kidnapping of Miguel Angel Blanco

In July 1997, ETA kidnapped and held hostage a young PP councillor, Miguel Angel Blanco, as he was waiting for a train in Ermua station. The condition for his release was that all ETA prisoners be immediately relocated nearer their families. What stunned the country was the unrealistic nature of the demand and the time limit given, 48 hours, and the ruthlessness with which the terrorists carried out their threat. The result was a wave of revulsion and anti-ETA sentiment throughout Spain, including in the Basque country. It marked a watershed for the PNV. Up to that point their nationalism had consisted of an acceptance of the institutional status quo as laid down by the Constitution and a determination to argue for change by persuasion and peaceful means. It had been the underpinning philosophy of the pact between Basque nationalist parties and the main national parties at Ajuria Enea in 1988. Now, ironically, with ETA and its allies on the ropes, the PNV departed from this constitutionalist consensus and sought an alliance among all the nationalist parties, including the anti-constitutionalist HB. Their fear was that the backlash against ETA as a result of the assassination would extend to Basque nationalism in general and sweep them away with it.

The PNV's change of strategy came at a time when the radical Basque movement had lost all claim to popular support in Basque society as a whole (de la Granja and de Pablo 2000: 161) and the determination of the government and other political groupings, including the PNV and EA, had been to isolate HB. HB even lost control of its flagship council in Mondragón (Fusi 2001: 841). There had even been a reaction against the ETA military command on the part of some radical Basques. This was accompanied by renewed police and judicial pressure. The killing inspired a movement of opposition within moderate Basque circles and leading intellectuals were moved to establish forums which openly opposed the self-determination strategy (*soberanismo*) adopted by the PNV. One such was the Foro de Ermua, established in February 1998 by figures including Fernando Savater and Jon Juaristi, and which characterized itself as a civic movement in opposition to the 'Basque fascism of ETA and HB'. Nonetheless, much of the powerful popular impact of the 'spirit of Ermua' was dissipated not least because of its politicization by supporters of the PP (de la Granja and de Pablo 2000: 162).

5.9   The Estella Pact

The PNV revived a strategy originally proposed in 1994 by one of its MPs Juan María Ollora, and it was now repackaged by the *lehendakari* José María Ardanza. The Ardanza Plan represented an important advance in the debate in its assertion, in defiance of radical Basque ideology, that the Basque problem was a problem internal to Basque society and not a conflict between it and the rest of Spain. It also affirmed the impossibility of defeating ETA by police means alone, and emphasized the Basques' right to self-determination. The result was a radical realignment of forces in the Basque Country with the division between democratic constitutionalists (among them the PNV, PP and PSOE) and the anti-constitutionalists (HB and supporters) that had characterized the Ajuria Anea Pact of 1988 now being replaced by a confrontation between nationalists and anti-nationalists.

The effect of all this was to change the PNV's stance from an ambivalently pragmatic one in which it accepted the regionalist system set up by the Constitution while not renouncing its aspirations towards independence or *soberanismo*, to a much more unequivocal advocacy of the latter and the principle of self-determination, hitherto the preserve of the radical Basques (*abertzales*) aligned with HB and ETA. In addition to the fear of an anti-Basque backlash, other factors influenced the change in the PNV's strategy. In the summer of 1998, the main nationalist parties in the three 'historic' regions, the Galician Nationalist Bloc (*Bloque Nacionalista Galego*, BNG), CiU and PNV, had signed the Barcelona Declaration which argued for a plurinational state. The Basque nationalists were also following closely developments in Northern Ireland, where an agreement had been signed on Good Friday 1998 which itself was the result of a strategy of dialogue begun in 1993 by the moderate nationalist leader of the SDLP, John Hume, with Sinn Fein, widely recognized as the political wing of the IRA. The immediate political result of the change in the PNV strategy was that in June 1998 the Socialist PSE-PSOE abandoned their participation in government with the moderate nationalists.

The project of dialogue with the extremists ran directly counter to the set policy with regard to ETA of Aznar and his government, which was characterized by a desire to eradicate the movement by police means. Important in this was not only Aznar's ideological intolerance of nationalism but also, no doubt, his personal experience in 1995 of being a victim of an ETA attack which had very nearly ended his life. Furthermore, the government's tactic had been having considerable success. During Jaime Mayor Oreja's period as Interior Minister arrests of suspected members of ETA and imprisonments rose steeply. Cooperation with France improved, thus depriving ETA members of one of their principal escape routes (Tusell 2004: 193–4). Ten days before the murder of Miguel Angel Blanco, Spain had witnessed the end of one of the longest ever kidnappings when a prisons official, José Ortega Lara, was freed by a police operation. Accused of being a mouthpiece of ETA, the newspaper, *Egin*, was closed down by judge Baltasar Garzón in July 1998 and the whole web of finance supporting the movement was under investigation. In December 1997 the entire leadership of HB was tried and jailed for including ETA in an electoral video the previous year. The initial approach concerning dialogue came from HB and occurred at a moment of weakness in the organization. The approaches led on 12 September 1998 to the signing of the Estella Pact in which the overall aim was declared to be full sovereignty for the Basque Country by what was termed a 'process of national construction'. The only party of national status to sign was the communist United Left (IU). Since the pact also included a formal condemnation of violence, it was followed four days later by a declaration of truce by ETA.

The Estella Pact formally set the PNV at odds with not only the main constitutionalist parties but the Constitution itself. By declaring its *soberanista* credentials it was rejecting the existing institutional arrangements and the Guernica Statute which had allowed it to govern in the Basque Country over the previous 20 years. HB had never accepted these and so one of its (and ETA's) demands was that there should be some movement towards a pan-Basque institutional body that would include not only the Basque Country, but also Navarra and the French Basque provinces, i.e. the territory to which the radical Basques like ETA aspired. This eventually came about in February 1999 when the Udalbiltza was set up in Pamplona, consisting of representatives of all the town councils in the greater Basque territory. It was never widely supported, particularly from the French side, but amazingly it managed to secure finance from the Basque Regional government in 2000.

The pact came into existence a matter of weeks before the regional elections in the Basque Country in October 1998 and the effect on these was to polarize the voting pattern. The moderate parties, in this case the partners in government over the preceding 12 years, the PNV and the Socialists, lost votes and seats. On the other hand the radical Basques of EH (the new formation covering HB for the elections) and the hardline conservative PP gained votes. The new leader of the PNV, Juan José Ibarretxe, formed a government of coalition which was wholly nationalist, with the help of EH in December 1998. In May 1999 EH formalized its support by signing a pact of government with the PNV and its partner EA, though it made clear it would only attend parliament to discuss the 'construction of the future nation'.

The attitude of Aznar's government was to be suspicious of the motivations behind the truce but to attempt to show some degree of response. Hence by September 1998 Aznar had held meetings with all the constitutional parties to discuss the situation and even designated a team to engage in discussions with ETA about how the armed campaign could be brought to a definitive end. An unsuccessful meeting was eventually held in Zurich on 19 May 1999. There was even some movement of prisoners closer to home, a major demand in the Miguel Angel Blanco affair. However, Aznar and his government, particularly Mayor Oreja, were careful to cast doubt on the truce, calling it a *tregua-trampa*, a truce that was no more than a trick to allow ETA to regroup and rebuild its capacity for a future return to violence. This was understandable in that throughout the period of the truce secondary violence in the form of street disturbances (*kale borroka*) continued unabated, cynically condoned by the *abertzales*. In 1999 there were 318 incidents of some sort, usually incendiary bombs targeting public buildings (Fusi 2001: 844). Needless to say, the government throughout was strenuous in its refusal to accept the viability of the demands behind the truce which it saw as entirely anti-constitutional. During the truce, though not connected, the jailed members of HB were released by the Constitutional Court in July 1999.

Politically, the Estella Pact merely favoured the parties on the extremes. Following the 1998 Basque elections, in June 1999 there were two major sets of elections, council and regional, where the impact of the Estella Pact could be analysed. The council elections revealed a greater polarization of the vote with recorded rises for *Eusko Herritarok* (EH), the name HB's supporters assumed to elude the ban, and the PP. In the Navarra regional elections the Union of the People of Navarre (*Unión del*

Pueblo Navarro, UPN), traditionally affiliated with the PP, saw its vote rise substantially; the PSOE vote held steady and EH's vote, while it rose from the previous elections (15.6 per cent from 9.2 per cent), remained firmly in the minority. Thus the fallout of the Estella Pact was simply a country that was more divided than ever between nationalists and non-nationalists and with no major political advance to show for it. When in November 1999 ETA finally called off its truce, the reasons it gave made no mention of the government and its treatment of prisoners but rather were directed at its moderate nationalist partners, the PNV and EA, who had been unprepared to take the next step in the process, initiated with the founding of Udalbiltza, which was the election of a parliament for the greater Basque region, *Euskal Herria*, a proposal which even their moderate Basque associates found 'bizarre' (de la Granja and de Pablo 2000: 175).

5.10   Crisis of the PSOE

The success of Aznar's first term is due undoubtedly to the effective and stable handling of the economy, but an important factor also was the parlous state that the other parties, especially the Socialists, found themselves in. After an initial stage when they were convinced that Aznar's government would not survive, in June 1997 their leader González took the decision to resign and activate the necessary renovation. The other parties also had difficulties. IU went into decline after the high point reached in the 1996 elections when, under Julio Anguita, it managed to win 2.6 million votes, its best result in a decade. Even the regional parties, as we have seen with the PNV, and with the possible exception of the Bloque Nacionalista Galego, underwent a period of uncertainty.

For the Socialists the problem was a lack of anyone with González's charisma and telegenicism. His decision took the party by surprise and his replacement, Joaquín Almunia, a former Employment Minister and a supporter of Felipe, was seen as a steady pair of hands but hardly a vote-winner. In addition, there was a sense of him having been imposed by González and the party elite (Méndez Lago 2005: 187). Perhaps to counter this and boost his authority, Almunia took the decision that the party would hold primary elections to choose the candidate for Prime Minister, and these were held in April 1998. A rival candidate emerged in the figure of Josep Borrell, another former minister in González's government, who had a more charismatic appeal for the public but was less popular than Almunia at party level.

The result of the primaries was a clear victory for Borrell, with 55 per cent of the vote compared to 44 per cent for Almunia, and if matters had rested there the fortunes of the party might have revived, particularly as holding the primaries had been a popular and democratic initiative (Méndez Lago 2005: 187). However, despite a promise to resign from the leadership of the party if he lost the primaries, Almunia decided to carry on and the result was a phenomenon referred to as *bicefalía*, leaving the party with no single clear leader to resolve internal disputes and front the party in the run-up to the elections. While Borrell had his own office and team as prime-ministerial candidate for the party, it was Almunia who was holding meetings with Aznar in the Moncloa Palace.

Borrell's impact was short-lived. He succeeded in giving the party a lead in the opinion polls but had an undistinguished performance in a crucial State of the Nation debate in May 1999. Several days later, on the eve of the European elections, he resigned over a minor issue of corruption concerning two former colleagues, which, although it did not affect him directly, could have had an indirect impact on the party's fortunes given the history of corruption over the previous decade. His resignation was an act of integrity which reflected well on him and the party but it left the PSOE with no choice but to accept Almunia as the prime-ministerial candidate, a decision Almunia would admit as his 'major mistake' (Colomer 2001: 491).

Still, the Socialists managed to narrow the PP's lead in the European elections and the gains made by the PSOE at a local and regional level owing to pacts, particularly with IU, paved the way for an electoral strategy the following year which would prove disastrous for both parties. IU's fortunes were obviously affected by its decision to support the Estella Pact in the Basque Country but in Cataluña, the local branch of the party, *Iniciativa per Catalunya* (IC), had entered a pact with the Catalan Socialists under the popular leader, Pasqual Maragall, and managed to make a severe dent in Pujol's hitherto unassailable position, forcing him to pact with the local Catalan PP to remain in power in 2000.

The PSOE–IU electoral pact was a failure both in its execution and its results. Initially, the idea was that the IU would withdraw its candidates for the Congress in the 32 constituencies where it had never won a parliamentary seat (out of the overall 52), thus leaving a clear field for the Socialist candidate. In return the PSOE would facilitate IU victories in the Senate. This was then reduced to eight constituencies, those where the combined vote at the previous election would have given the Socialists a greater number of seats. Then, after a joint electoral programme was negotiated in which PSOE had to include some of the more radical proposals of the Communists, it was decided that IU would fight all constituencies and be guaranteed a third of the winnable seats in the Senate. The effect was the worst of both worlds. The Socialists lost their winning strategy for the Congress and also suffered the negative impact among their moderate voters of a manifesto which was more leftist than they would have liked. Similarly, the Communist coalition undoubtedly alienated its more radical sympathizers with the pact (Colomer 2001).

Aznar's victory in 2000 was spectacular on the surface (see Appendix 8). His party won an overall majority with 183 seats in parliament and more votes, 10.3 million, than those won by the Socialists in their landslide victory in 1982. However, the turnout, especially on the left, was low as a result of a lack of confidence in the Almunia ticket, but also in the light of the unquestionable success of Aznar's first term. The economy in 2000 was booming and Spain had just had its first full term of government, the longest in its democratic history, without industrial unrest. The absolute majority spelt the end of a need for pacts with their moderating influence and, indeed, Aznar's second term was marked by a drift to the right. Certainly the government felt less constrained to meet the needs of nationalists and this was seen when, in advancing the devolution of powers to the regions in 2001 with the health services, it became clear that the new government's aim was to create a uniform system and also to place a limit on the process of transfer of powers.

It also felt more confident in rebuffing the regions' claims for greater representation and participation in the Community arena and with regard to the Basque crisis, the policy of treating it as purely a security issue was maintained. The PP even felt confident enough to try to develop its own alternative nationalist vision by adapting the Habermasian concept of 'constitutional patriotism' adopted by the party at its 2002 Party Congress – in the PP's terms, a 'political updating of a form of loyalty to Spain', the plural Spain of the Constitution which is inclusive, as distinct from the exclusivist peripheral nationalisms, and which attempts to create 'a new confidence in the Spanish national project' (Núñez Seixas 2005: 133–4). It was the same attempt at re-creating a sense of Spanish nationalism, out of favour since its association with the Franco regime, which led Aznar's government to approve the siting of a huge Spanish flag in the Plaza de Colón in Madrid in 2002.

The election victory for Aznar was a huge blow to the PSOE, which lost 16 seats in parliament. Almunia resigned immediately and, as a result, the party was effectively without a leader for four months, governed by an emergency team led by the veteran Andalusian President, Manuel Chaves. Nonetheless, it paved the way for the profound reassessment of the party's position that had not happened in 1996 owing to the relative complacency over Aznar's narrow victory (Méndez Lago 2005: 186). Essentially the Socialists were seen to have lost contact with the reality of Spanish society, as, for example, in their attacks on the PP's patently successful handling of the economy. As Colomer notes, they 'developed a negative campaign,

denouncing some entrepreneurs' big profits and even improvised a proposal to penalise the most profitable companies with
a new, retrospective tax, which met with widespread rejection'
(2001: 493).

5.11   The Second Term, 2000–4

While the absolute majority and the disarray of his rivals effectively gave Aznar *carte blanche* he nonetheless proposed to
continue to be conciliatory, though now it was no longer out of
need. He promised a politics that was 'centrist, reformist and
based on dialogue' (Tusell 2004: 284). Indeed, with both the
major regionalist groups, the PNV and CiU, the situation was
now reversed. In the Basque Country, the PNV's radical stance
with the Estella Pact had weakened it and strengthened the PP.
In Catalonia, the boot was now on the other foot as a weakened
Pujol needed the support of the local PP to survive. The reasons
for moderation were several. The PP still wanted to appeal to
the sociological centre of Spanish society and it knew that the
PSOE's difficulties would not last forever. Thus in spite of being
regularly perceived as a right-wing party, the PP did not have to
suffer from 'bilateral competition' as it had no extreme right-
wing party to contend with and therefore sensibly aimed to steal
support from its centre-left socialist rivals (Astudillo and García-
Guereta 2006: 415).

In his investiture speech on 25 April 2000 Aznar committed
himself to a series of reforms regarding electoral regulations to
guarantee stability, party financing to ensure greater transparency and a reduction of costs and a review of the public
audiovisual media. He also promised parliamentary reform and
progress on the perennial issue of reform of the Senate. The
reformist aims were, according to Tusell, quickly forgotten and
in many cases never even attempted (2004: 285). Instead, the
power of the absolute majority was wielded in areas such as
education and justice.

In education the reforms affected both the higher and

secondary sectors. In the first term, the PP's ideological nationalism had been evident in the controversy over the teaching of
Humanities, where the government proposed a stronger
'national' curriculum, a move clearly aimed at those regions
which the government suspected of promoting their own
'nationalist' agenda, especially in the teaching of Spanish
history. By his second term, Aznar felt more confident about
tackling reform of the Socialists' education system, dominated
by the LOGSE. In both this area and that of university reform,
the government courted controversy by trying to implement a
substantial overhaul of the system with minimal, if any, consultation. The most controversial aspect of the Quality in
Education Act (LOCE), which had a markedly reactionary style
to its proposals, was the role of religion in education.

At the third level, the introduction of a University Act (Ley
Orgánica de Universidades, LOU) in December 2001 had the
laudable aim of wishing to improve the process of recruitment
of new young staff and create more mobility in a sclerotic
system which for years had suffered from a type of 'internal
recruitment' known as *endogamia*. The law aimed to make
recruitment more rigorous and competitive. However, it was
bitterly opposed by 61 out of 68 university heads, although
welcomed by others who saw the need for greater transparency.
As Tusell notes, it was not so much that reform was not seen as
necessary, as dissatisfaction with the government's high-handed
approach as well as the omission of increased financial investment in the sector (2007: 438). In terms of university entrance
the reforms did away with the national examination, the *selectivi-
dad*, and placed more emphasis on the marks achieved in the
bachillerato at secondary school, a move that was interpreted as
indirectly favouring the private-school sector and its clients.

Immigration was another area that revealed the more illib-
eral nature of Aznar's second-term government. By this time, it
was recognized that immigration in Spain was not a passing
problem but a structural trend and needed a more considerate
and constructive legal framework. To this end, a new Aliens Act,
with more focus on the integration of immigrants, had been

drafted in 2000 which had achieved a wide political consensus, only for the PP to withdraw support at the eleventh hour because of a split in its own ranks over concessions to immigrants' rights (Jiménez 2000). After the elections awarded them an absolute majority, a more draconian version of the 2000 Aliens Act (*Ley de Extranjería*) was passed in January 2001, which the government justified in terms of needing to meet the criteria set by Brussels. This made distinctions between rights of legal and illegal immigrants and between immigrants and native Spaniards, subsequently challenged in the Constitutional Court, resulting in 11 of its articles being declared unconstitutional in March 2003. Its main feature, in addition to the attempt to control the inflow of immigrants, was to reach agreement with origin countries. Also, the period of residence required to seek regularization was increased from two to five years. The following year Aznar used developments in other EU countries as a reason for further reform of the law.

The government did seek consensus with the Socialists in some areas and this was facilitated by the PSOE's election in 2000 of a new leader, José Luis Rodríguez Zapatero, and his determination to be conciliatory where possible. Thus Zapatero, under a certain amount of criticism from his own followers, proposed an Anti-Terrorism Pact (*Pacto por las Libertades y contra el Terrorismo*), which was eventually signed in December 2000, though without the wider parliamentary participation envisaged by the Socialists who particularly wanted the involvement of the PNV. It was a response to the end of the ETA truce in 1999 and the return to violence in 2000 and its intention was to avoid terrorism being used as a political football. The pact was in fact opposed by the majority of the other parties led by the IU and while the CiU supported its ten principles it refused to sign the agreement because of the introduction which explicitly criticized the moderate Basque Nationalist Party for its involvement in the Estella initiative.

The other area where cooperation was achieved was reform designed to tackle the overpoliticization of the Judiciary. The controlling body, the *Consejo General del Poder Judicial*, had prior to

1985 been composed of a mixture of candidates elected by Parliament and the legal associations, eight and twelve, respectively. The conservative bias of the latter meant that many of the Socialists' reforms were blocked and so, under a new law, appointment was exclusively in the control of politicians and reflected the political composition of Parliament at the time. This, of course, did not remove politicization but simply made it more 'democratic' on the surface but in practice, especially in a situation of absolute parliamentary majority, gave the government full control of appointments. In 2001 the PP and PSOE agreed a compromise in which the members would still be appointed by Parliament but only 8 directly – the other 12 had to be appointed from a list of 36 candidates proposed by the legal associations. As Christopher Ross notes, 'rather than removing political influence, this delicate compromise is really an attempt to balance its different forms' (2002: 264).

5.12   Economy in the Second Term

Growth in the Spanish economy dropped from 4 per cent to under 3 per cent by the end of 2001, partly as a result of the fallout from the events of 11 September in the USA. However, it continued to grow above the European average, 2.5–3 per cent compared to 0.4 per cent for the period 2000–3 (Tusell 2004: 422). After managing to reduce inflation to under 2 per cent during the first term, higher oil prices caused it to rise again from 1999, reaching nearly 4 per cent in 2002 (*The Economist* 2004). Unemployment was nearing European levels, but while job creation continued, the Socialists, now under the leadership of Rodríguez Zapatero, were able to score effective political points by criticizing the poor quality, and frequently short duration, of these new jobs. Still, there was evidence that the government was achieving a decrease in the extent of temporary employment, down from 33.8 per cent in 1996 to 30.6 per cent in 2004 (Astudillo and García-Guereta 2006: 412). The increased cost of housing and the rise in private debt constituted other black spots (Ross 2004: 186). But by 2002 the country's finances were returned to a balance from a deficit of 7 per cent in 1995 (Astudillo and García-Guereta 2006: 412). The government depended on its objective of a zero deficit as the key to activating the economy and producing employment in the longer term, but its emphasis on such narrow fiscal policy meant that it failed to fully exploit the benefits of the bonanza leading *The Economist* to conclude that 'Spain's splendid record of economic growth in 1996–2003 owed as much to the EU as to the government's management' (2004: 10).

5.13   Foreign Policy: the EU and the Iraq War

It was natural that Spain's position and status in Europe should change under Aznar's PP. The party had spent six years in opposition largely critical of the Socialists' handling of European membership. Aznar's own approach would be dictated by a variety of factors: one would be his own political make-up and instincts, especially his attitude to his European neighbours and his relations with his political counterparts. Another was the nature and composition of the People's Party which was far from homogeneous politically and certainly encompassed a range of views on Europe. Finally, there was Aznar's essential pragmatism, what Powell refers to as 'his "deeds, not words" approach to politics in general', but also his patriotism that ensured, on the one hand, a disinterest in the visionary dimension of the European project but, on the other, a determination to get the maximum benefit from it for Spain (Powell 2001b: 17).

The wide range of ideological standpoints that found a home in the People's Party ensured that a unified view on Europe was difficult to achieve (Closa and Heywood 2004: 46). The more moderate, ex-UCD members of the party tended to be Europhiles whereas those on the right felt less guilt about Spain's Francoist past and saw no need to regard Europe as a solution. Some members of the PP even cultivated a very British kind of Euroscepticism in imitation of their admired Conservative friends (Powell 2001b: 11). The challenge for Aznar was to mark his distances from the community policy of his predecessors, despite the fact that there was strong pressure from the Christian Democrat wing of the party, especially in the form of the EU Commissioner Abel Matutes, for a non-partisan approach to Spain's relationship with Europe. However, unlike González, Aznar was not a fan of the Union nor was he at ease in Community circles, despite a chapter in his memoirs being entitled 'In the Vanguard of Europe' (Aznar 2004). His isolation in Europe and his distance from France and Germany might be put down to the fact that his counterparts at the time were the social democrat leaders Jospin and Schröder, with the latter of whom he clashed over many issues (Closa and Heywood 2004: 120), but it allowed the otherwise relatively unknown Aznar to parade the European stage as a significant leader of the right. In addition by the late 1990s the Franco-German partnership had lost much of the power it had a decade earlier. In some ways the more 'ideologically-inspired nationalism' of Aznar clashed with the practicalities of Community membership, resulting in an inconsistent approach to policy. Certainly in constitutional terms, Aznar, rather than closer integration, was much more committed to defending the identity of the individual nation-state, hence his support of the concept of a Europe of Nations (*Europa de las Patrias*) based on cooperation rather than integration (Aznar 2004: 187). On other aspects of European policy the PP chose continuity with previous Socialist policy, as in the commitment to a deepening of the structures and strengthening of the role of the EU in external affairs. Similarly, Aznar shared González's policy of staunch defence of Spain's interests with regard to the two crucial areas of funding and enlargement.

While from the opposition benches he had attacked González for his demeaning attitude to European subsidies, especially at the Edinburgh Summit in 1992, once in power himself Aznar was determined not to lose any advantages that Spain might gain from membership. The differential approach was that the PP would be more attentive to Spanish concerns and needs rather than follow what they saw as the slavishly pro-European policy of the Socialists. His period in office also coincided with a greater move towards enlargement rather than integration in EU. The inclusion of the East European nations inevitably meant that attention shifted away from the south Mediterranean states as the most economically needy.

Europe's need to advance on enlargement offered Aznar the opportunity to drive a hard bargain over cohesion and structural funds. This was not easy for him as Spain had without question made enormous strides towards economic convergence with its community neighbours, as evidenced by its determination to be in the first group of entrants into the EMU. Nevertheless, in the Berlin summit of 1999 Aznar successfully fought for the level and the distribution of Cohesion Funds to be maintained until 2006, amounting to a net gain of 1.2 billion euros per year, successfully arguing that the Spanish economy, while constituting 6.6 per cent of the Community's GDP, actually contributed 7.1 per cent to the budget (Powell 2001a: 583). Likewise at the Nice conference in December 2000, a more confident Aznar was successful in negotiating retention of Spain's power of veto in respect of funds for the period 2007–13 (Powell 2001b: 16).

Spain has often been thought of as opposed in principle to enlargement, occasionally with a 'stubbornness bordering on intransigence' (Closa and Heywood 2004: 130). During Aznar's term of office the EU underwent its second major enlargement since 1986, involving the ten Eastern European countries (Poland, Latvia, Hungary, Lithuania, Slovenia, Malta, Cyprus, Estonia, the Czech Republic and Slovakia) for which public opinion in Spain seemed largely in favour. Indeed, Eastern expansion seemed to evoke greater sympathy and support in Spain than the Nordic enlargement had done in 1995. The view then expressed by the Spanish Foreign Minister, Josep Piqué, was that it would help the new members consolidate democracy in their own countries but also create a formidable economic force and aid the fight against terrorism (Closa and Heywood 2004: 133).

Aznar's position, much as González's had been in 1995, was to affirm support but seek to ensure that Spain's status as a large-to-medium player in Europe was not undermined. Since accession Spain had been a 'big' player in the Commission with two commissioners like the 'big four' countries of Germany, France, Italy and the UK. In the Council of Ministers it was a medium player, with eight votes compared to the big four's ten. In the Nice treaty negotiations, Aznar's government attempted to ensure that geographical equilibrium was maintained. He was not entirely successful, and in return for giving up one commissioner he demanded the same votes on the Council as the leading countries, but in the end had to be content with 27 votes, two less than Germany, France, Italy and the UK, but the same number as the recently admitted Poland. However, in Spain, as Closa and Heywood observe, Aznar was criticized for what was seen 'as his narrow-minded defence of the number of votes, his failure to secure his aim of achieving the strength of the "Big Four" on the issue of the blocking minority, and his failure to avoid a reduction in the share of Spanish MEPs' (2004: 130). It has been pointed out, however, that the most crucial stage of the negotiations on enlargement was successfully realized under the Spanish presidency in 2002 (Closa and Heywood 2004: 120–1).

Some incidents cast the government in a very poor light internationally, none more so than the Isla Perejil crisis in July 2002. Six Moroccan soldiers had landed on this uninhabited rock, over which Spain has had territorial rights since 1668, and the Spanish government acted promptly to 'recapture' the island, sending four warships. As John Hooper remarked, 'ludicrous' though it was, the incident 'represented the first unilateral military action undertaken by Spain since the return of democracy' under a leader who 'hungered for a more prominent international role for his country' (2006: 197). This opportunity would soon be provided by the Iraq War in 2003. Despite opposition to the war by two-thirds of the Spanish population, Aznar was determined to involve his country. In his memoir of his presidency, the chapter dealing with this concerns 'Spain's role in the world' and links it with the events of 11 September (Aznar 2004: 143).

It was in the second term that Aznar's natural Atlanticism emerged most fully. In 1998 he had already supported the US bombing of Iraq and the year before had strengthened Spain's involvement with NATO by joining the military structure. For a country that still spent only 1.2 per cent of GDP on defence, 0.7 per cent less than its European NATO neighbours, Aznar clearly saw national security as guaranteed by loyalty to NATO (*The Economist*, 2004; Herrero de Miñón 2000: 46). In January 2001, the two countries had signed a bilateral declaration, and when George Bush visited Europe for the first time in June 2001, he made Madrid his first port of call. Undoubtedly the events of 11 September 2001 facilitated this siding with America and, along with Tony Blair, Aznar was to become one of America's most ardent allies in the war on terror. Alastair Campbell in his diaries noted how 'Aznar was really pushing the importance of the transatlantic alliance' in the run-up to the war with Iraq (Campbell 2008: 679).

Aznar's urge to please America took priority over his relationship with the electorate and with parliament as he rejected any need for a parliamentary debate, claiming that the purpose of the modest Spanish contingent of 1300 troops was principally 'peacekeeping and post-war reconstruction' (Encarnación 2008: 64), whereas the opposition claimed it was 'logistical support'. At the meeting with Bush in Crawford, Texas on 22 February 2003, days before the conflict, Aznar is unconditional in his support, though wishing for a second UN resolution. In September 2007 *El País* published a transcript of their conversation and at one point, intriguingly, Aznar claims that what he was doing was a 'very profound change for Spain and the Spanish, changing the policy that the country had followed for over 200 years'. The explanation of what he meant can be found in his memoirs where, speaking of his support of the US in Iraq, he says, 'In the last two hundred years, our country had not assumed international responsibilities ... Since the disaster of the Napoleonic invasion, Spain was expelled from European politics in the Congress of Vienna in 1815. Since then, save one or two exceptions, Spain has turned in on itself' (Aznar 2004: 151). Tusell interprets Aznar's policy as less an example of the pro-Americanism that characterized the Spanish right since the Franco regime than a concern for Spanish greatness, a sense of national cohesion and pride. Terrorism was a threat to that, and siding with the USA seemed to be the best protective measure. Ironically, for many, this route would lead to the tragic events of 11 March 2004.

5.14   Regionalist Problems

It has been noted how, in his second term, Aznar 'developed a new "nationalistic" policy profile' (Astudillo and García-Guereta 2006: 413). While in the first term this manifested itself in a promotion of an improved image of Spain abroad, especially among the EU partners, as a competent and financially solid economy, in the second term this ideology could be directed more towards the nationalist movements within Spain. In particular Aznar wanted, with a final transfer of powers to the regions, to bring the process to a definitive end, one in which all Spanish regions would have virtually the same level of responsibility, what Moreno refers to as the 'latent federalization' in the Spanish system (2005: 68). Relations between the PP and the CiU had been strained by issues such as the controversy over remarks by the King in an award ceremony to the effect that the Spanish language had never been 'imposed' on anyone and, more importantly, the government's National Water Plan (*Plan Hidrológico Nacional*) in 2001. The PP won the latter battle against the initial opposition of the Catalans to Aznar's plan to divert water from the Ebro to Catalonia and the dry southern regions. Jordi Pujol, the Catalan President, had proposed a nationalistic alternative in which water would come from the Rhône in France, thus reinforcing 'Catalan links with France and neighbouring Mediterranean countries, rather than increasing Catalonia's dependence on Spain' (McFall 2002: 49).

In the May 2001 Basque regional elections, the nationalists still won an overall majority and the PNV and their minority partner EA won 33 seats, 7 up on the previous occasion and a 6.5 per cent rise in their vote. One of the victims was EH, the electoral front for Batasuna, which saw its vote and seats halved, unsurprising given the continued violence of ETA, assassinating a PP Senator on 6 May and posting a letter bomb to a journalist the day after the election. Of the national parties the PP improved and consolidated its position as second political force in the region while the PSOE saw its vote slip by one seat. The results marked a victory for the PNV's Ibarretxe and dashed the hopes of an anti-nationalist front winning out in the region. Arnaldo Otegi, leader of EH, while admitting the damaging effect of ETA's campaign for the radical party, saw the vote as an overwhelming rejection of the PP and its proposed leader for *lehendakari* (President of the Basque Region) Jaime Mayor Oreja.

By March 2003 the CiU proposed a reform of the Catalan Statute that incorporated much of the *soberanista* rhetoric of the Basques (see **5.9**), including the possibility of a 'free-association' relationship with the rest of Spain. In the Basque Country, given the polarized vote that had resulted from the Estella Pact, the PNV under its *lehendakari*, Juan José Ibarretxe, tried to seize the initiative away from the radicals by promoting the idea of self-determination. This eventually evolved into a full-blown 'plan' for a compromise between the (for the Basques, unacceptable) constitutional status quo and full independence: a regime of free association, announced in September 2002. Relations had been further strained when the PP, earlier in March, pushed for a Political Parties Act (*Ley de Partidos Políticos*) which allowed the banning of any party which failed to respect 'democratic principles and human rights'. The only parties that opposed the vote in parliament in May 2002 were the PNV, EA and the BNG. The target of the law was Batasuna (previously HB), but the PNV and the majority of Basque public opinion saw it as anti-nationalist. The result would eventually mean that in March 2003 Batasuna was banned by the Spanish Supreme Court.

The Ibarretxe Plan, as it was known, envisaged a Basque

State in charge of its own security and international affairs within a 'confederal arrangement whereby the Basque Country and Spain would enter into a free association' (Lecours 2005: 23). In this context the Basque Country would have virtually unlimited control over its own affairs, with no interference from the Madrid government, most crucially in judicial matters. The Spanish government would retain control over Spanish nationality, immigration and the right to asylum, defence and the armed forces, production of arms, monetary system, customs and import duties and international relations (though Basques would have direct representation in the EU), as well as 'common legislation to guarantee the defence of the essential contents of fundamental rights'. Institutional relations between them would be regulated by a Basque Country-State Bilateral Commission. The idea was that it would be put to a referendum of the Basque people on condition that there was a cessation of violence by ETA. Given the absence of any such long-term commitment on the part of ETA, the success of the Plan seems unlikely, though Ibarretxe has always insisted that neither ETA nor the central government should be an obstacle to progress in the Basque peace process. More serious for the Ibarretxe Plan's future was the radical opposition of the main non-Basque parties and even the equivocal support of some Basque parties. It won initial support from the PNV's minority partners, EA and EB, the Basque branch of the national party the IU, though the former saw it as a step towards independence and the latter as a refinement of the current constitutional arrangement (Keating and Bray 2006: 355). There was support from Aralar, a breakaway party of Batasuna that is radical but rejects violence, but not initially from Batasuna, hardly surprising, since 'the proposal seems to exclude outright independence as exemplified by its central concept of "co-sovereignty"' (Lecours 2005: 24), and it still reserved a role for the King of Spain as head of state. When it came to the vote in the Basque Parliament, Batasuna strategically spread its votes between the no and the yes camps to simultaneously register criticism and facilitate its approval (Keating and Bray 2006: 356).

Nonetheless, Ibarretxe's Plan could never prosper while the PP was in power, with its staunch anti-nationalist stance and its vigorous attempt at promoting its own brand of Spanish 'constitutional patriotism' (see **5.10**). The security forces' successes against the terrorists and the decline in street violence in the Basque Country seemed to reinforce the government in its convictions. The Plan might have had a future within the context of a strong European movement in support of the regions, but it coincided with the EU's problems over ratification of the Constitution and the debate over Europeanness which put paid to any hope of 'identification with Basqueness' (Keating and Bray 2006: 361).

5.15   Revival of the Socialists and the Fall of the PP

By 2002 Spain seemed to be at ease with the Government and Aznar looked to have achieved his aim of extending the party's control over the centre ground (Tusell 2004: 376). He also seemed confidently in control of his plans for the future. Though many in the party wanted the Prime Minister to renege on his promise not to stand for a third term, the PP's 2002 Congress confirmed his decision to stand down at the next election, a cabinet reshuffle in July set up the likely successors and towards the end of the year Aznar prepared his legacy with the inauguration of his neoconservative think-tank, the *Fundación de Análisis y Estudios Sociológicos* (FAES). However, several events occurred in that year which indicated a change in the mood of the country. On 20 June 2002 the Spanish trade unions organized a strike in protest against the government's changes in the scheme for unemployment benefit which linked receipt of benefit to acceptance of offers of work. The fact that the reform was introduced by decree-law, known popularly as a *decretazo*, seemed further evidence of the PP's high-handedness. Added to this was increased opposition to the government's almost slavish adherence to US policy regarding Iraq, as a result of which the Socialists were regularly ahead in the opinion polls. The PSOE won the regional and local elections in May 2003. Within the PP, after announcing to his party Congress in 2002 that he was not standing for re-election, in September 2003 Aznar named his successor as Mariano Rajoy, a personal uncontested choice that was much criticized at the time.

The government's reputation was badly damaged by the Prestige disaster in November 2002. An ageing petrol tanker got into difficulty in a storm off the Galician Costa da Morte and was ordered by the Spanish government to head out to sea. When it eventually sank in over 3500 metres of water the effects of its seepage on a coastline rich in prized seafood was devastating and far worse than if it had been contained within a limited area near the coast. The anger of Spaniards and Galicians was directed towards both the national and regional PP governments, not only for their incompetent handling of the disaster but the insensitive attitude demonstrated by their leading figures. Aznar did not visit the region until over a month after the sinking. In December approximately 50,000 people (police estimates put it at 15,000) protested in Barcelona and demanded his resignation. Fraga, leader of the regional government at the time, was discovered to have been out hunting at the time of the disaster and made matters worse by trying to deny it. While undoubtedly the incident had some impact on the results of the next regional elections in 2005, where for the first time in 15 years the PP lost its hold on government to a coalition of socialists and nationalists, it was less than one might expect. The PP remained the most voted party in the region losing only 35,000 votes, but this, combined with a significant rise in the Socialist vote, boosted perhaps by Zapatero's victory in 2004, provided the narrow margin for change. In March 2009, in a controversial and much contested decision, a Spanish judge cleared the PP government of blame for its decision to send the sinking tanker out to sea.

Meanwhile, Zapatero's star was rising. He had been attributed victory by the polls in the Debates on the State of the Nation in 2001 and 2002, though Aznar seemed to gain the upper hand again in 2003. The surveys showed that over the period of Aznar's second term, the PP's popularity dropped by 8 per cent and that of the Socialists under Zapatero rose by 7 per cent.

The elections of 14 March 2004 were overshadowed and some would say determined by the bomb explosions that occurred in Madrid three days earlier. While Moreno is correct that 'a direct cause-effect relationship between the attacks and the defeat of the Popular Party in the general election held three days later cannot be mechanically drawn' (2005: 65), the discovery that they were carried out by Islamist terrorists and that Osama Bin Laden had since October 2003 threatened Spain, among others, with retaliation for supporting the USA in its 'unjust' war against Iraq explains why Aznar's government went to such lengths to have everyone believe that ETA was responsible. What made matters much worse for the PP, of course, was that their efforts to maintain the possibility of ETA responsibility well beyond the limits of its own and even public knowledge quickly seemed to be electorally motivated.

It was undoubtedly this and not so much the actual Iraq policy of the government that mobilized an unusually large turnout, 76 per cent. As noted earlier, according to Charles Powell Spanish elections can be divided into those that were for 'continuity' and those that were for 'change', with usually in the latter a higher turnout, 75–80 per cent compared to around 70 per cent for the former (Powell 2001a: 619). Since, as Tusell points out, abstentionism tends to be among the left, the increased turnout and government's appearance of trying to manipulate the truth meant that, despite the undeniable successes of the government, the 2004 poll was an election for change. As Moreno points out, 'the usual behaviour of electors in times of crisis generally translates into rallying round the incumbent government' (66) but on this occasion, the PP was seen as to be partly to blame for the crisis. So concerned was the government that linkage to Spain's involvement in Iraq would prove an electoral disaster, it attempted to undermine that link until the election was safely won. The UN Security Council even passed a resolution in which the attack was attributed to

ETA at the urging of the Spanish government, requiring subsequently an apology from the Spanish UN ambassador (Moreno 2005: 66, n.4).

While the government tried to redeem itself by establishing a parliamentary enquiry, its image was only further tarnished by the persistence of its ministers, especially Angel Acebes, and of Aznar himself, in perpetuating the suspicion of a link between the Islamist terrorists and ETA. Rather than a desire for uncovering the truth, they revealed an enduring obsession with defending their own position and undermining the democratic legitimacy of the Socialists' electoral victory. Hence it was not the bomb attack itself but their response to it that sealed their electoral fate.

5.16   Conclusion

Any assessment of the two governments of José María Aznar must rest on the point we made at the beginning of this chapter, which is that their principal success was economic. In his memoirs Aznar ends by summing up his achievements and warning of dangers. Among the former he clearly sees Spain's international role as an example of the success of his government. What he calls 'Spain's new position on the international stage' is the result, he writes, of his foreign policy which in turn is an extension of our domestic policy: the defence of freedom and the fight against terrorism (Aznar 2004: 274). While he can be criticized for a certain lack of imagination or possibly willingness in seeking political solutions to the Basque problem, one must admire Aznar's tenacity in standing up to and pursuing ETA. In addition, for all his reputation for arrogance, Aznar is to be admired for his disciplined adherence to his promise to only serve two terms and for the smooth handling of the process of succession, yet another example of his firm hold on his party. As for his legacy, that is harder to determine. According to *The Economist* in 2004, 'democratic Spain has won the respect of other countries [and] some have attributed this to the assertive leadership of Mr Aznar'. As examples, it cites the breaking of ties with France and Germany, the alliance with the UK and the USA and brooking 'no nonsense from countries such as Morocco when they provoked him' (2004: 4). Others might see the same pattern of anti-Europeanism, dubious alliances and militaristic posturing as having completely the opposite effect on Spain's international reputation. The journal is perhaps on safer ground when it continues 'after years on the fringes of international respectability, Spain has certainly started to count in the world ... yet the respect given to his country beyond its borders derived not so much from his strutting on the world stage as from the fact that Spain had become a country that worked'. While Aznar and his ministers can certainly take some credit for this, his period in power has perhaps fallen short of the 'second transition' that he heralded.

6

ZAPATERO IN POWER

6.1 Introduction

The 2004 victory of Jose Luis Rodríguez Zapatero could not have occurred in a context of greater controversy nor greater tragedy, and this was destined to colour virtually the whole of his first term in office. In the run-up to the elections the majority of polls showed Zapatero's PSOE to be in line for a close defeat at the hands of the People's Party under Mariano Rajoy, Aznar's hand-picked successor, with 43 per cent of the vote compared to 36 per cent for the Socialists (Méndez Lago 2005: 191; Colomer 2005: 151). Tusell points out, however, that since Zapatero took over the leadership of his party in 2000, the PP's popularity rating had gone down by 8 per cent, whereas the Socialists' had risen by 7 per cent. Furthermore, as we will mention below, to interpret the election results purely in terms of a reaction to the 11 March bomb attacks would both contradict the evidence of research into voting behaviour on the day (Moreno 2005; Bali 2007; Lago and Montero 2006) but also underestimate the enormous work done by the PSOE under Zapatero in developing an innovative social project and connecting with a wide range of minority and marginal groups which clearly gave him their support on 14 March (Kennedy 2007: 191). Still, that is not to deny that 11 March 2004 did have enormous impact, not only in electoral terms but at all levels of society in Spain and, unusually for a Spanish election, had profound international repercussions.

Certainly the opposition to the Iraq War was a major factor of discontent in the country as a whole. The government of José

María Aznar had already charged the atmosphere in the latter stages of his second term of office. In addition to the tensions with the regional governments of Catalonia and the Basque Country over his refusal to even contemplate dialogue on nationalist issues, he had taken Spain into the Iraq War without consultation with parliament, let alone the Spanish people. In a meeting with Zapatero on 2 February 2003 to discuss their stance, Aznar asked the leader of the opposition to support him in the same way that he had supported González during the 1991 invasion. Zapatero refused to accept the comparability of the situations and exhorted Spaniards to protest, which they did in force towards the end of February (Campillo 2004: 333).

6.2   Renewal in the PSOE

Zapatero had taken over the leadership of the Socialist Party in July 2000 after the resignation of Joaquin Almunia and in the wake of the party's crushing defeat by Aznar in the 12 March elections of that year. His appointment as Secretary-General of the party certainly led to a rise in its fortunes. Almunia's tenure, between 1997, when González resigned, and the elections of 2000, had been characterized as a period when 'internal power struggles hindered the much needed process of organisational and ideological renewal necessary to win elections' (Méndez Lago 2005: 187). The leadership election pitted him against Rosa Díez, a Basque politician who had been a successful MEP but was not a national MP; Matilde Fernández, who was a remnant of the *guerrista* branch of the party, a throwback to the past who still gave the raised fist as a greeting (Tusell 2004: 296); and one powerful and popular regional 'baron', José Bono, 17 years in the Presidency of Castilla-La Mancha. Of the four candidates for the leadership, Zapatero was not only the youngest and least associated with previous Socialist govern- ments, but also seemed the least ideological. His concern was for unity and renewal (Méndez Lago 2005: 189). Rather like his UK counterpart, Tony Blair, he was given (also ironically by a former Deputy Prime Minister, in this case Alfonso Guerra) the nickname 'Bambi'. In Zapatero's case it was thought to be due to his wide-eyed and rather innocent expression. But, as with early Blair, it also implied a certain political naivety. However, as demonstrated by his stance on Iraq, the opposite of Blair's, he quickly emerged as a principled leader determined to impose order in the party but also seek a consensual approach to politics by way of contrast with Aznar's authoritarian image. Ironically, many of his policies proved deeply divisive. As Tusell pointed out, unlike the previous situation of the PSOE prior to 1982, Zapatero from 2000 onwards set himself the task of carrying out a 'useful opposition' (Tusell 2004: 298).

This conciliatory approach began in opposition when he showed a willingness to collaborate with the conservative government on a range of issues, including the fight against terrorism, by signing up to the Anti-Terrorism Pact and, in May 2001, a Justice Pact, which included the thorny issue of the appointments to the General Council of Judges (*Consejo General del Poder Judicial*, CGPJ) (see **5.11**). Similarly, within the EU he showed flexibility over voting rights. Once elected, although opposed in principle to the Ibarretxe Plan for the Basque Country, one of his first actions was to telephone the Basque President, a contrast to Aznar, who had not spoken to Ibarretxe in the previous two years. In his election manifesto Zapatero outlined three main areas to be tackled: one was greater cooperation in the EU, the second was 'strengthening the cohesion within a plural Spain' and the third was 'citizenship', improving the rights and welfare of Spaniards (PSOE 2004: 9–10). The manifesto also stressed the need to improve the political climate, 'participation, dialogue, consensus'; however, the circumstances of the political transition in 2004 made such an aim virtually impossible.

6.3   The Madrid Bomb, 11 March 2004

At 7.34 a.m. on the morning of 11 March 2004, three rucksacks exploded on a train as it was pulling in to Atocha station during the busy rush hour. Moments later, four other explosions occurred on a train just outside the station at Calle Téllez. Shortly after, two bombs went off at the El Pozo del Tío Raimundo station and one at the Santa Eugenia station, both on the same line from Alcalá de Henares to Madrid-Atocha. The result was devastation that led to 191 deaths and over 1800 injured. The damage and injuries would have been vastly increased but for the fact that the train was slightly late reaching Atocha and was not actually inside the station when the bomb went off. Amid the chaos the first questions started to be asked as to who were the authors. Almost everyone suspected ETA.

The ensuing drama will be remembered for two collective actions of opposing sorts. On the one hand, the extraordinary display of solidarity and united response to a horrendous tragedy given by the people of Madrid. Private cars were used as ambulances, an improvised hospital was set up in a leisure centre, ordinary *madrileños* came on to the streets to help the emergency forces and provide blankets. The queues to donate blood were surplus to requirements.

On the other side of the spectrum, the response of the government, once it had recovered from the initial shock, seemed quickly to turn to the consequences for the general elections to be held three days later. The initial suspicion, natural in the circumstances and shared by all, even the opposition leader, Zapatero, that it was ETA soon became an insistent certainty relayed to all the information services through press conferences, interviews and, amazingly, even direct telephone calls to the newspaper editors from Aznar himself. There were signs too that there was an eager participation by the media as the 'so-called conspiracy theory that attributed the jihadist-style bombings to ETA, the Socialist Party, and foreign intelligence services, without offering any empirical evidence, was spread by a coalition of media supportive of the PP' (Sampedro and Seoane Pérez 2008: 341). Such an insistence on the part of the government to attribute the outrage to ETA, in spite of the numerous doubts and indicators to the contrary that in the course of the first day started to emerge, suggested a collective awareness on the part of the Aznar team that the elections could be won or lost on this issue. ETA involvement would galvanize the nation behind a government which had fought hard to weaken the organization and reduce it to its current parlous state. If, as evidence seemed to show, it was the work of Islamists, the Spanish would not fail to link the bomb to Spain's participation in the Iraq War, for which polls revealed a clear 90 per cent opposition (Colomer 2005: 152).

Aznar's government was soon forced to recognize that there were two lines of enquiry but while he and his ministers, including Foreign Affairs minister Ana Palacios, who appeared on the BBC programme *Breakfast with Frost* on the Sunday of polling, insisted that the ETA hypothesis was 'still strong in the investigation', the police and figures like Baltasar Garzón knew from late Thursday that the Islamist line was the more likely. On the afternoon of 11 March, a white van was found near Alcalá de Henares station. It contained seven detonators and a tape of recitations of the Koran. By the end of the day, *Al-Quds al-Arabi*, a London-based Arabic newspaper, claimed to have received a five-page email from Abu Hafs al-Masri's brigade, claiming its 'death squad' had managed to attack 'one of the pillars of the crusade alliance, Spain'. While this organization was dismissed by some as unreliable, at the same time, Arnaldo Otegi, leader of Batasuna, was insisting that ETA was not to blame. Certainly it did not follow their modus operandi, which usually involved a warning. Much discussion centred on the explosives used. Usefully for the security forces an unexploded bomb was found in an abandoned bag and it allowed them to confirm that the explosive used was a Spanish made Goma-2 ECO and not the Titadyn normally associated with ETA (Yoldi and Rodríguez 2007). The SIM card of a mobile found at the scene allowed police to make initial arrests of three Moroccans on Saturday 13 March. By 3 April, members of the special GEO force were closing in on a flat in Leganés used by seven suspected authors of the attack, including their leader, an Algerian Allekema Lamari, when they committed suicide by exploding a bomb, as a result of which one GEO member died.

Subsequent investigations on the remains of the seven showed some had links with Al Qaeda.

As the news gradually filtered out and in spite of the People's Party's attempt to keep alive the flagging hypothesis that the bomb may have been the work of ETA, public anger grew. On 13 March, the traditional *jornada de reflexión* when, according to electoral custom in Spain, no public campaigning is allowed, there were massive demonstrations at the headquarters of the People's Party. For Rajoy and his team these were seen as politically motivated demonstrations rather than mere outpourings of discontent. While there were insinuations from the PP of a mobile-texting campaign deliberately initiated among socialist supporters to ensure that the electoral discomfiture of the governing party was kept to a maximum this was most likely a 'non-party initiative' (Colomer 2005: 154). The result the following day was that the PSOE swept to victory, if not with an absolute majority, at least with a comfortable lead over the opposition, especially considering the recent history of the Socialist Party and the relative success, barring the Iraq controversy, of the Aznar government and in particular its handling of the economy.

6.4 The 2004 Election

The theory that the Socialists would not have won the elections of March 2004 had it not been for the bomb is given some weight if it is remembered that, in spite of the negative fallout from the Prestige disaster in 2002 and the impact of Spain's involvement in Iraq, the party was still unable to clinch major electoral breakthroughs. The Socialists had tried to make the war a central issue in the regional and local elections of 25 May 2003 but in the end local issues dominated. As an example, the Socialists' opposition to the PP's National Hydrological Plan according to which water from the Ebro would be transferred to the dry south-east led, on the one hand, to victory in the Aragón regional elections but to a loss of seats in the southern region of

Murcia. The PSOE managed to win over 100,000 more votes than the PP. Nonetheless, the latter still managed to dominate the regional elections, with Aragón its only setback.

Still, overall the panorama was good for the PSOE. In the local elections for the first time since 1993 it won a majority of the votes, although suffering losses in the important centres of Barcelona and Madrid. In the regional elections in Madrid, the Socialists, with 47 seats, at first looked set to win power in coalition with the United Left, a total of 56 seats over the 55 of the PP, until two Socialist regional MPs, Eduardo Tamayo and María Teresa Sáez, absented themselves from the vote, eventually deserted the party and allowed Esperanza Aguirre of the PP to resume control of that important region in a rerun of the election (Campillo 2004: 338–9).

Nonetheless, if Zapatero's aim to create a more harmonious climate for Spanish politics might have been utopian in normal circumstances, in the aftermath of the 11 March bomb it was entirely unrealistic and proved unattainable. For one thing, the bomb had managed to obscure any notion of electoral legitimacy for the new government. The PP simply refused to accept that it had not been robbed of the right to govern by, first, Islamist terrorists who, in their eyes, had influenced the democratic process of a Western country, and then the PSOE, who were able to make political capital out of the tragedy. As a result they refused to accept Zapatero as a rightful prime minister. Secondly, the PP would not relinquish the conviction that ETA was in some way involved with the attack and that the accusations of electoral manipulation were unfounded.

This led to Zapatero's subsequent term of office being overshadowed by the ongoing investigation into the bomb, first in the form of a parliamentary commission, then the actual court case itself, during which time the PP never missed an opportunity to peddle the ETA hypothesis and simultaneously cast doubt on the Socialists' right to be in power in the first place. Some would say it also explains the obsessively negative attitude adopted by the PP in opposition. The bitterness felt in the PP camp at having victory so cruelly, in the broadest sense of the term, snatched from their grasp, unfortunately permeated into all levels of political activity over the next four years and prevented any hope of constructive political activity on any issue.

In what the leading Madrid daily, *El País*, billed as the 'saddest elections in Spanish history', a turnout of over 77 per cent – the third largest of the democratic era – voted Zapatero into power with 42.64 per cent of the vote, compared to 37.64 per cent for the governing PP (see Appendix 9). This translated into 164 parliamentary seats, 12 short of an absolute majority. Nonetheless, the 16-seat advantage over the PP ensured that Zapatero's Socialists would be safe from parliamentary challenges to its future policies, though it would rely on parliamentary support from the Communist IU and the left-wing Catalan nationalist party, the ERC, whose 5 and 8 votes, respectively, took the Socialists, with 164, to 177, one over the absolute majority figure. The PP lacked any obvious allies other than, perhaps, the Canaries Coalition (CC) to provide sufficient support to challenge the new government in parliament. Furthermore, most parties, including the CC, shared the reprobation of the PP for apparent manipulation of information in the days following the bomb. The victory of the socialists was not wholly determined by the bomb attack but the signs are that it mobilized wavering voters or potential non-voters into turning out to express their anger, above all at the government's seeming attempt to manipulate information. 'The terrorist attacks encouraged 1.6m people who had decided abstaining to vote; also another 1m people changed their vote, mostly from IU or other parties in favour of the PSOE' (Colomer 2005: 154). According to Colomer, the result was a consequence of a greater polarization in Spanish society between the two main parties, much the same as had happened in 1982. In this case the 'PSOE received a clear mandate from voters to put an end to terrorist threats, including ETA's, as well as avoid risky interventions in international politics' (2005: 155).

6.5 The 11-M Commission

The 11-M Commission was set up on 27 May and presented its conclusions, which were approved by all parties except the People's Party on 30 June 2005. The principal conclusions were damning for Aznar and his party. The Commission found that Aznar's government had underestimated the Islamist threat to Spain and was unprepared for the attacks. It also eliminated any suspicion of involvement by ETA but, crucially, the Commission found that the Aznar government had manipulated information in the days between the bombing and the polls for electoral purposes.

One of the unfortunate features of the tragedy and its repercussions was the emergence of not only new victims' associations but their increasing politicization. In the wake of the bombing the mother of one of the victims, Pilar Manjón, became a powerful spokesperson and helped set up a group called the *Asociación 11-M Afectados por el Terrorismo*. She herself had been a member of the communist trade union, CC OO, and her group was seen as highly critical of the government of the PP. On the other hand, a group called the *Asociación de Víctimas del Terrorismo* (AVT), which had been founded in 1981 and, according to its website, aims to offer aid to 'all the victims of terrorism who have been abandoned and sidelined by the State, as well as large sectors of Spanish society', assumed much greater activism after the Madrid bomb, taking a much more hardline, anti-Zapatero stance. It sides with the PP in emphasizing the priority of the fight against ETA and, for example, vehemently opposes Zapatero's policy, for which he won parliamentary approval on 17 May 2005, to contemplate talks with ETA providing there is a cessation of violence. The AVT advocates full implementation of the Anti-Terrorism Pact (see **5.11**), a point which marks its coincidence with the stance of the conservative opposition. The AVT, particularly under its former leader Francisco José Alcaraz, was even criticized by one of Spain's leading authors, Javier Marías, for its aggressive adoption of the rhetoric and ideology of the extreme right (Marías

2007). Yet another group, the *Asociación de Ayuda a las Víctimas del 11–M*, is also seen as pro-PP and supportive of the conspiracy theories generated by that party and its media supporters.

In the end, the trial found 21 people guilty and acquitted 7 others. The major upset was that one of the suspected masterminds, Rabei Osman Sayed Ahmed, known as 'the Egyptian', was one of those acquitted, although he heard the verdict from an Italian prison where he was held for belonging to an international terrorist organization. Victims' associations were unhappy with the acquittals and the light sentences given to some of the defendants, which they planned to appeal. Politically, the verdict had something to please both sides. On the one hand, the court ruled out categorically any involvement of ETA, which pleased those on the left. On the other hand, the court also found no evidence that the attack was related to the war in Iraq, an accusation levelled at the PP by the Socialists and which they resented as making them morally responsible.

6.6   Social Issues

One of the areas where the new administration of Zapatero has made its mark has been the determination to extend equality in society. Paul Kennedy notes how 'the PSOE has utilised social democratic *and* social liberal elements to implement a domestic policy which has focused on the extension of civil and gender rights' (2007: 191). In this area a major influence on Zapatero has been the Princeton academic, Philip Pettit, and his theories of freedom and 'non-domination'. According to Pettit, freedom is the state of not being dominated by anyone else (Kennedy 2007: 190). Pettit himself describes his philosophy of 'civic republicanism' as a respect for 'all communities, identities, collectives and ideas as they all contribute to avoiding domination by some over others' (Jiménez 2008).

Zapatero's first policy decisions were directed at women's rights. He showed his own personal commitment to gender equality by appointing the first cabinet in Spanish history with an equal weighting of male and female ministers, and in addition, the appointment of a woman, María Teresa Fernández de la Vega, as Deputy Prime Minister; secondly, his government's first legislative move was a law concerning the acute social problem in Spain of domestic violence. When Zapatero took over, it was calculated that approximately 600 women had died in the previous eight years as a result of gender violence and according to the government's *Instituto de la Mujer* (Institute for Women), there were 2 million Spanish women suffering abuse. In the year of the law's introduction it was reported that 72 women had been beaten by their partners, 57,000 had lodged formal complaints to the police and 30 women had been killed by partners (Fuchs 2005). In April the government approved a bill with four aims: prevention, protection of victims, supporting the recovery of victims and penalties for aggressors. The law came into effect on 28 December 2004. It provides for the setting up of over 400 special courts to deal specifically with cases of gender violence, over 380 extra officers to protect women under threat and harsher penalties for perpetrators (Fuchs 2005).

An important step in Zapatero's equality agenda was the law that permitted homosexual marriage. The law (*Ley por la que se modifica el Código Civil en materia de Derecho a Contraer Matrimonio*) took effect on 1 July 2005. It allowed gay people the same rights as heterosexuals including, controversially, the right to adopt children, making Spain only the fourth country to do so after Holland, Belgium and Canada. The law was passed with opposition only from the PP and some members of the Catalan CiU. Rajoy defended his party from accusations of homophobia, aligning the PP with the majority of European countries where a union between homosexuals is legal in every way but stops short of using the term 'marriage' or permitting joint adoption. He pointed out that only Belgium and Holland call such homosexual unions marriages. There were some conservative defections from this official party policy, notably the MP and former Health Minister Celia Villalobos, and outside parliament, the mayor of Madrid, Alberto Ruiz Gallardón, a leader on the more liberal wing of the party. The law, as its name implied, had the effect of modifying 16 articles of the Civil Code, many of which involved a mere word change from husband and wife or father and mother to the terms spouse and progenitor. The law attracted strenuous opposition from the Catholic Church, which led a massive protest rally in Madrid on 18 June, despite the fact that polls regularly show that over 60 per cent of Spaniards support the law.

On 15 March 2007, the government, with all-party support except for the PP, passed an Equality Act (*Ley Orgánica para la Igualdad efectiva de Mujeres y Hombres*) aimed at improving the gender balance at all levels, but particularly in employment. Companies with over 250 employees have to negotiate an equality scheme and aim within eight years to have at least 40 per cent women on their Boards of Directors. Maternity conditions are improved and there is greater recognition of paternity leave, set at two weeks but with the intention that by 2013 it would be four weeks. Electoral lists would also have to observe the 40 per cent women rule. The objections from the PP were mainly that the law had fallen short and they would have preferred paternity leave to start at 30 days and longer periods of maternity leave for women, but they objected to the gender constraint on electoral lists which they saw as anti-constitutional. Further equality measures included the Dependency Act (*Ley de Dependencia*) which came into force on 1 January 2007 and was designed to give support to families, particularly women, who had to care for elderly or disabled relatives. Another was a law, the *Plan Integral para la conciliación de la vida laboral-familiar*, intended, as the name indicated, to aid Spaniards in achieving the work–life balance.

In addition to the equality laws, Zapatero's government also made radical proposals concerning abortion, divorce and Church–State relations which naturally ensured opposition from the PP and the Church. On abortion, Zapatero has been cautious. The communist coalition IU made the extension of the abortion law a condition of its support in the 2008 elections, but Zapatero called for a debate to decide how this should be reflected in the electoral programme. The last debate among socialists occurred in 1998 when a fourth criterion for abortion

– as a result of a personal, social or family conflict – and specifying stages of development when abortion could take place, was passed by the party but defeated in parliament. Following attacks and prosecutions by PP-controlled authorities against clinics practising abortions, Zapatero's government in 2009 moved to reform the 1985 law. The proposal would bring Spain closer to its European neighbours by permitting unconditional terminations up to the 14th week and terminations thereafter under certain conditions up to the 22nd week.

On the issue of divorce, in June 2005, the government introduced reforms to speed up the process, popularly known as the *divorcio exprés*, removing the need for couples to undergo the year-long period of separation prior to legal proceedings taking place. In addition the need to attribute responsibility for the failure of the marriage is removed, thus eliminating the 'guilt' factor common to the experience. A procedure which usually took two years can now take as little as ten days and a maximum of six months. The year following the change in legislation the divorce rate rose by 74.3 per cent, with the previous alternative, separation, experiencing a similar decline (70.7 per cent).

The consequence of these laws is to confirm Spain as one of the most socially progressive countries in Europe. Laws such as the one on divorce and gay marriage were overwhelmingly popular with the public but set Zapatero's government on a collision course with the Catholic Church. The reforms were criticized by Pope Benedict during Zapatero's initial audience with him in Rome in 2004 and repeated during the papal visit to Spain in July 2006. Nonetheless, the contradiction of the popular appeal of the laws in this still predominantly Catholic country illustrated the changing nature of Spanish society and its relationship to the official Church.

6.7   Regional Reform

On the issue of the regions, Zapatero's readiness to address smouldering nationalist concerns by pushing the boundaries of the Constitution managed to ruffle many feathers both outside and inside his party but illustrated his reasoning that 'extending greater regional autonomy is the only effective way to keep restive regions such as Catalonia within Spanish borders' (Encarnación 2008: 157). The Socialists' election manifesto promised statutory reform that complied with the Constitution and received a high degree of democratic consensus. Noticeable from the language of the manifesto is the implication that such changes should be activated 'desde el Estado', i.e. from the central government. The clear implication is that the government will not simply bow to nationalist pressure (PSOE 2004). Once in power, Zapatero called a meeting to discuss regional issues, the first since 1997, and made it an annual event.

As expected, the main pressures for reform were coming from the Catalans and the Basques but in very different ways. While the Basque *lehendakari*, Juan José Ibarretxe, had from 2002 applied pressure with his Ibarretxe Plan (see **5.14**), categorically rejected by all the national parties, in Catalonia, Zapatero had to contend with a regional government which since 2003 had been run by a coalition of the Catalan Socialist party (PSC), a radical nationalist republican party (ERC) and the local branch of the communist party, IC/Verds (formerly the PSUC). The PSC, led by Pasqual Maragall, had since 1996 espoused an unthreatening 'differential federalism', one which tries to combine federalism with recognition of Catalonia's regional distinctiveness, the 'differential fact' (see **3.8**), as opposed to the asymmetrical devolution set out in the Constitution, and as opposed to 'the multinational Spain that figures so strongly in the programs of the ERC and CiU' (McRoberts 2001: 88). In the 2003 Catalan elections, with Pujol's retirement, there was a mood for change, and Maragall and Carod-Rovira's more radical call for 'a new federal constitution for Spain which recognized the rights of the historic nations to self-government rather than the concessions of autonomy allowed to the seventeen nations and regions under the 1978 Constitution' (Payne, 2004: 249) had greater appeal to the electorate.

A socialist victory in 2004 provided a welcome change from

Aznar's intransigence when it came to regional matters. The reformed Catalan Statute was passed in a referendum on 18 June 2006 with over 73 per cent in favour and only 20.5 per cent against. The Statute was supported by the moderate nationalists of the CiU, the socialists of Maragall's *Partit dels Socialistes de Catalunya* (PSC) and the *Iniciativa per Catalunya Verds*. It was opposed by two parties on opposing ends of the spectrum, the PP and the hardline nationalists, the ERC. The latter, with whom Maragall shared government, found the final version, hammered out between the leader of the CiU, Artur Mas, and the Prime Minister, a much too watered-down version of the draft passed by the Catalan parliament on 30 September 2005.

One of the sticking points was the description of Catalonia as a 'nation'. In the final version, the government, which had refused the use of the term in the body of the statute, allowed it in the Preamble, thus depriving of it of any legal force in the eyes of central government. Other issues were finance and the refusal to allow the regional government to take control of areas such as the airport. However, it grants more control over immigration, taxation and the courts and most controversially specifies that the region's powers come not from the Spanish Constitution but from the Catalans themselves. The conservative PP opposed the whole principle of the statute and the risks that the reform posed as a prelude to a further weakening of the Spanish state. Nonetheless, the PP leader in Catalonia, Josep Piqué, expressed a lack of concern with the final version, unlike his Madrid colleagues, who preferred to keep up the pressure of criticism on Zapatero for his negotiations with nationalists. Rajoy had even made the issue of Catalonia's denomination as a nation in the Preamble the principal motive for a demonstration in the capital on 3 December 2005 and an appeal concerning the new statute was made by the PP to the Constitutional Court. Within the PSOE the Statute was opposed by the Defence Minister, José Bono, who eventually resigned from government. Before doing so he had had to sack a leading general, José Mena Aguado, who earlier in the year had insisted in a speech that the draft of the Statute at the time might justify the army intervening to preserve the integrity of the Spanish State as laid down by Article VIII of the Constitution.

With regard to the Basque question, Zapatero's approach differed radically from his predecessor's. Aznar's first term, when he relied on support from the Basque and Catalan parties, had seen a 14-month ETA truce from 1998 to 1999 whose failure was attributed to the government's intransigence, and in 2000 there were 23 assassinations by ETA, mainly of Socialist and PP politicians in the Basque Country. In part, Aznar's hardline stance could be justified by the shift in alignments brought about by the Estella Pact in 1998 which ranged the nationalist parties much more confrontationally against all the 'constitutionalist' parties. The Anti-Terrorism Pact signed in December 2000 at the behest of the PSOE bound them to reject any political negotiation with ETA and in 2001 Aznar's government had for the first time managed to secure a unanimous decision by all 15 members of the EU to declare ETA a terrorist organization. In 2002 investigations by Garzón had led to the seizure of HB's assets, the arrest of its leaders and the banning of the party in 2003.

After the defeat of the moderate Ardanza Plan in 1998, power in the PNV shifted to the more radical sector within the party led by the new *lehendakari* Juan José Ibarretxe. His strategy was to push for a political path to the extreme nationalist aim of outright independence for an enlarged Basque territory. Hence, what became known as the Ibarretxe Plan argued for a new model of Spanish–Basque relations outside the existing constitutional arrangement and involved a system of 'free association'. This proposal was rejected by the PP and PSOE alike and prompted the government, with the support of the Socialists, to introduce a controversial Political Parties Act (*Ley de Partidos Políticos*) in 2002 which 'established a judicial procedure making illegal any party that gave real and effective political support to violence or terrorism', a move which targeted specifically Batasuna and its various electoral guises. Complementing this political isolation of ETA was continued police action which had succeeded in netting most of the leadership of the terrorist group. As a result, prior to the 2004 elections ETA was both substantially weakened, but for that very reason suspected of planning renewed attacks to regain its reputation. In May 2003 two police officers died in an ETA bomb attack in Sanguesa, just south of Pamplona.

6.8   Tackling the Problem of ETA

Zapatero tried to break the deadlock partly created by the Anti-Terrorism Pact itself by pushing a proposal through parliament in May 2005 that allowed the government to enter into talks with ETA once violence had been renounced. The intention was that talks with ETA would involve no political concessions but solely the fate of the more than 700 ETA prisoners scattered round Spain and France. Political progress would be sought in a separate set of talks among the parties with the aim of improving autonomy and reforming the existing Autonomy Statute approved in 1979. It was in this climate that ETA declared a permanent ceasefire in March 2006 which was cautiously welcomed by Zapatero but treated with suspicion by the opposition, who viewed it as no more than a tactical pause and held firm to their preference for a reliance on police operations. While the terrorists' statement made no explicit demands it had a clear tone of expectation that political progress would result, as it exhorted the politicians to 'respond positively' to the organization's gesture. The aim was 'to drive the democratic process in the Basque Country so that through dialogues, negotiation and agreement, the Basque People can achieve the political change it needs ... constructing a democratic framework ... recognising its rights as a people and ensuring in future the development of all political options'. The Basque right to self-determination was evident in the words: 'At the end of the process, Basque citizens should have their say and decide on their future' (*El Mundo*, 23 March 2006).

The concept of a twin process, one between the government and ETA to resolve purely 'technical' issues such as prisoners, and one between political parties to seek a long-term solution, was not a new one. As far back as 1983, it was suggested by the then *lehendakari*, Carlos Garaikoetxea, and Mario Onaindia, the leader of Basque Country Left (*Euskadiko Ezkerra*), but was rejected by the left wing of the Basque nationalist movement. However, Arnaldo Otegi embraced the idea in the so-called Anoeta Declaration, made by Batasuna in November 2004, and subsequently Zapatero's government managed to have Parliament accept a similar proposal in 2005. The important issue was that ETA should not be seen as a participant in dialogue on a political solution.

The permanence of the truce was belied when in December 2006 ETA, frustrated by lack of progress, planted a bomb in Terminal 4 of Madrid Airport. There was a warning, but still two Ecuadorean nationals were killed. The organization delayed until early June 2007 to declare the ceasefire over. 'Minimum conditions for a continuation of the negotiation process' were lacking, according to their statement, and it criticized the government for responding to the end of armed activities with 'arrests, tortures and persecutions'. Their statement also condemned the recent local elections in which the representatives of Batasuna were excluded. There had been press reports of the first talks between the government and ETA in December 2006 in a European capital, but a theft of guns by the group in Nîmes in October had led to speculation that an end to the truce was imminent. The process had been hampered by an extension by two years of the ban on Batasuna imposed in January 2006 by Judge Marlaska. Thus, the aim of the process by which the radical Basque left was to be drawn into the political process as ETA retreats had been weakened.

Zapatero's handling of the truce was severely criticized by the conservative opposition, who saw him as being too compliant with the terrorists. When in the summer of 2007 a notorious ETA prisoner, Iñaki Juana de Chaos, guilty of 25 murders but in prison for lesser offences, began a hunger strike and was allowed out on house arrest, this was seen as another example of pandering to the extremists, as was the government's apparent reluctance to apply the Political Parties Act against groups like the Basque Nationalist Association (*Asociación Nacionalista Vasca*, ANV) and the Communist Party of the Basque Lands (*Partido Comunista de las Tierras Vascas*, PCTV), seen as flags of convenience for the currently illegal Batasuna. The failure of the peace process may have been responsible for the Socialists' narrow defeat in the May 2007 local elections, a result that over the years has proved a good indicator of general election results. Nonetheless, the government had throughout 2007 a good record of concerted pursuit of ETA and considerable success. In July three members of ETA, including the head of logistics, were arrested, making a total of 18 members of the organization detained in the space of two months. In addition, the absence of the ceasefire meant that the opposition can no longer attack the government for betrayal of the victims through negotiations with their killers. The killing of two policemen in the French resort of Capbreton in December 2007 marked the first assassinations since the formal breakdown of the truce.

In response to the killings on 1 December 2007 there was unprecedented unity of all parties in parliament, as well as trade unions and employers' organizations, as they signed up to a text entitled 'For Freedom, For the Defeat of ETA' (*Por la libertad, para la derrota de ETA*). Nevertheless the difficulty of the main two parties in drafting the text illustrated the underlying rifts. A phrase such as 'ETA has never nor will ever manage to make democracy bend' was removed, as the 'has never' conflicted with the standard PP discourse according to which the Zapatero government had 'surrendered' to the terrorists during the 2005–6 truce. Similarly the government's wish to insert a phrase saying 'we will support the government's efforts to end terrorism' had to be changed to 'efforts to defeat ETA', thus showing clearly the difference between the PSOE's focus on finding a solution and the PP's insistence on outright victory. Zapatero was to say in 2007 that his prediction of the end of ETA was one of the two mistakes he reckoned he made in his term of office, the other being the rather more pedestrian error of setting a precise date for the arrival of the high-speed train in Barcelona.

Regional elections in Galicia and the Basque Region on 1 March 2009 produced a reverse for the nationalist groupings. For the first time in the democratic period the PNV was ousted from power (though remaining the most voted party) owing to the pact between the Basque PP and the PSE-EE to allow Patxi López, leader of the Basque Socialists, to assume the position of *lehendakari* with a minority Socialist government. In Galicia the brief period of Socialist–Nationalist coalition came to an end with the return to power of the Galician PP under Alberto Núñez Feijóo.

6.9   The Economy under Zapatero

Aznar's period in office had, from the economic point of view, been quite a success and until the worldwide recession of 2008, Zapatero had managed to build on that success. Aznar inherited a 22 per cent unemployment rate in 1996 and had reduced it by half by the time he left office. Under Zapatero it continued to drop, reaching 8 per cent in 2007, close to the 7.2 per cent EU average (*The Economist* 2008). At the end of Aznar's term Spain was creating on average 45 per cent of jobs in the EU and under Zapatero job creation continued to grow, more than Germany, France and the UK combined, with total employment reaching 20 million in 2007 compared to 12 million in 1993. When Aznar left the growth rate was 3 per cent and by the end of Zapatero's first term it was still around double that of the rest of Europe. It was Aznar's ambition to make Spain a member of the G-8, and some would say it had more right to be there than Canada. In 2007 Zapatero was able to boast that Spain's growth rate exceeded all the members of the G-8 and placed Spain as the eighth largest economy. Aznar fought to take Spain into the Eurozone and benefited from the economic stability that brought, but at least he was disciplined to conform to EU strictures and he was obsessive about attaining a perfectly balanced budget. Zapatero continued to keep tight control of public finances with the result that in 2006 Spain's growth was 3.9 per cent, the fastest since 2000.

Much of the success of the economy is due to the contribution both legally and illegally (calculated at around 30 per cent of the total) of the over four million immigrants in Spain. While there are continuing problems of integration, social tensions and concern about the government's failure to spell out a clear immigration policy, still the government's stance has been to stress the economic benefits. Government figures show that since the first wave of 600,000 'regularized' immigrants in Zapatero's first government, by December 2008 the number of immigrants affiliated to the social security system in which they are still net contributors had risen to just under 2 million. Immigrants boost the economy by working in the care sector thus allowing Spaniards, especially women, to work themselves. For the government their contribution in taxes exceeds by 20 per cent their cost in terms of public services (Matlack 2007). In the 2008 general election campaign Zapatero's central message was that immigrants' contributions of 9000 million euros to the system funded 900,000 pensions in Spain. A report in 2006 prepared by the government and two leading banks showed that between 1996 and 2006 immigrants had contributed 30 per cent to the country's GDP, rising to 50 per cent over the second half of the period (Ministerio de la Presidencia 2009: 152).

However, by the end of 2008, with the recession biting in Spain and unemployment levels rising to almost 11 per cent, the highest in the EU, there was developing concern about the burden on the unemployment benefit system of approximately 250,000 unemployed immigrants. For this reason, a scheme was introduced in November 2008 to encourage unemployed immigrants to return home with the inducement of a part advance payment of benefit. The condition was they should surrender permits and not return within three years. By March 2009 the scheme, which applies to 19 countries with which Spain has social security agreements, had attracted nearly 4000 immigrants, most from Ecuador and the rest from Colombia and Argentina. The official target is 100,000.

6.10 The PP in Opposition

Given the circumstances of the PP's loss of the elections in 2004, it is perhaps not unexpected that its role in opposition was marked by a resigned acceptance of the decision of the electorate. The PP parliamentary spokesperson, Eduardo Zaplana's oft-repeated remarks in November 2004 that the Aznar government had lost the election due to a 'remote-controlled attack' set the tenor for the party as a whole and especially its leader, Mariano Rajoy, who devoted most of his efforts to trying to undermine Zapatero's position. In an approach that recalls the *acoso y derribo* of González practised earlier (see **4.5**) the PP has harried Zapatero from the outset, perhaps most contentiously refusing their cooperation on anti-terrorist policy on which traditionally parties try to show consensus. In December 2007 the PP tried for the fourth time to have the 2005 policy on permitting talks with ETA in absence of violence revoked and found itself once again alone and accused of disloyalty to the government and other parties and, even worse, the now customary taint of using terrorism as a political football. The PP presented a motion requesting removal of the statute of limitations on terrorist acts, the outlawing of the PCTV and ANV (see **6.8**) and the revoking of the 2005 resolution. The policy of the PP was to argue for the return to the 2000 Anti-Terrorism Pact. The inclusion in the pact of a statement criticizing the cooperation between Basque nationalist parties as a result of the pan-nationalist Estella Pact signed in September 1998, meant that the Anti-Terrorism Pact had not attracted the support of other political parties (Mata 2005: 89).

Above all, the PP tried to argue that Zapatero's government had undermined the unity of the post-Transition consensus, the secret of Spain's successful democratization. However, this criticism sat awkwardly with the PP's difficulty in officially condemning the military uprising in 1936, something that only occurred in 2002 and which it had explicitly refused to do in 1999. Much of the PP's approach in opposition has been directed at presenting itself in a populist way as the practical, common-sense party, allied with the daily concerns of the man and woman in the street in the face of the Socialists' radical ideological agenda. Ironically, in most issues the party has shown itself to be out of step, not only with other political parties but also the majority of Spanish citizens. As Encarnación observes, 'every "radical" policy implemented by Zapatero (the withdrawal of Spanish troops from Iraq, the recovering of the historical memory, same-sex marriage and gender equality in government and the workplace) was a campaign promise made to the electorate during the 2004 elections' and 'the bulk of Zapatero's agenda is very much in synch with the public's wishes' (2008: 162).

6.11   Church and State

One of the major casualties of the Zapatero governments has been Church–State relations. Such difficulties are not new and were a characteristic of the González governments where the issues of divorce, abortion, church financing and religion in schools led to a permanent state of tension and yet, according to Hooper, 'more than half the country's practising Catholics and a fifth of its daily communicants voted for the Socialists at the 1982 general election' (2006: 103). However, Zapatero's radical reforms have caused alarm of a different order. Part of the problem has been the direction taken by the Spanish Church itself. As Hooper points out, as a result of the Church's positive role towards the end of the Transition and its links with democratic forces, it was in 'an ideal position to make itself a force for reconciliation and unification', yet what happened was that it 'gradually, haltingly shifted itself to the point at which it was, and is, seen by many as the People's Party at prayer: an institution reflecting the outlook of only one half of Spanish society' (2006: 102–3). The appointment of Antonio Rouco Varela as Archbishop of Madrid in 1994, and then President of the Episcopal Conference in 1999 signified an important move towards the right in the Church's leadership, interrupted only from 2005–8 when the more liberal Ricardo Blázquez Pérez occupied the post.

Conflict with the Church was inevitable when Zapatero decided on his package of social reforms relating to gay marriage, abortion, divorce and the teaching of religion in schools. While its opponents would accuse the government of anti-clericalism, Zapatero's stance was that he was merely implementing and extending the separation of Church and State laid down in the 1978 Constitution but which is belied by the continued substantial financial support given to the Church from government, calculated at approximately 40 million euros per year, and which it receives on top of the voluntary contributions of Spaniards calculated at 90 million euros in 2004. There are regular attempts on the part of the Socialist government to move the Church to a self-financing basis.

Education has always been a battleground between the main parties. Studies have pointed to it as the legislative area in Spain where consensus is least likely between government and opposition (Mújica and Sánchez Cuenca 2008). Within education, the teaching of religion has tended to be the focus for most of the conflict. Since an agreement signed in 1979 between the Vatican and the Spanish government, they are committed to offering religious teaching in all state schools. The Socialists under González were the first to make it a voluntary subject of study and not permit marks obtained from it to count towards university entrance. The PP under Aznar reversed that and once again Zapatero made it voluntary. Zapatero, however, went further with his promotion of Citizenship Education, a new obligatory subject phased into schools from 2008. Its opponents on the right object to the subject's advocacy for many of the radical reforms that the Socialists introduced into society, especially those relating to sexual equality.

What has alarmed some observers is what they see as an over-politicization of the Church in Spain and the frequent coincidence of the Church and the People's Party in street protests, leading some to talk of the two 'working in tandem' (Encarnación 2008: 154). Shortly before the March 2008 elections, the Bishop of San Sebastián, Juan María Uriarte, was prompted to issue a warning to his colleagues to avoid showing any 'party preference' and to 'respect the independence of the democratic process', though he was careful to add that the clergy could give ethical guidance that might help a voter make up his or her mind. The high point was a demonstration in the capital called by the Archbishop of Madrid, Rouco Varela, on 30 December 2007 'in defence of the Christian family'. The bishops targeted the government's legislation on gay marriage, the 'quickie divorce' (*divorcio exprés*), Education for Citizenship and proposals on abortion. For some, particularly alarming given the evident secularization of Spanish society over the democratic period in line with other western democracies, was the comment made by a Valencian cardinal that laicism leads to the dissolution of democracy. However, it was the Bishops' injunction, at their Episcopal Congress about one month before the elections, that no Spaniard should vote for a party that negotiates with terrorists that most enraged the Socialist government since, as they were quick to point out, this would eliminate every president throughout Spain's short democracy. Furthermore, it was pointed out that when Aznar engaged in talks with ETA in Switzerland in 1999, he had been accompanied by none other than the then Bishop of Zamora, Juan María Uriarte.

6.12 Foreign Policy

In terms of foreign policy Zapatero resumed the line established by Felipe González by giving precedence to the EU and Latin America, over Aznar's gravitation towards the USA and Britain. He has indicated that foreign policy will assume a larger role in his second term of office. The distancing from the USA was initiated with his decision, the first after assuming office, to honour his election promise to withdraw troops from Iraq. Aznar had pulled back at the last minute from sending troops for the invasion itself but its support troops, totalling 1300, constituted the sixth largest in Iraq. Zapatero had originally promised to withdraw them if the UN had failed to take control of Iraq by the 30 June, but in the aftermath of the bomb attack he ordered their immediate return on 18 April, thereby pleasing his voters with a rapid compliance with his promises and risking the accusations of surrendering to terrorism that followed from figures such as the US Defence Secretary, Donald Rumsfeld. Zapatero was always keen to emphasize that Spain remained committed to international cooperation in peacekeeping with more than 3000 Spanish troops deployed from Afghanistan to the Balkans (Sciolino 2004). Surveys showed that Spain was the European country most opposed to the Iraq War (Campillo 2004: 335; Colomer 2005: 152). Zapatero balanced this decision with a constructive contribution to the international debate on increased tension between Islamic nations and the West when, speaking at the UN General Assembly in September 2004, he announced a proposal for an 'alliance of civilizations' to foster dialogue and cooperation.

Zapatero had already attracted American criticism when in 2003 at the celebrations for the *Día de la Hispanidad* (12 October) he refused to stand up as the American flag passed and did not disguise it was 'to keep coherence with the majority of the Spanish people who are against the war' in Iraq. The sea-change in Spain's relationship with the USA after Aznar's attempt to cultivate the friendship was compounded and deepened by Zapatero's explicit aim to improve Spain's relationship with its near European neighbours, France and Germany, and to improve its engagement with the EU. Finally, again much to the detriment of Madrid–Washington relations was Zapatero's determination to renew and improve relations with Spain's Latin American partners, and in particular those regimes which had fallen foul of Aznar's pro-American vision.

Since victory in the March 2008 elections and especially since the arrival of the more progressive Barack Obama in the White House after the November 2008 elections, hopes of an improved relationship with the USA were rekindled. This was temporarily jeopardized by the abrupt way that Spain

announced its decision to withdraw peacekeeping troops from
Kosovo in March 2009, attracting criticism from all sides as well
as an official US statement expressing 'deep disappointment' at
the decision. Spain is one of the few Western countries not to
recognize Kosovo's independence from Serbia. So while the
moral coherence of the government's position was not disputed,
concern was expressed at the clumsy management of decision.
Diplomatic fences were mended the following month at a meeting in Prague, when Obama declared himself a 'friend of
Zapatero' and announced a new era of collaboration with
Spain.

Regarding the EU, Zapatero had made it his declared policy
to improve relations with France and Germany. More surprising was his willingness to give way in the discussions over EU
voting rights. Aznar's government had been strongly opposed
to the double-majority voting system. However, Zapatero has
been a strong supporter of enlargement. In May 2004
Zapatero conveyed to his German and French counterparts his
willingness to accept the principle of 'double majority' voting
as long as the percentages were adjusted to preserve the weighting agreed at the Nice Treaty. Support for the EU Constitution
was also set as a priority, and in February 2005, Spain was the
first EU country to hold a referendum which, while poorly
attended with only 42 per cent participation, approved the text
with over 76 per cent in favour and only 17 per cent against. It
received cross-party support in the parliament the following
April.

However, Zapatero's support for the EU did not find the
expected reward when it came to dealing with the crisis of
immigration. Despite the undoubted economic benefits of
planned and controlled immigration (see **6.9**), it also constitutes
a grave humanitarian challenge. While not the only country
affected, Spain since 2000 has been the most targeted European
country, with unprecedented inflows of illegal immigration
especially to the Canary Islands. For Zapatero, this is not solely
a Spanish problem but affects the Community as a whole.
Nonetheless, there was scant support from Brussels for his calls

for action with many EU countries, including France and Germany, judging Spain's emergency amnesty in 2005 for over 600,000 immigrants as a cause of the increase. It led in September 2006 to a serious spat between Zapatero and Sarkozy, only for the French President to introduce a similar measure the following year. Spain did become the primary net beneficiary of funds assigned by the Union to deal with immigration, calculated at €87 million, in 2007. Nonetheless, the expansion of the EU to 27 members presents Spain with major challenges as it will undoubtedly cease to be a net beneficiary of EU funds (calculated as €3500 million in 2006) and become a net contributor.

However, Zapatero has worked hard on two fronts that have always figured highly on Spanish governments' agendas: Latin America and the Maghreb. Such links date back to the Franco regime when the dictator hoped that North Africa and Latin America would provide an outlet for imperial ambitions. The former was thwarted by history, but the bonds between Hispanic countries as a counter to the isolation from its European neighbours were more deep-rooted. After the loss of empire in the Disaster of Cuba in 1898, the progressive elements in Spanish society, the Regenerationists, set their sights on Europe as Spain's future while the more conservative forces looked back nostalgically to Latin America, but *hispanismo*, 'the idea of a transatlantic spiritual community as an external projection of the Spanish nation', remained intrinsic to both traditions (Balfour and Quiroga 2007: 32).

As far as contemporary relations with Morocco are concerned, these had suffered under Aznar, particularly as a result of the Isla Perejil (Parsley Island) incident in 2002. Hence, diplomatically, it was chosen as the first foreign visit of Zapatero's prime ministership. Relations with Morocco have always been fraught, and the ongoing conflict in the Western Sahara has seen Spain more often on the side of the Polisario in the dispute over the territory. Ceuta and Melilla, Spain's remaining enclaves in North Africa, still rankle with the Moroccan regime. Nonetheless, the two countries are linked by a set of crucial issues, ranging from immigration through security to agricultural produce that require that they get on. Moroccan Islamists were involved in the 11 March bomb and the same group was thought responsible for the 2003 Casablanca bomb. Thus united as victims, Zapatero was eager to improve relations and police cooperation between the two countries. He is also committed to lobbying within the EU for aid to Morocco. However, he has also been staunch in his defence of the North African enclaves, Ceuta and Melilla, as Spanish, paying them a visit, much to Morocco's displeasure, in January 2006. This was followed by a much publicized and equally controversial visit by the Spanish monarchs, their first visit since Juan Carlos assumed the throne, in 2007.

Zapatero's fostering of links and support with Latin America has to be seen in the context of his parallel distancing from the USA, which represented a reversal of his predecessor Aznar's approach. Less concerned with *hispanismo* perhaps and more with the fact that Spain has 'become the leading investor in the Southern Cone, second only to the United States in the Latin American region as whole [where its] $80 billion invested in Latin America counts for half of all EU investment in the region between 1992 and 2001' (Chislett 2003: 12). Zapatero courted early controversy when in 2005 he sold military equipment worth €1.3 billion (£900 million) and consisting of 10 C-295 transport planes, four coastal patrol corvettes and four smaller coastguard patrol boats to Hugo Chávez, the USA's *bête noire*. He defended his decision on the basis that the material was mainly to help combat terrorism and drug-trafficking. Zapatero and the King later clashed with Chávez, and Juan Carlos famously told the Venezuelan leader in no uncertain terms to 'shut up' ('¿Por qué no te callas?') on the last day of the Ibero-American Summit in Chile in 2007, though it did little to damage long-term relations. Zapatero established good relations with the Presidents of Brazil and Argentina and promised support for plans to improve links between Mercosur and the EU (Encarnación 2008: 160).

6.13   Historical Memory

After the Aznar years, when the PP made every conceivable effort to block, delay and disparage the various movements seeking retribution and reparation for injustices carried out during the Civil War and during the regime (Encarnación 2008: 143–4), progress on the issue at last became a possibility when the PSOE reached government and another of Zapatero's early decisions was to set up a commission to look at compensating victims of the Franco regime. On 1 June 2004 the Spanish Parliament passed a proposal that the plight of the victims of the Civil War be re-examined and some system of reparation be introduced, providing money for exhumation and reburial. An Interministerial Commission to Study the Plight of Civil War Victims (*Comisión Interministerial para el Estudio de la Situación de las Víctimas de la Guerra Civil*) was set up, led by the Deputy Prime Minister, María Teresa Fernández de la Vega, with the brief of looking at revising the decisions of the Francoist courts, the identification of victims in mass graves, the opening of archives, the removal of symbols from the Franco period and the moral and economic recognition of the victims. In the light of slow progress, two parties, the IU and the radical Catalan ERC, made their own proposal in parliament in late 2005. Their aim, however, was only the recognition of the Republican victims. The final version that in December 2006 entered its last parliamentary phase was a more moderate and inclusive version of the original proposal, though it still was opposed by the PP and, while obtaining majority support among Spaniards, caused deep divisions. The conservative opposition saw the law as divisive and reopening old wounds. Critics on the left thought it did not go far enough.

One of the most controversial points referred to the sentences meted out by the Francoist courts, which parties on the left wished to see annulled and compensation granted to the descendants. The Socialist government preferred a compromise arrangement whereby the Francoist courts were declared illegitimate and thus opened the door to victims or their families to seek reparation through the courts. Should they do so, the law prevents Francoist legislation being used as a legal justification for rejecting their claims. An Association for the Recovery of Historical Memory (ARMH), set up by Emilio Silva in 2000 with the express purpose of uncovering the unmarked graves, had by 2005 recovered over 500 bodies of Republicans killed and calculated that around 30,000 disappeared during the war and the subsequent regime. It is estimated that the recovery of historical memory movement has led to the creation of over 160 associations (Encarnación 2008: 140).

The law was denounced in March 2007 by another group, *Foro por la Memoria*, which saw it as an attempt, along with the 1977 Amnesty Act and what is known as the 'pact of silence' during the Transition, to grant impunity to the Franco regime. The beatification of 498 martyrs of the Civil War on 28 October 2007 was interpreted by many as a sign of the Church's displeasure at the Act. In the end, the Historical Memory Act, *Ley de Memoria Histórica*, was finally passed by Congress on 31 October 2007. Its main provisions are: the exhumation, identification and reburial of bodies found in anonymous graves; investigation of human rights abuses during the war and its aftermath, compensation to victims, and arrangements regarding the public display of Francoist symbols and monuments. It sums up its intentions as 'closing those wounds still open in Spaniards ... deepening the spirit of reunion and concord of the Transition'.

One of the consequences of the movement was that in 2006 relatives of murdered relatives on the Republican side placed a death notice (*esquela*) in the national newspaper *El País*, both as a reminder but also in reparation. However, it activated a series (a war or *guerra*, as it was termed) that in its tit-for-tat nature served as a sad reminder of the conflict itself (Tesón 2006). Another controversial but possibly necessary consequence was the counter-revisionist movement in which a number of authors offered much-criticized but editorially successful attempts to debunk what they see as the myths of historical orthodoxy about Franco and the Civil War. The most high-profile of these is the former GRAPO activist turned historian, Pío Moa, whose writings present the right-wing narrative which stressed the Republic's responsibility for the Civil War (Stradling 2007: 442–57; Labanyi 2007: 112).

Omar Encarnación has highlighted the likely genesis of this movement of recovery of historical memory in the 1996 prosecution brought against Augusto Pinochet, the former Chilean dictator, by the Spanish judge Baltasar Garzón, suggesting in some way the affair 'sensitized the public about the artificial line that the democratic transition had drawn between the past and the present' (2008:132). He points, too, to the series of anniversaries that Spain experienced from 2000 commencing with the 25th anniversary of Franco's death that year (Encarnación 2008: 139). That same judge continued to ruffle feathers in 2008 by seeking access to local authority and church records in an attempt to establish the manner of death of the victims of the Franco regime. Such killings were not recorded with the same meticulousness as those of the victims of the Republicans. The hope was to allow descendants to claim compensation if, as is thought, their ancestors were killed illegally, but Garzón's actions also opened the door to prosecutions of those responsible and still alive, a prospect that will truly test Spain's commitment to uncovering the past.

6.14   The 2008 Election

Zapatero fought his second elections on 9 March 2008 against the same opponent, Mariano Rajoy. The election was preceded by a brutal ETA assassination of a former Socialist councillor, Isaías Carrasco, in the Basque town of Mondragón. In these elections it was clear that what was coming under scrutiny was the economic policy of the government. The dominance of social policies in the first term had drawn the accusation from the opposition that the Socialists had 'done nothing' on the economic front other than keep the efficient machine that Aznar had bequeathed them ticking over. Rajoy's complaint was that an opportunity had been missed to build on a wonderful legacy. By the time of the election the recession was on the horizon, Spain's growth had slowed, prices were rising and the all-important construction sector was in crisis, and the politicians mocked Zapatero for refusing to admit the country was heading towards recession, though by July he had.

The election was won by the Socialists, increasing their number of seats slightly from 164 to 169, still 7 short of an overall majority (see Appendix 10). The PP could take some comfort from Rajoy improving its performance and ending with 153 seats, 5 more than in 2004. The ERC and IU lost seats most likely to the phenomenon of the 'useful vote', tactical voting for the larger leftist party to keep the PP out. The participation rate was almost the same as in 2004 (75.3 per cent) which, according to Powell's equation, made it 'an election of change'. It may have been that the Socialists, aware that abstention tends to hurt them more than the right, did all they could to mobilize their voters, but there was also the sense that, given the shadow over the 2004 vote, it wanted a clear legitimation at the polls this time round (Field 2008: 2). The campaign was enlivened by two television debates, the first since the two encounters between González and Aznar in 1993. The difficult negotiation that preceded them and the refusal by the opposition party, the PP, to allow the public channel, RTVE, to host either, revealed the failure of repeated government promises, including Zapatero's, to eliminate political bias in the public channel (Sampedro and Seoane 2008). Polls indicated that Zapatero came out top in both, as did his veteran Economy Minister, Pedro Solbes, in his joust with the PP's Manuel Pizarro. The smaller parties complained about their exclusion from the debates; however, it can be seen to reflect (possibly even contribute to) a trend in Spain towards a two-party system. As Field shows, from 1989 elections have shown a progressive concentration of the vote in the two main parties, from 65 per cent to the 84 per cent of 2008. Because of the distorting effect of the D'Hondt electoral system used this is even greater in terms of parliamentary representation. Currently, the PSOE and the PP between them control 92 per cent of the seats (Field 2008: 2). Zapatero failed to win the investiture vote first time around when absolute majority support is needed but was elected on the second round with a simple majority, becoming the first PM since democracy to have to resort to the second round following general elections.

6.15　National Identity in a Multicultural Society

As Mary Vincent observes, Spain has retained much of its cultural singularity, especially in those areas that seem to enhance the quality of its citizens' lives – its eating culture, its evening stroll, the centrality of family life – while modernizing in those other areas that ensure it is integrated into the modern world of business and high finance. Similarly Spain has acquired the characteristics and problems of a modern Western democracy – one of Europe's lowest birth rates, advancing secularization and multiculturalism, and both the increasing need for immigration and the social cost of its illegal forms (2007: 236–7).

There is no doubt that immigration has had a profound effect on Spanish society. By 2005 its immigrant community stood at 8.7 per cent, putting Spain ahead of France and just behind Germany in the European immigration tables. Zapatero's government has attempted to balance progressive encouragement of immigration with administrative control. If European surveys in the 1990s, which showed that over half of respondents saw immigration as a problem, placed Spain in the group who felt it was not a big problem (Lahav 2004: 1167), the 2007 Eurobarometer reveals that 43 per cent of Spaniards think the fight against illegal immigration should be an EU priority, compared to a Community average of 29 per cent. Where earlier surveys put Spain's intolerance level towards immigrants at 10 per cent, this has increased to 30 per cent since 2000. In recent surveys immigration has been overtaken by economic issues and terrorism, but it remains a constant concern of Spaniards.

The El Ejido riot in 2000 was an isolated case of racial conflict and in general Spain is adapting well to multiculturalism. The 2004 bomb did not provoke any discernible anti-Muslim backlash. Although there is still a tendency to link immigrants with crime and their presence is disproportionately high in activities such as prostitution, the fact that many immigrants are Hispanic in origin has tended to aid integration (Chislett 2008: 12; Díez Medrano 2005: 145). While immigrants often encounter hostility based on the common assumption that they divert employment away from the local unemployed, it is more often linked to the prejudice that they are principally responsible for crime and drug-trafficking (Corkill 2000: 54). In 2006 a Centre for Sociological Research (CIS) survey showed that immigration had overtaken terrorism as Spaniards' second major concern after unemployment and a 2007 European survey kept it in second place, this time behind terrorism and quite a distance ahead of housing and unemployment (Eurobarometer 67, 2007).

Integration remains a problem, especially in the education system, which has brought the multicultural nature of Spanish society into sharp relief. Over 600,000 pupils from other countries are enrolled and the figure rises by around 80,000 per year. Regional governments, now responsible for their own education systems, have to develop pedagogical policies aimed at integration, usually a mixture of integration and, controversially, segregated tuition, especially for the Spanish language, in special 'reception classes' (*aulas de acogida*). In addition, substantial effort and investment are being made in training pupils and teachers in 'interculturality'. The long-term perspective is concerning. Recent studies show that a disproportionate number of pupils from immigrant communities leave the education system before university, raising fears of a future ethnically stratified society.

What effect this multicultural trend in Spanish society will have on the sense of national identity is difficult to predict. Spaniards have always had a troubled relationship with the concept of nationality. Despite Spain being considered by some as one of the earliest nation-states, Spanish nationalism has never been strong, a fact bemoaned in the 1920s by Ortega y Gasset in his *Invertebrate Spain* and commonly attributed to the failure of the liberal state-building project in the nineteenth century (Conversi 1997: 110–11; Mar-Molinero and Smith 1996b). According to this school of thought, during Europe's 'age of nationalism' in the nineteenth century, while other countries experienced a nationalist resurgence, Spanish nationalism had to compete with the emerging local nationalisms on its periphery. A sense of patriotic sentiment is often traced to the rising of Spaniards against Napoleon in 1808 and to this effect Spain celebrated in 2008 the bicentenary of a time when, according to the President of the Madrid Region, 'Spaniards rose up against the most powerful army in the world in the name of freedom and national sovereignty' (*El País*, 1 January 2009). Kamen, among others, have stressed how the 'notion of a "national" cause in the uprising of Spaniards in 1808 was, in perspective, pure myth' in that most of the targets of the 'patriotic' rioters were Spaniards (Kamen 2008: 2–3; Alvarez Junco 2008).

Balfour and Quiroga, on the other hand, make clear that prior to the 1800s there was undoubtedly a clear sense of Spanishness identified with Catholicism and opposition to external enemies, usually the northern Protestant nations (2007: 18–25). This nationalism survived the nineteenth century, in both liberal and conservative versions, and re-emerged under Franco, as a combination of National Catholicism, political centralism and a xenophobic sense of Spanishness (*hispanismo*). By the 1960s the regime's wish to belong to Europe and the need to present an acceptable face to foreigners made such ideas unfashionable and the concept of Spanish nationalism was contaminated by identification with the regime (Núñez Seixas 2005: 122).

In the democratic period Spain's position within the EU has provided a kind of solution, allowing it to leapfrog the national level and embrace an ideologically neutral European identity, but without necessarily losing the national and local affiliations. Thus rather than a crisis of identity, Spain through the simultaneous processes of 'modernisation, decentralisation and Europeanisation' has developed a 'group of overlapping circles of collective identity' (Stapell 2007: 182). Spain has evolved into an affluent cosmopolitan post-national society characterized culturally by 'postmodern hybridity' (Labanyi 2002b: 9). There are numerous signs, too, of the growing ethnic diversity of Spain's new multicultural society penetrating the cinema and television in ways that range from sympathetic solidarity to the perpetuation of racial stereotypes. However, at least, as Isabel Santaolalla argues, their presence 'could be seen to encourage – even if unintentionally in many cases – a re-examination of Spain's attitudes to its Others' (2002: 68).

Problems continue to linger. Spaniards still seem reluctant to accept their Muslim past. As Balfour and Quiroga note, the 'endurance of the concept of the Moor as the alien that defines what Spanishness is not, and therefore links the nation to Christianity, may come as a surprise in a society that has dramatically secularized its habits in the past thirty years' (2007: 118–19). They suggest that while contemporary Spanish national identity has been rebranded by both right and left as 'civic, constitutional and democratic', the 'latent ethnic components of Spanishness come to the fore when it is a question of integrating non-Christians into the national community' (2007: 119). A 2005 study reveals that, on the whole, Spaniards are tolerant towards immigrants, in favour of tightening control of illegal immigration but extending rights of citizenship to legal immigrants (Díez Medrano 2005: 144). How these attitudes evolve under pressure from economic recession and increased competition for jobs is the real test of Spain's tolerance levels.

6.16 Conclusion

On one level, the elections of 2008 had served as a judgement on Zapatero's first term in office in which one could say he scored a modest pass mark. On another more symbolic level, the elections were a final legitimation of the 2004 election result, over which had hung, as no doubt was intended, the shadow of the PP's slurs and accusations. Zapatero had wanted his government to usher in a new era of consensus politics, a change from the *crispación* or mood of confrontation that had characterized previous governments. Sadly, this did not happen and the period from 2004 to 2008 was one of the most bitter and most divisive periods of Spain's democratic history. Nonetheless, while the PP and their allies both in the Church and among some of the new movements that had grown up in the wake of the country's recent terrorist history represented substantial segments of Spanish society, justifiably concerned with the pace and radical nature of some of the changes that were being introduced, still it seems that the Socialists were in tune with the majority of Spaniards.

Zapatero has proved his credentials as a competent and progressive leader with a wide vision for change in Spanish society, above and beyond the mere search for economic prosperity and extension of individual freedoms that marked his predecessor. He showed too an ability as a relative newcomer on the international scene to make an impact with his proposal of an 'alliance of civilizations' in 2004. Aznar's successor in the party, Mariano Rajoy, has struggled to instil a similarly convincing but alternative vision and certainly some of his party's attempts, such as the defence of a new constitutional patriotism seen in street demonstrations of flag-waving in the company of church dignitaries, seem too reminiscent of a former era to find wide acceptance. However, as the country heads towards the end of the first decade of the new millennium amid a global financial crisis, Zapatero will perhaps be judged less on his idealistic vision of a new society than on how he and his team handled the gravest economic challenge faced by Spain in the democratic period.

CONCLUSION

The preceding chapters have charted Spain's progress from the trauma and devastation of the Civil War, where it was by turns the stage of the 'last great cause' and testing ground for a larger international conflict, to a situation today where Spain is if not at, then at least very near to the centre of contemporary world events. In that process, many of the standard myths of Spain have been laid to rest. A country famed for its unreliability and economic backwardness has from the late 1980s been one of the great economic success stories of Europe. Prior to the recent global banking crisis the outstanding success was Banco Santander, seen as an example of that 'combination of international ambition and risk-aversion [which] is characteristic of Spanish business' (*The Economist* 2008: 18).

As nations gathered in 2008 to discuss the crisis, France and the USA, the two prime movers of Spain's international isolation in the 1940s, were the strongest defenders of Spain's right, as the world's eighth-largest economy, to participate in the G-20 summit of the world's richest nations and emerging economies. In 2007 Zapatero took a certain amount of satisfaction from announcing that Spain had overtaken Italy in terms of per capita GDP, subsequently contested by the Italian Prime Minister, Romano Prodi, wielding figures produced by the IMF. Eurostat figures confirmed that Spain occupied ninth position among the 27 member states, above Italy for the second successive year. None of this, however, has insulated Spain from the effects of that crisis. In fact, in 2009 the Finance Minister, Pedro Solbes, predicted a shrinkage in the economy of 1.6 per cent which would make Spain's plight one of the worst in the EU and unemployment at 18 per cent, with 4 million out of work, places Spain once again among the worst in that category. The economic theory that Spain's economy tends to converge with its European neighbours at times of expansion while diverging at times of recession may be proved correct yet again (Harrison and Corkill 2004: 3).

While Spain's seemingly linear progress out of dictatorship to democracy and full integration into the political, social and economic structures of Western Europe may appear reasonably clear, as our introduction indicated, that very progress has led to the emergence of new perspectives which cast doubt on or at least call for a rethinking of the linear simplicity of that narrative (Pérez Serrano 2007). One formulation of this is made by Fernando León Solís in an article analysing two newspapers, one national (*El País*) and another regional/nationalist (*Avui*), and their discourse on the Transition. On the one hand, the national discourse represents the Transition as a successful stage in the past which Spain has surmounted, and quotes novelist and former Culture Minister under Felipe González, Jorge Semprún, saying that 'Spain has overcome all the problems of the transition except terrorism.' On the other, for *Avui*, a newspaper linked to the moderate Catalan nationalist coalition CiU, the Transition 'despite the achievements ... is still not the past, it is still present' and even, projecting into the future, regarded as 'promising' (León Solís 2003: 54). Thus, where the Transition from a national perspective might be seen as a 'mission accomplished', for the attention of historians, the view from the nationalist periphery is still very much one of a work in progress.

One illustration of this in contemporary Spain relates to the Spanish Constitution. Many in Spain, particularly those on the Right, regard the Constitution as the untouchable bedrock of the country's democracy. Others recognize the need for reform, especially as large sections such as that outlining the process of devolution have been superseded by events. As Vincent says, the Constitution's 'elaboration testified to the resolution of several historic cleavages' (2007: 215). It was one of the key manifestations of the strategy of consensus, the principle of *convivencia* that marked the success of the Transition (Edles 1998: 101). It is as though tampering with it might risk unravelling the whole process, and yet reform is required. One relatively straightforward modification planned by the current government is to change Article 57 to permit a female heir to the throne, so eliminating the one case of sexual discrimination permitted by the Constitution (Tamames 1995: 100–1).

The issue of the Constitution draws attention to the one area of domestic politics which is politically unresolved, that is, regional devolution and the problem of the nationalisms, and it is not only in the context of Basque terrorism, although that inevitably is its most dramatic manifestation. As Pérez Serrano points out, it is no coincidence that a more critical debate on the success of the Transition's model for decentralization, and other matters, was opened up in the wake of Aznar's electoral victory in 2000 and the Right's determined promotion of a more robust Spanish nationalist agenda (2007: 72–3). For the Spanish right the 1978 Constitution, by allowing an open-ended devolution system, the *proceso autonómico*, unleashed a monster which is threatening to cause the break-up of Spain (Balfour and Quiroga 2007: 105–6). Their aim is to put a halt to the process and sets them at odds with the nationalists, whose strategy is to push at the constitutional boundaries in a limitless search for increased autonomy. The moderate Catalans seem content to do so within the Constitutional structure, as long as the principle of 'self-determination' is recognized, and this is reflected in Article 3 of the reformed Catalan Statute of 2006 which says that Cataluña's 'political and geographic space' is within Spain and Europe.

The Basques, even the moderate members of the PNV, are now bent on independence (*soberanismo*), for which Ibarretxe's plan for free association is merely a halfway house. The Socialists' support for the reform of the Catalan Statute and for the principle of constitutional reform in general was countered by the PP's new version of Spanish nationalism. As Balfour and Quiroga point out, this concept of 'constitutional patriotism' tries to reconcile, on the one hand, a postmodern emphasis on plurality and diversity where even immigrants can find accommodation in a loyalty to the Constitution with, on the other, a discourse redolent of Francoism, Spain as a 'political nation forged over the course of a long historical trajectory' (2007: 116). Neither can appeal truly to the immigrant nor the nationalist; indeed, 'constitutional patriotism primarily aimed not to integrate peripheral nationalists into a common Spanish project but to create a solid alternative to them' (Balfour and Quiroga 2007: 93). Nor will those nationalists, so concerned for their *hecho diferencial*, be satisfied with the Socialist project of creeping federalism which would erase any such differential marks. Therefore, in this area of domestic politics the prospect of a resolution in the future seems remote. Nonetheless, as Vincent rightly says, while the 'open questions as to the status of the regions, the role they played in Europe and the extent of devolved powers remained live issues', it is also the case that 'these questions have as much salience in Belgium as in Spain and also find some resonance in Britain', and she concludes that if Spain is in no better position to solve them than her neighbours, she is 'in no worse a position either' (2007: 238).

What will be more problematic is the search for reconciliation and closure in the matter of historical memory. Here the division is of necessity on a more national scale, cutting across all regions and all classes, much as did the original Civil War. As Davis points out, the success of the Transition with its pact of forgetting was that it 'rested on a version of Spain's history that views the civil war as a conflict between two Spains, Republican and Nationalist, in which atrocities were committed on both sides and according to which the war is best forgotten' (2005: 876; Aguilar 1999), even though this conflicts with evidence that while the Republican violence was largely unplanned and against the will of government, the repression by Francoist terror was 'programmed, thought-out and intentional' (Richards 1998: 32). It is easy to see how the alternative reading according to which a legitimate, progressive government was plunged into reaction and repression by an illegal military coup was suppressed in order to 'placate the political right' (Davis

2005: 877), and how to revive it has the potential to reopen old wounds as those on the right maintain. But it is equally obvious that for as long as those relatives of the victims of Francoist repression are unable to have their equivalent of the *Causa general* that the dictator inaugurated in 1942, according to which 'those rightists killed by the left were identified and buried with honour and dignity' (Preston 2006: 9–10), then the existing wounds will continue to fester.

One corollary of the Francoist *Causa*, as Preston points out, was an element of retribution, albeit arbitrary, in that the process of identification was 'often followed by acts of extreme violence against the local left' (2006: 10). Davis indicates how the initial 'impulse behind the activation of memory politics in Spain was towards truth rather than justice', but that there has developed a demand for 'justice in a moral or historical sense' (2005: 879). Towards the end of 2008, Judge Baltasar Garzón published a document in which he accused the Franco regime of responsibility for 114,000 deaths, naming 35 suspected perpetrators, including Franco. The action was a test case since all those named were, like the Caudillo, dead and therefore no trials would result but possibly open the way to future prosecutions against living suspects. In what would have been a momentous challenge to the tradition of the Transition, the judge caused alarm in government circles with a request for the exhumation of 25 graves, with a view to possibly prosecuting the perpetrators of the deaths. After an appeal by the public prosecutor, Garzón agreed to hand jurisdiction for such investigations over to the regional courts. The prosecutor's appeal was based on the principle that the 35 accused were covered by the 1977 Amnesty Act, whereas Garzón claimed to be basing his accusation on Human Rights legislation.

The Socialist government's invoking of the Amnesty Act, a key element in the Transition's narrative of forgetting, to block Garzón's investigation suggests that Davis's hope that the new Socialist administration 'less directly dependent than previous PSOE governments, in terms of their own claims to power and legitimacy, on the shared story of the Transition' might be well placed to 'sponsor a reworking of that story, a controversial yet cathartic process that, it seems, can no longer be avoided' (2005: 879) is unlikely to be fulfilled. The move angered the Socialists' supporters among the intelligentsia, such as Ian Gibson and Juan Goytisolo.

Despite this, it remains the case that the Socialist government of José Luis Rodríguez Zapatero has done more than any previous administration to address this sensitive issue. It has refused the counsel of the right to leave matters as they were, or, indeed, the Archbishop of Madrid, Rouco Varela, who called for forgetting 'on the basis of reconciliation and forgiveness' (*ABC*, 24 November 2008), but equally resisted those further on the left who pressed for more radical reform of the 2007 law, and in so doing Zapatero has sought the path of direct observance of a law that in itself was a hard-won compromise between competing extremes. The emphasis the law places on individual initiatives, supported by the authorities, may, in the circumstances, be the best solution for all concerned, since official promotion of public remembrance even by liberal democratic states can, as Graham observes, have the effect of altering the nature of the remembrance. 'Memory work that emanates from civil society is inherently more healing and more useful in terms of building a democratic culture' (Graham 2005: 146).

Happily Spain is a stable, liberal democratic society and will undoubtedly be able to cope with this and the other challenges that face it in the future, but in a sign of how enduring is the memory of the conflict that ended in 1939 and the power it continues to exert at the beginning of the twenty-first century, the historian and government advisor, José Alvarez Junco, interviewed in *El País* in September 2008 about the recovery of memory, urged prudence: 'Spain's institutions are solid, stable. They don't seem to be under any danger or threat but the tragic events of seventy years ago were such that one must not tempt fate.'

Appendices: Election Results, 1977–2009*

Appendix 1 General Election, 15 June 1977

Census	23,583,762		
Voters	18,590,130	78.8%	
Abstention	4,993,632	21.2%	
Parties	**Votes**	**%**	**Seats**
UCD	6,310,391	34.5	166
PSOE	5,371,866	29.4	118
PCE	1,709,890	9.4	19
AP	1,504,771	8.2	16
PDC	514,647	2.8	11
PNV	296,193	1.6	8
PSP–US	816,582	4.5	6
UC-DCC	172,791	1.0	2
EC–FED	143,954	0.8	1
EE-IE	61,417	0.3	1
CAIC	37,183	0.2	1
CIC	29,834	0.2	1

* *Sources*: Appendices 1–10: tables compiled using data from the Spanish Interior Ministry (http://www.elecciones.mir.es/MIR/JSP/resultados); Appendix 11: Basque Government (http://www.euskadi.net/elecciones)

Appendix 2   General Election, 1 March 1979

Census	26,836,490		
Voters	**18,259,192**	**68%**	
Abstention	**8,577,298**	**32%**	
Parties	**Votes**	**%**	**Seats**
UCD	6,292,102	35.0	168
PSOE	5,477,037	30.5	121
PCE	1,940,236	10.8	23
CD	1,070,721	6.0	10
CiU	483,446	2.7	8
PNV	275,292	1.5	7
PSA–PA	325,842	1.8	5
HB	172,110	1.0	3
UN	379,463	2.1	1
ERC	123,448	0.7	1
EE	85,677	0.5	1
UPC	58,953	0.3	1
PAR	38,042	0.2	1
UPN	28,248	0.2	1

Appendix 3   General Election, 28 October 1982

Census	26,846,940		
Voters	**21,469,274**	**80.0%**	
Abstention	**5,377,666**	**20.03%**	
Parties	**Votes**	**%**	**Seats**
PSOE	10,127,392	48.3	202
AP-PDP	5,548,107	26.5	107
CiU	772,726	3.7	12
UCD	1,425,093	6.8	11
PNV	95,656	1.9	8
PCE	846,515	4.0	4
CDS	604,309	2.9	2
HB	210,601	1.0	2
ERC	138,118	0.7	1
EE	100,326	0.5	1
FN	108,746	0.5	0
PSA–PA	84,474	0.4	0
UPC	35,013	0.2	0

Appendix 4   General Election, 22 June 1986

Census	29,117,613		
Voters	20,524,858	70.49%	
Abstention	8,592,755	29.5%	
Parties	**Votes**	**%**	**Seats**
PSOE	8,901,718	44.1	184
AP-PDP-CL	5,247,677	26	105
CDS	1,861,912	9.2	19
CiU	1,014,258	5	18
IU	935,504	4.6	7
EAJ-PNV	309,610	1.5	6
HB	231,722	1.2	5
EE	107,053	0.5	2
CG	79,972	0.4	1
PAR	73,004	0.4	1
AIC	65,664	0.3	1
UV	64,403	0.3	1

Appendix 5   General Election, 29 October 1989

Census	29,604,055		
Voters	20,646,365	69.7%	
Abstention	8,957,690	30.26%	
Parties	**Votes**	**%**	**Seats**
PSOE	8,115,568	39.6	175
PP	5,285,972	25.8	107
CiU	1,032,243	5.0	18
IU	1,858,588	9.1	17
CDS	1,617,716	7.9	14
EAJ-PNV	254,681	1.2	5
HB	217,278	1.1	4
PA	212,687	1.0	2
UV	144,924	0.7	2
EA	136,955	0.7	2
EE	105,238	0.5	2
PAR	71,733	0.4	1
AIC	64,767	0.3	1
ERC	84,756	0.4	0
CG	45,821	0.2	0

Appendix 6   General Election, 6 June 1993

Census	31,030,511		
Voters	23,718,816	76.4%	
Abstention	7,311,695	23.56%	
Parties	**Votes**	**%**	**Seats**
PSOE	9,150,083	38.8	159
PP	8,201,463	34.8	141
IU	2,253,722	9.6	18
CiU	1,165,783	4.9	17
EAJ-PNV	291,448	1.2	5
CC	207,077	0.9	4
HB	206,876	0.9	2
ERC	189,632	0.8	1
PAR	144,544	0.6	1
EA-EUE	129,293	0.6	1
UV	112,341	0.5	1
CDS	414,740	1.8	0
BNG	126,965	0.5	0
PA	96,513	0.4	0

Appendix 7   General Election, 3 March 1996

Census	32,531,833		
Voters	25,172,058	77.4%	
Abstention	7,359,775	22.62%	
Parties	**Votes**	**%**	**Seats**
PP	9,716,006	38.8	156
PSOE	9,425,678	37.6	141
IU	2,639,774	10.5	21
CiU	1,151,633	4.6	16
EAJ-PNV	318,951	1.3	5
CC	220,418	0.9	4
BNG	220,147	0.9	2
HB	181,304	0.7	2
ERC	167,641	0.7	1
EA	115,861	0.5	1
UV	91,575	0.4	1
PA	134,800	0.5	0
ChA	49,739	0.2	0

Appendix 8   General Election, 12 March 2000

Census	33,969,640		
Voters	23,339,474	68.71%	
Abstention	10,630,166	31.29%	
Parties	**Votes**	**%**	**Seats**
PP	10,321,178	45.24	183
PSOE	7,918,752	34.71	125
CiU	970,421	4.25	15
IU	1,263,043	5.54	8
EAJ-PNV	353,953	1.55	7
CC	248,261	1.09	4
BNG	306,268	1.34	3
PA	206,255	0.90	1
ERC	194,715	0.85	1
IC–V	119,290	0.52	1
EA	100,742	0.44	1
ChA	75,356	0.33	1

Appendix 9   General Election, 14 March 2004

Census	34,571,831		
Voters	26,155,436	75.66%	
Abstention	8,416,395	24.34%	
Parties		**% vote**	**Seats**
PSOE	11,026,163	42.64	164
PP	9,763,144	37.64	148
CiU	835,471	3.24	10
ERC	652,196	2.54	8
EAJ-PNV	420,980	1.63	7
IU	1,284,081	4.96	5
CC	235,221	0.86	3
BNG	208,688	0.8	2
ChA	94,252	0.37	1
EA	80,905	0.32	1
Na-Bai	61,045	0.24	1

Appendix 10   General Election, 9 March 2008

Census	35,073,179		
Voters	25,900,442	73.85%	
Abstention	9,172,737	26,15%	
Parties		**% vote**	**Seats**
PSOE	11,289,335	43.64	169
PP	10,278,010	40.11	154
CiU	779,425	3.05	10
EAJ-PNV	306,128	1.20	6
ERC	298,139	1.17	3
IU	969,946	3.80	2
BNG	212,543	0.82	2
CC-PNC	174,629	0.65	2
UpyD	306,079	1.20	1
Na-Bai	62,398	0.24	1

Appendix 11 Basque Regional Elections, 1980–2009

Party	1980 %	1980 Seats	1984 %	1984 Seats	1986 %	1986 Seats	1990 %	1990 Seats	1994 %	1994 Seats	1998 %	1998 Seats	2001 %	2001 Seats	2005 %	2005 Seats	2009 %	2009 Seats
PNV[1]	38.1	25	42.01	32	23.71	17	28.49	22	29.84	22	28.01	21	42.72	33	38.67	29	38.56	30
PSE-EE[2]	14.21	9	23.07	19	22.05	19	19.94	16	17.13	12	17.6	14	17.9	13	22.68	18	30.7	25
PP	4.77	2	9.36	7	4.86	2	8.23	6	14.41	11	20.13	16	23.12	19	17.4	15	14.1	13
EA[3]					15.84	13	11.38	9	10.31	8	8.69	6					3.69	1
EB-B (IU)[4]	4.02	1							9.15	6	5.68	2	5.58	3	5.37	3	3.51	1
UAl[5]							1.41	3	2.73	5	1.26	2						
UPD																	2.15	1
HB/EH[6]	16.55	11	14.65	11	17.47	13	18.33	13	16.29	11	17.91	14	10.12	7	12.44	9		
EE[7]	9.82	6	7.98	6	10.88	9	7.78	6										
CDS					3.54	2												
UCD	8.52	6																
Aralar[8]															2.33	1	6.03	4
Total		60		75		75		75		75		75		75		75		75

[1] The PNV governed the Basque Region alone from 1980 to 1986, from 1986 to 1998 in coalition with the PSE (briefly with EA and EE from 1990 to 1994) and from 1994 to 1998 in coalition with the PSE and the EA. The EB joined the government coalition after the 2001 elections. In 2009 this nationalist tripartite government coalition gave way to a minority government run by PSE-EE under Patxi López with support of the Basque PP.

[2] The PSE-EE is the Basque branch of the national Socialist Party (PSOE).

[3] The EA formed after a split in the PNV in 1986. It was a partner in government with the PNV from 1998 to 2009. In the 2001 and 2005 elections it campaigned jointly with the PNV in the PNV–EA coalition.

(continued overleaf)

4   The EB is the Basque branch of the national coalition United Left (IU). It formed a coalition with the Basque Green Party (Berdeak) in 1994 and in 2004 changed its name to Ezker Batua-Berdeak (EB-B).

5   UAI (Alava Unity) formed from a split with the PP in 1989. It supports the rights of the province of Alava and its identity with Castile.

6   The HB formed in 1978 as a political support party for ETA. It assumed the name EH from 1998 to 2001. Since 2001 it labelled itself Batasuna and was banned in 2003. In 2005 the Communist Party for the Basque Land (Partido Comunista de las Tierras Vascas, PCTV-EHAK) is commonly understood to have been a front for Batasuna and it gained 12.5% of the vote and 9 seats. It too was banned in 2009.

7   The EE, founded in 1977, includes some members of ETA (politico-military) which abandoned violence and dissolved in 1982. It joined the government coalition with the PNV and the EA in 1991 and merged with the PSE in 1991 to form the PSE-EE.

8   Aralar formed in 2000 as a splinter from the HB/EH. It is radical Basque but condemns violence.

BIBLIOGRAPHY

Abella, Carlos, *Adolfo Suárez: el hombre clave de la transición* (Madrid: Espasa, 2006).

Aguilar, Miguel Angel, 'Los medios de comunicación', in Tusell, 2000, pp. 181–208.

Aguilar, Paloma, 'The Memory of the Civil War in the Transition to Democracy: The Peculiarity of the Basque Case', in Heywood, 1999, pp. 5–25.

Aguilar, Paloma, 'Justice, Politics, and Memory in the Spanish Transition', in Barahona de Brito, 2001, pp. 92–118.

Aguilar, Paloma, *Memory and Amnesia: The Role of the Spanish Civil War in the Transition to Democracy* (Oxford: Berghahn Books, 2002; original Spanish edn 1996).

Allen, John L., *Opus Dei: Secrets and Power inside the Catholic Church* (London: Penguin/Allen Lane, 2005).

Alvarez Junco, José, 'La verdad histórica contra las pasiones', *El País*, 2 February 2008.

Alvarez Junco, José and Adrian Shubert, *Spanish History since 1808* (London: Arnold, 2000).

Anson, Luis María, *Don Juan* (Barcelona: Plaza y Janés, 1994).

Ardagh, John, *France Today* (London: Penguin, 1988).

Ashford Hodges, Gabrielle, *Franco: A Concise Biography* (London: Weidenfeld & Nicolson, 2000).

Astudillo, Javier and Elena García-Guereta, 'If It Isn't Broken, Don't Fix It: The Spanish Popular Party in Power', *Southern European Society and Politics*, 11:3–4 (September–December 2006), pp. 399–417.

Aznar, José María, *España: la segunda transición* (Madrid: Espasa Calpe, 1995).

Aznar, José María, *Ocho años en el Gobierno: una visión personal de España* (Barcelona: Planeta, 2004).

239

Bibliography

Balfour, Sebastian, 'Spain: From 1931 to the Present', in Carr, 2000, pp. 243–82.

Balfour, Sebastian (ed.), *The Politics of Contemporary Spain* (London: Routledge, 2005a).

Balfour, Sebastian, 'The Reinvention of Spanish Conservatism: The Popular Party since 1989', in Balfour, 2005b, pp. 146–68.

Balfour, Sebastian and Alejandro Quiroga, *The Reinvention of Spain: Nation and Identity since Democracy* (Oxford: Oxford University Press, 2007).

Balfour, Sebastian and Paul Preston (eds), *Spain and the Great Powers in the Twentieth Century* (London: Routledge, 1999).

Bali, Valentina A., 'Terror and Elections: Lessons from Spain', *Electoral Studies*, 26 (2007), pp. 669–87.

Barahona de Brito, Alexandra, Carmen González Enríquez and Paloma Aguilar (eds), *The Politics of Memory: Transitional Justice in Democratizing Societies* (Oxford: Oxford University Press, 2001).

Barrera, Carlos, *Periodismo y franquismo: de la censura a la apertura* (Barcelona: Ediciones Internacionales Universitarias, 1995).

Barrera, Carlos, *Historia del proceso democrático en España: tardofranquismo, transición y democracia* (Madrid: Editorial Fragua, 2002).

Barton, Simon, *A History of Spain* (London: Palgrave, 2004; 2nd edn 2009).

Beevor, Antony, *The Battle for Spain: The Spanish Civil War 1936–39* (London: Weidenfield & Nicolson, 2006).

Bernecker, Walther L., 'Monarchy and Democracy: The Political Role of King Juan Carlos in the Spanish *Transición*', *Journal of Contemporary History*, 33:1 (1998), pp. 65–84.

Blaye, Edouard de, *Franco and the Politics of Spain* (London: Pelican, 1976).

Boyd, Carolyn P., *Historia Patria: Politics, History, and National Identity in Spain, 1875–1975* (Princeton: Princeton University Press, 1997).

Brooksbank Jones, Anny, *Women in Contemporary Spain* (Manchester: Manchester University Press, 1997).

Burns, Jimmy, *Barça: A People's Passion* (London: Bloomsbury, 1999).

Cabrera, Mercedes and Fernando del Rey, *The Power of Entrepreneurs: Politics and Economy in Contemporary Spain* (New York: Berghahn Books, 2007).

Callahan, William J., 'The Spanish Church: Change and Continuity', in Townson, 2007, pp. 182–94.

Campbell, Alastair, *The Blair Years* (London: Arrow, 2008).

Bibliography

Campillo, Oscar, *Zapatero: Presidente a la primera* (Madrid: La Esfera, 2004).

Carr, Raymond, *Modern Spain 1875–1980* (Oxford: Oxford University Press, 1980).

Carr, Raymond, *The Spanish Tragedy: The Civil War in Perspective* (London: Phoenix Press, 1986).

Carr, Raymond, 'What was Francoism like?', Second Ramón Pérez de Ayala Lecture (30 November 1995, University of Southampton).

Carr, Raymond (ed.), *Spain: A History* (Oxford: Oxford University Press, 2000).

Carr, Raymond and Juan Pablo Fusi, *Spain: From Dictatorship to Democracy* (London: George Allen & Unwin, 1979; 2nd edn 1981).

Carrillo, Santiago, 'The Consensus-building Role of the Communist Party', in Threlfall, 2000, pp. 53–60.

Chislett, William, *Spanish Direct Investment in Latin America: Challenges and Opportunities* (March 2003), ww.realinstitutoelcano.org

Chislett, William, *Image and Reality: Contemporary Spain*, Working Paper 45/2008, www.realinstitutoelcano.org

Clark, Robert P., *The Basques: The Franco Years and Beyond* (Reno: University of Nebraska Press, 1979).

Closa, Carlos and Paul Heywood, *Spain and the European Union* (Basingstoke: Palgrave Macmillan, 2004).

Coca Hernando, Rosario, 'Towards a New Image of Women under Franco: The Role of the Sección Femenina', *International Journal of Iberian Studies*, 11:1 (1998), pp. 5–13.

Colomer, Josep M., 'The Spanish "State of Autonomies"', in Heywood, 1999, pp. 40–52.

Colomer, Josep M., 'The 2000 General Election in Spain', *Electoral Studies*, 20 (2001), pp. 463–501.

Colomer, Josep M., 'The General Election in Spain, March 2004', *Electoral Studies*, 24 (2005), pp. 149–56.

Conversi, Daniele, *The Basques, the Catalans and Spain: Alternative Routes to Nationalist Mobilisation* (London: Hurst & Co., 1997).

Corkill, David, 'Race, Immigration and Multiculturalism in Spain', in Jordan and Morgan-Tamosunas, 2000, pp. 48–57.

Cornelius, Wayne A., 'Spain: the Uneasy Transition from Labor Exporter to Labor Importer', in *Controlling Immigration: A Global Perspective*, ed. Wayne Cornelius, Philip Martin and James Hollifield (Palo Alto: Stanford University Press, 2004), pp. 387–429.

Bibliography

Coverdale, John F., *Uncommon Faith. The Early Years of Opus Dei (1928–1943)* (Princeton, NJ: Scepter, 2002).

Davis, Madeleine, 'Is Spain Recovering its Memory? Breaking the *Pacto del Olvido*', *Human Rights Quarterly*, 27 (2005), pp. 858–80.

de la Granja, José Luis and Santiago de Pablo, 'La encrucijada vasca: entre Ermua y Estella', in Tusell, 2000, pp. 153–79.

Delgado, Irene and Lourdes López Nieto, 'Spain', *European Journal of Political Research*, 28 (1995), pp. 473–6.

de Madariaga, Salvador, *Spain* (London: Jonathan Cape, 1942).

Díaz, Elías, 'Ideologies in the Spanish Transition', in Heywood, 1999, pp. 26–39.

Díez Medrano, Juan, 'Nation, Citizenship and Immigration in Contemporary Spain', *International Journal on Multicultural Societies*, 7:2 (2005), pp. 133–56.

The Economist, 'Who Speaks for Spain', 11 March 1989, pp. 1–22.

The Economist, 'The Second Transition', 24 June 2004, pp. 1–18.

The Economist, 'The Party's Over', 8 November 2008, pp. 1–22.

Edles, Laura Desfor, *Symbol and Ritual in the New Spain: The Transition to Democracy after Franco* (Cambridge: Cambridge University Press, 1998).

Ellwood, Sheelagh, *Franco* (Profiles in Power) (London: Longman, 1994).

Encarnación, Omar G., *Spanish Politics: Democracy after Dictatorship* (Cambridge: Polity, 2008).

Enders, Victoria Lorée, 'Problematic Portraits: The Ambiguous Historical Role of the *Sección Femenina* of the Falange', in *Constructing Spanish Womanhood: Female Identity in Modern Spain*, ed. Victoria Lorée Enders and Pamela Beth Radcliff (New York: State University of New York Press, 1999).

Esenwein, George and Adrian Shubert, *Spain at War: The Spanish Civil War in Context 1931–39* (London: Longman, 1995).

Farrell, Mary, 'Spain in the New European Union', in Balfour, 2005a, pp. 215–24.

Field, Bonnie N., 'The Parliamentary Election in Spain, March 2008', *Electoral Studies* (2008), pp. 1–4, doi:10.1016/j.electstud.2008.07.001

Folguera Crespo, Pilar, 'La Mujer', in *Historia de España. La Epoca de Franco (1939–75): Sociedad, vida y cultura* (Madrid: Espasa Calpe, 2001).

Fuchs, Dale, 'Spain Acts to Stop Domestic Violence', *Guardian*, 30 June 2005.

Bibliography

Fuente, Ismael, *El caballo cansado: El largo adiós de Felipe González* (Madrid: Temas de Hoy, 1991).

Fusi, Juan Pablo, *Franco: autoritarismo y poder personal* (Madrid: El País, 1985a).

Fusi, Juan Pablo, 'El boom económico español', *Cuadernos Historia 16*, no. 34 (Barcelona: Grupo 16, 1985b).

Fusi, Juan Pablo (ed), *Franquismo: el juicio de la historia* (Madrid: Temas de Hoy, 2005).

Fusi, Juan Pablo, José María Jover Zamora and Guadalupe Gómez-Ferrer (eds), *España: Sociedad, Política y Civilización (SIGLOS XIX–XX)* (Madrid: Areté, 2001).

Fusi, Juan Pablo and Jordi Palafox Gámir, *Historia de España 14: La España de Juan Carlos I. Transición y democracia (1975–1999)* (Madrid: Espasa, 1999).

García Viñuela, Enrique, 'Reforming Campaign Finance in the Nineties: A Case Study of Spain', *European Journal of Law and Economics*, 25(3), 2008, pp. 177–90.

Gibbons, John, *Spanish Politics Today* (Manchester: Manchester University Press, 1999).

Gillespie, Richard, 'The Spanish General Election of 1996', *Electoral Studies*, 15(3), August 1996, pp. 425–31.

Gilmour, David, *The Transformation of Spain: From Franco to the Constitutional Monarchy* (London: Quartet, 1985).

Graham, Helen, *The Spanish Civil War: A Very Short Introduction* (Oxford: Oxford University Press, 2005).

Graham, Helen and Jo Labanyi (eds), *Spanish Cultural Studies: An Introduction* (Oxford: Oxford University Press, 1995).

Grugel, Jean and Tim Rees, *Franco's Spain* (London: Arnold, 1997).

Guerra, Alfonso, *Dejando atrás los vientos: memorias 1982–91* (Madrid: Espasa Calpe, 2006).

Gunther, Richard, José Ramón Montero and Joan Botella, *Democracy in Modern Spain* (New Haven: Yale University Press, 2004).

Gunther, Richard, Giacomo Sani and Goldie Shabad, *Spain after Franco: The Making of a Competitive Party System* (Berkeley: University of California Press, 1988).

Harrison, Joseph and David Corkill, *Spain: A Modern European Economy* (Aldershot: Ashgate, 2004).

Hermet, Guy, 'Spain under Franco: The Changing Character of an Authoritarian Regime', *European Journal of Political Research*, 4 (1976), pp. 311–27.

Bibliography

Herrero de Miñón, Miguel, 'Política exterior', in Tusell, 2000, pp. 41–54.

Heywood, Paul, *The Government and Politics of Spain* (Basingstoke: Palgrave Macmillan, 1995).

Heywood, Paul (ed.), *Politics and Policy in Democratic Spain* (London: Frank Cass, 1999).

Heywood, Paul, 'Corruption, Democracy and Governance in Spain', in Balfour, 2005a, pp. 39–60.

Hooper, John, *The New Spaniards* (London: Penguin; 2nd edn 2006).

Hopewell, John, *Out of the Past: Spanish Cinema after Franco* (London: BFI Books, 1986).

Jiménez, Juan Carlos, 'Balance económico de un fin de siglo', in Tusell, 2000, pp. 55–69.

Jiménez, Lidia, 'El gran reto de Zapatero será su relación con la Iglesia: entrevista con Philip Pettit', *El País*, 15 March 2008.

Jordan, Barry and Rikki Morgan-Tamosunas (eds), *Contemporary Spanish Cultural Studies* (London: Arnold, 2000).

Judt, Tony, *Postwar: A History of Europe since 1945* (London: Pimlico, 2005; 2nd edn 2007).

Juliá, Santos, 'The Socialist Era, 1982–1996', in Alvarez Junco and Shubert, 2000, pp. 331–44.

Juliá, Santos, 'La sociedad', in Fusi, 2005, pp. 69–143.

Kamen, Henry, *Imagining Spain: Historical Myth and National Identity* (New Haven and London: Yale University Press, 2008).

Keating, Michael and Zoe Bray, 'Renegotiating Sovereignty: Basque Nationalism and the Rise and Fall of the Ibarretxe Plan', *Ethnopolitics*, 5:4 (2006), pp. 347–64.

Kennedy, Paul, 'Phoenix from the Ashes. The PSOE Government under Rodríguez Zapatero 2004–2007: A New Model for Social Democracy?' *International Journal of Iberian Studies*, 20:3 (2007), pp. 187–206.

Labanyi, Jo (ed.), *Constructing Identity in Contemporary Spain: Theoretical Debates and Cultural Practice* (Oxford: Oxford University Press, 2002a).

Labanyi, Jo, 'Introduction: Engaging with Ghosts; or, Theorizing Culture in Modern Spain', in Labanyi, 2002b, pp. 1–14.

Labanyi, Jo, 'Memory and Modernity in Democratic Spain: The Difficulty of Coming to Terms with the Spanish Civil War', *Poetics Today*, 28:1 (Spring 2007), pp. 89–116.

Lago, Ignacio and José Ramón Montero, 'The 2004 Election in Spain: Terrorism, Accountability, and Voting', *Taiwan Journal of Democracy*, 2:1 (July 2006), pp. 13–36.

Lahav, Gallya, 'Public Opinion Toward Immigration in the European Union: Does it Matter?', *Comparative Political Studies*, 37:10 (2004), pp. 1151–83.

Lannon, Frances, *Privilege, Persecution and Prophecy: The Catholic Church in Spain 1875–1975* (Oxford: Oxford University Press, 1987).

Lannon, Frances, 'Catholicism and Social Change', in Graham and Labanyi, 1995, pp. 276–82.

Lecours, André, 'The Plan Ibarretxe: A New Formalism', *McGill International Review* (Fall 2005), pp. 22–6.

Leitz, Christian, 'Nazi Germany and Francoist Spain, 1936–1945', in Balfour, 1999, pp. 127–50.

Leitz, Christian and David J. Dunthorn (eds), *Spain in an International Context, 1936–1959* (New York: Berghahn Books, 1999).

León Solís, Fernando, 'The Transition(s) to Democracy and Discourses of Memory', *International Journal of Iberian Studies*, 16:1 (2003), pp. 49–63.

Linz, Juan José, 'An Authoritarian Regime: Spain', in *Politics and Society in the Twentieth Century*, ed. Stanley Payne (New York, 1976), pp. 160–207.

Low, Robert, *La Pasionaria: The Spanish Firebrand* (London: Hutchinson, 1992).

Magone, José M., *Contemporary Spanish Politics* (London: Routledge, 2004).

Malefakis, Edward, 'The Franco Dictatorship: A Bifurcated Regime?', in Townson, 2007, pp. 248–54.

Mar-Molinero, Clare and Angel Smith (eds), *Nationalism and the Nation in the Iberian Peninsula: Competing and Conflicting Identities* (Oxford: Berg, 1996a).

Mar-Molinero, Clare and Angel Smith, 'Myths and Realities of Nation-Building in the Iberian Peninsula', in Mar-Molinero and Smith (eds), 1996b, pp. 1–30.

Marías, Javier, 'Un país demasiado anómalo', *El País*, 21 January 2007.

Marín, José María, Carme Molinero and Pere Ysás, *Historia de España: Historia contemporánea. Historia política 1939–2000* (Madrid: Istmo, 2001).

Martín Aceña, Pablo and Elena Martínez Ruiz, 'The Golden Age of Spanish Capitalism: Economic Growth without Political Freedom', in Townson, 2007, pp. 30–46.

Martín de la Guardia, Ricardo M., 'La sociedad española a finales de siglo', in Paredes, 2004, pp. 1028–46.

Martínez, Jesús A. (coord.), *Historia de España: siglo XX, 1939–1996* (Madrid: Cátedra, 2003).

Mata, José Manuel, 'The Weakness of Democracy in the Basque Country', in Balfour, 2005b, pp. 81–105.

Mateos, Abdón and Alvaro Soto, *El final del franquismo, 1959–1975: La transformación de la sociedad española*, Colección Historia de España, no. 29 (Madrid: Temas de hoy, 1997).

Matlack, Carol, 'How Spain Thrives on Immigration', *Spiegel Online*, 10 May 2007.

Maxwell, Kenneth and Steven Spiegel, *The New Spain: From Isolation to Influence* (New York: Council on Foreign Relations Press, 1994).

McDonough, Peter, Samuel H. Barnes and Antonio López Pina, *The Cultural Dynamics of Democratization in Spain* (London: Cornell University Press, 1998).

McFall, Annie, 'The *Plan Hidrológico Nacional*: A Missed Opportunity or a Wily Exercise in Pragmatic Governance?', *International Journal of Iberian Studies*, 15:1 (2002), pp. 40–54.

McRoberts, Kenneth, *Catalonia: Nation Building without a State* (Oxford: Oxford University Press, 2001).

Méndez Lago, Mónica, 'The Socialist Party in Government and in Opposition', in Balfour, 2005a, pp. 169–97.

Ministerio de la Presidencia, Secretaría de Estado de Comunicación *2004–8: Balance de Legislatura* (December 2007).

Ministerio de la Presidencia, *España hoy 2009*, http://www.la-moncloa.es/Espana/EspaniaHoy, accessed March 2009.

Moreno, Luis, 'The Madrid Bombings in the Domestic and Regional Politics of Spain', *Irish Studies in International Affairs*, 16 (2005), pp. 65–72.

Mújica, Alejandro, and Ignacio Sánchez-Cuenca, 'Consensus and Parliamentary Opposition: The Case of Spain', *Government and Opposition: An International Journal of Comparative Politics*, 41:1 (2008), pp. 86–108.

Nash, Mary, 'Pronatalism and Motherhood in Franco's Spain', in *Maternity and Gender Policies: Women and the Rise of European Welfare States 1880s–1950s*, ed. Gisela Bock and Pat Thane (London: Routledge, 1994), pp. 166–77.

Newton, Michael with Peter Donaghy, *Institutions of Modern Spain: A Political and Economic Guide* (Cambridge: Cambridge University Press, 1997).

Núñez Seixas, Xosé-Manoel, 'From National-Catholic Nostalgia to Constitutional Patriotism: Conservative Spanish Nationalism since the early 1990s', in Balfour, 2005a, pp. 121–45.

Pack, Sasha D., *Tourism and Dictatorship: Europe's Peaceful Invasion of Franco's Spain* (London: Palgrave, 2006).

Pack, Sasha D., 'Tourism and Political Change in Franco's Spain', in Townson, 2007, pp. 47–66.

Palomares, Cristina, *The Quest for Survival after Franco: Moderate Francoism and the Slow Journey to the Polls* (Brighton: Sussex Academic Press, 2004).

Palomares, Cristina, 'New Political Mentalities in the *Tardofranquismo*', in Townson, 2007, pp. 118–39.

Paredes, Javier (ed.), *Historia contemporánea de España s.XIX–XX* (Barcelona: Ariel, 2004).

Passmore, Kevin, *Fascism: A Very Short Introduction* (Oxford: Oxford University Press, 2002).

Payne, John, *Catalonia: History and Culture* (Nottingham: Five Leaves, 2004).

Payne, Stanley, *Franco's Spain* (London: Routledge & Kegan Paul, 1967).

Payne, Stanley, *The Franco Regime 1936–1975* (London: Phoenix Press, 1987).

Payne, Stanley, *Franco: el perfil de la historia* (Madrid: Espasa Calpe, 1994).

Payne, Stanley, *Fascism in Spain: 1923–1977* (Wisconsin: University of Wisconsin Press, 1999).

Pereira Castañares, J.C. and P.A. Martínez de Lillo, 'Política exterior, 1976–2004', in Paredes, 2004, pp. 1000–27.

Pérez-Díaz, Víctor M., *The Return of Civil Society* (Cambridge, MA: Harvard University Press, 1993).

Pérez Serrano, Julio, 'La Transición a la democracia como modelo analítico para la historia del presente: un balance crítico', in Quirosa-Cheyrouze y Muñoz, 2007, pp. 61–76.

Powell, Charles, *España en democracia 1975–2000: Las claves de la profunda transformación de España* (Barcelona: Plaza y Janés, 2001a).

Powell, Charles, 'Fifteen Years On: Spanish Membership in the European Union Revisited', November 2001b, http://www.ces.fas.harvard.edu/publications/docs/pdfs/Powell.pdf

Powell, Charles and Pere Bonnin, *Adolfo Suárez* (Barcelona: Ediciones B, Cara y Cruz, 2004).

Powell, Jonathan, *Great Hatred, Little Room: Making Peace in Northern Ireland* (London: Bodley Head, 2008).

Prego, Victoria, *Así se hizo la transición* (Barcelona: Plaza y Janés, 1995.

Prego, Victoria, 'La Transición según Victoria Prego', *Anales de la Real Sociedad Económica de Amigos del País de Valencia* (University of Valencia, 1995–6), pp. 155–66, http://www.uv.es/rseapv/web.shtml

Prego, Victoria, *Presidentes* (Barcelona: Plaza y Janés, 2000).

Preston, Paul, *The Triumph of Democracy* (London: Methuen, 1986).

Preston, Paul, *Franco* (London: Fontana, 1995a, 1st edn 1993).

Preston, Paul, *The Politics of Revenge: Fascism and the Military in Twentieth-century Spain* (London: Routledge, 1995b, 1st edn 1990).

Preston, Paul, 'Franco's Foreign Policy', in Leitz and Dunthorn, 1999, pp. 1–18.

Preston, Paul, *Juan Carlos: A People's King* (London: HarperCollins, 2004).

Preston, Paul, *The Spanish Civil War: Reaction, Revolution and Revenge* (London: HarperCollins, 2006).

Preston, Paul, *El gran manipulador: la mentira cotidiana de Franco* (Barcelona: Ediciones B, 2008).

PSOE, *Merecemos una España mejor: Programa electoral. Elecciones Generales 2004* (Madrid: PSOE, 2004).

PSOE, *Comprometidos con una España mejor: balance de un año de gobierno, 2005* (Madrid: PSOE, 2005).

Pujas, Véronique and Martin Rhodes, 'Party Finance and Political Scandal in Italy, Spain and France', *West European Politics*, 22:3 (July 1999), pp. 41–63.

Quirosa-Cheyrouze y Muñoz, Rafael (coord.), *Historia de la Transición en España: Los inicios del proceso democratizador* (Madrid: Biblioteca Nueva, 2007).

Radcliff, Pamela, 'Associations and the Social Orgins of the Transition during the Late Franco Regime', in Townson, 2007, pp. 140–62.

Ramonet, Ignacio (ed.), *Fidel Castro: My Life* (London: Penguin, 2007).

Resina, Joan Ramon, 'Short of Memory: The Reclamation of the Past Since the Spanish Transition to Democracy', in *Disremembering the Dictatorship: The Politics of Memory in the Spanish Transition to Democracy*, ed. Joan Ramon Resina (Amsterdam: Rodopi, 2000), pp. 83–126.

Richards, Michael, *A Time of Silence: Civil War and the Culture of Repression in Franco's Spain 1936–1945* (Cambridge: Cambridge University Press, 1998).

Bibliography

Richardson, Nathan E., *Postmodern* paletos*: Immigration, Democracy and Globalization in Spanish Narrative and Film, 1950–2000* (London: Bucknell University Press, 2002).

Rodríguez Braun, Carlos, 'De la agonía a la agonía', in Tusell and Sinova, 1992, pp. 51–66.

Romero Salvadó, Francisco J., *Twentieth-century Spain: Politics and Society in Spain, 1898–1998* (London: Macmillan, 1999).

Romero Salvadó, Francisco J., *The Spanish Civil War: Origins, Course and Outcomes* (Basingstoke: Palgrave Macmillan, 2005).

Ross, Christopher, *Contemporary Spain: A Handbook* (London: Arnold; 2nd edn 2002).

Ross, Christopher, *Spain 1812–2004* (London: Arnold, 2004).

Ross, Christopher, Bill Richardson and Begoña Sangrador Vegas, *Contemporary Spain* (London: Hodder; 3rd edn 2008).

Ruiz, David, *La España democrática (1975–2000): Política y sociedad* (Madrid: Síntesis, 2002).

Salmon, Keith, *The Modern Spanish Economy: Transformation and Integration into Europe* (London: Pinter, 1995).

Sampedro, Víctor and Francisco Seoane Pérez, 'The 2008 Spanish General Elections: "Antagonistic Bipolarization" Geared by Presidential Debates, Partisanship and Media interests', *Press / Politics*, 13:3 (2008), pp. 336–44.

Sánchez Cervelló, Josep and Iván Tubau, *Felipe González* (Barcelona: Cara y Cruz, 2004).

Sánchez Marroyo, Fernando, *La España del siglo XX: Economía, demografía y sociedad* (Serie Historia de España XX) (Madrid: Istmo, 2003).

Santaolalla, Isabel, 'Ethnic and Racial Configurations in Contemporary Spanish Culture', in Labanyi, 2002a, pp. 55–71.

Shubert, Adrian, *A Social History of Modern Spain* (London: Routledge, 1990).

Sciolino, Elaine, 'Spanish Premier Says Troops Will Not Return to Iraq', *New York Times*, 7 May 2004.

Soto, Alvaro, 'La crisis del régimen, 1969–75', in Mateos and Soto, 1997, pp. 68–95.

Soto, Alvaro, 'Política social. Relaciones con los sindicatos', in Tusell, 2000, pp. 71–96.

Soto, Alvaro, *Transición y cambio en España 1975–1996* (Madrid: Alianza, 2005).

Stapell, Hamilton M., 'Reconsidering Spanish Nationalism, Regionalism, and the Centre-Periphery Model in the Post-Francoist

Bibliography

Period, 1975–1992', *International Journal of Iberian Studies*, 20:3 (2007), pp. 171–85.

Stradling, Robert, 'Maoist Revolution and the Spanish Civil War: "Revisionist" History and Historical Politics', *English Historical Review*, 122:496 (2007), pp. 442–57.

Suárez, Sandra, 'Mobile Democracy: Text Messages, Voter Turnout, and the 2004 Spanish General Election', http://electionupdates.caltech.edu/Suárez.pdf

Sullivan, John, *ETA and Basque Nationalism: The Fight for Euskadi 1890–1986* (London: Routledge, 1988).

Tamames, Ramón, *Introducción a la Constitución española (texto y comentarios)* (Madrid: Alianza, Ediciones del Prado, 1995).

Tesón, Nuria, 'Esquelas de las dos Españas', *El País*, 10 September 2006.

Thomàs, Joan María, 'Getting to Know Ramón Serrano Suñer: Reality and Invention, 1937–42', *International Journal of Iberian Studies*, 18:3 (2005), pp. 165–79.

Threlfall, Monica, *Consensus Politics in Spain: Insider Perspectives* (Bristol: Intellect, 2000).

Toharia, José Juan, 'La sociedad: la vieja y la nueva España', in Tusell and Sinova, 1992, pp. 67–76.

Townson, Nigel (ed.), *Spain Transformed: The Late Franco Dictatorship, 1959–75* (Basingstoke: Palgrave Macmillan, 2007).

Tremlett, Giles, *Ghosts of Spain: Travels through a Country's Hidden Past* (London: Faber, 2007).

Triana Toribio, Núria, 'A Punk called Pedro: *La Movida* in the Films of Pedro Almódovar', in Jordan and Morgan-Tamosunas, 2000, pp. 274–82.

Trythall, J.W.D., *Franco. A Biography*, with foreword by Raymond Carr (London: Rupert Hart-Davis, 1970).

Tusell, Javier, *La dictadura de Franco* (Barcelona: Altaya, 1996; original edn Alianza, 1988).

Tusell, Javier, *Historia de España: La transición española. La recuperación de las libertades*, Vol. 30 (Madrid: Historia 16, Temas de Hoy, 1997).

Tusell, Javier, *Historia de España en el siglo XX: IV La transición democrática y el gobierno socialista* (Madrid: Taurus, 1999).

Tusell, Javier (ed.), *El gobierno de Aznar: Balance de una gestión, 1996–2000* (Barcelona: Crítica, 2000).

Tusell, Javier, *El aznarato: el gobierno del Partido Popular 1996–2003* (Madrid: Santillana, 2004).

Tusell, Javier, *Spain: From Dictatorship to Democracy 1939 to the Present* (Oxford: Blackwell, 2007).

Tusell, Javier and Justino Sinova, *La década socialista: El ocaso de Felipe González* (Madrid: Espasa, 1992).

Vázquez Montalbán, Manuel, *La aznaridad: Por el imperio hacia Dios o por Dios hacia el imperio* (Barcelona: Mondadori, 2003)

Vázquez Montalbán, Manuel, *Crónica sentimental de la transición* (Madrid: Debolsillo, 2005).

Viñas, Angel, 'Breaking the Shackles from the Past: Spanish Foreign Policy from Franco to Felipe González', in Balfour and Preston, 1999, pp. 245–67.

Vincent, Mary, *Spain: 1833–2002. People and State* (Oxford: Oxford University Press, 2007).

Walsh, Michael, *The Secret World of Opus Dei* (London: Grafton, 1989).

Ward, John, *Latin America: Development and Conflict since 1945* (London: Routledge, 1997).

Welles, Benjamin, *Spain: The Gentle Anarchy* (London: Pall Mall Press, 1965).

Wert, José Ignacio, 'Opinión pública: encuestas y elecciones 1996–1999', in Tusell, 2000, pp. 209–33.

Woodworth, Paddy, *Dirty War, Clean Hands: ETA, the GAL and Spanish Democracy* (Cork: Cork University Press, 2001).

Woodworth, Paddy, 'Using Terror against Terrorists' in Balfour, 2005a, pp. 61–80.

Yoldi, José and J.A. Rodríguez, 'Los TEDAX descartaron que el explosivo fuera Titadyn desde el primer momento', *El País*, 15 March 2007.

INDEX

252

Index

Index

Index

Index

Index

Index